ETHICAL THEORY

T0372855

In this new kind of introduction to ethical theory, Daniel Muñoz and Sarah Stroud present 50 of the field's most exciting puzzles, paradoxes, and thought experiments. Over the course of 11 chapters, the authors cover a huge variety of topics, starting with the classic debate between utilitarians and deontologists and ending on existential questions about the future of humanity.

Every chapter begins with a helpful introduction, and each of the 50 entries includes references for further reading and questions for reflection. Among the entries are such classics as the Ring of Gyges, Jim and the Villagers, the Repugnant Conclusion, JoJo, "One Thought Too Many," the Miners Puzzle, the Gentle Murder Paradox, Nowheresville, the Experience Machine, and the Trolley Problem. The book also explores several more recent topics of interest, such as doxastic wronging and the ethics of AI, so that even advanced students are likely to discover something new. Each entry can be read on its own, and the writing is accessible and conversational throughout, making this an ideal resource for undergraduate teaching. Readers at any level can pick up this book and see for themselves how fascinating—and puzzling—ethical theory can be.

Key Features:

- Offers 50 puzzles, paradoxes, and thought experiments, with every entry including the following elements:
  - Presentation of the case
  - Discussion of responses to and implications of the case
  - A reading list which cites the classic presentation of the case and recommends several other treatments or responses
  - Questions for reflection

- Coverage of each of the 50 is self-contained, allowing students to quickly understand an issue and giving instructors flexibility in assigning readings to match the themes of the course.
- Additional pedagogical features include a general volume introduction as well as smaller introductions to each of the 11 larger, topic-oriented chapters.

Daniel Muñoz is Assistant Professor of Philosophy and Core Faculty in Philosophy, Politics, and Economics at the University of North Carolina at Chapel Hill, USA. He received his PhD from MIT in 2019, and is writing a book about the foundations of deontology entitled *What We Owe to Ourselves*.

Sarah Stroud is Professor of Philosophy and Director of the Parr Center for Ethics at the University of North Carolina at Chapel Hill, USA. She has published widely in ethical theory, moral psychology, and metaethics and was a co-editor (with Hugh LaFollette, Editor-in-Chief, and John Deigh) of *The International Encyclopedia of Ethics* (9 volumes; 2013).

PUZZLES, PARADOXES, AND THOUGHT EXPERIMENTS IN PHILOSOPHY

Imaginative cases—or what might be called puzzles, paradoxes, and other thought experiments—play a central role in philosophy. This series offers students and researchers a wide range of such imaginative cases, with each volume devoted to fifty such cases in a major subfield of philosophy. Every book in the series includes: some initial background information on each case, a clear and detailed description of the case, and an explanation of the issue(s) to which the case is relevant. Key responses to the case and suggested reading lists are also included.

Recently Published Volumes:

EPISTEMOLOGY
KEVIN MCCAIN

FREE WILL AND HUMAN AGENCY
GARRETT PENDERGRAFT

PHILOSOPHY OF LANGUAGE
MICHAEL P. WOLF

AESTHETICS
MICHEL-ANTOINE XHIGNESSE

PHILOSOPHY OF MIND
TORIN ALTER, AMY KIND, AND ROBERT J. HOWELL

BIOETHICS
SEAN AAS, COLLIN O'NEIL, AND CHIARA LEPORA

ETHICAL THEORY
DANIEL MUÑOZ AND SARAH STROUD

Forthcoming Volumes:

METAPHYSICS
SAM COWLING, WESLEY D. CRAY, AND KELLY TROGDON

For a full list of published volumes in **Puzzles, Paradoxes, and Thought Experiments in Philosophy**, please visit www.routledge.com/Puzzles,Paradoxes,andThoughtExperimentsinPhilosophy/book-series/PPTEP

ETHICAL THEORY

50 PUZZLES, PARADOXES, AND THOUGHT EXPERIMENTS

Daniel Muñoz and Sarah Stroud

NEW YORK AND LONDON

Designed cover image: Daniel Mayer– Dreamy Alien Studios / © Getty Images

First published 2025
by Routledge
605 Third Avenue, New York, NY 10158

and by Routledge
4 Park Square, Milton Park, Abingdon, Oxon OX14 4RN

Routledge is an imprint of the Taylor & Francis Group, an informa business

© 2025 Daniel Muñoz and Sarah Stroud

ISBN: 978-1-032-33517-9 (hbk)
ISBN: 978-1-032-33516-2 (pbk)
ISBN: 978-1-003-31996-2 (ebk)

DOI: 10.4324/9781003319962

Typeset in Bembo
by codeMantra

CONTENTS

INTRODUCTION

Ethical theory asks some big, lofty, ancient questions. What makes for a good life? Which kinds of actions are right and which are wrong? Are we morally responsible agents or mere puppets of our own desires?

These questions are so big, so lofty, and so ancient that it's sometimes hard to know where to start. That's where this book comes in. Our goal is to get you thinking about some of the deepest questions in ethics using three engaging and intuitive methods: puzzles, paradoxes, and thought experiments.

Over the course of 11 chapters, we dip into 50 cases and conundrums, each with references for further reading and a few questions for discussion. You'll find lots of certifiable classics: Plato's **Ring of Gyges** (#36), Parfit's **Repugnant Conclusion** (#50), Thomson's **Trolley Problem** (#6), and so forth. But we've also prioritized variety, and we hope that even experts will find at least one or two new puzzles to savor.

That said, this book is very much written as an introduction. It is also supposed to be enjoyable to read. Don't think of this as 50 encyclopedia entries. Instead of laying out the state of scholarly debate, these chapters are trying to get you intrigued, to spark in you *your own* interesting questions, hypotheses, and insights. Many entries include

DOI: 10.4324/9781003319962-1

"Responses" from philosophers trying to solve this or that paradox. But we leave the last word to the reader.

We hope that the book will be useful in undergraduate moral philosophy courses, either as a source of standalone readings or as a supplement to primary sources. But you don't have to be a philosophy major, much less a philosophy professor, to understand this book.

Each chapter, and even each entry, can be read completely on its own. That said, we have tried to note (in parentheticals) some of the more important connections between different entries, and we have tried to give the book a kind of thematic arc. We start (Ch. 1) with the most wonderfully simple theory of them all: *utilitarianism*, which says that we should always do what promotes the greatest happiness for all. After considering some of the classic counterexamples, we then turn to utilitarianism's traditional rival: *deontology*—which has its own tricky cases to deal with (Ch. 2) as well as more conceptual puzzles (Chs. 3–4). The middle of the book adds in a little of that human touch: partiality towards loved ones (Ch. 5) and the components of a good life (Ch. 6). From there, we embark on an adventure into more abstract issues having to do with the logic and psychology of morality: tragic dilemmas (Ch. 7), moral motivation (Ch. 8), the nature of moral responsibility (Ch. 9), and the significance of factual and moral uncertainty (Ch. 10). Finally, we turn towards the future (Ch. 11): conscious robots, the end of humanity, and the kind of world we should want for future generations.

Ethical theory—ancient and abstruse though it may be—is *awesome*. There are not many things in the world that are so fascinating and yet so close to everyday life. We hope that this book leaves you at least a little more fascinated than you were before.

UTILITY AND CONSEQUENCES

Suppose you had a decision to make in your life. It could be a big decision—where to go to college, what career to aim for—or a more minor decision, like how to spend the weekend. What would you base your decision on? Is it possible to characterize the criteria we use when we make choices in absolutely general terms?

One compelling general answer, which seems to apply equally to both big and small decisions, is that you would decide based on *which option you think would work out best*. In other words, you would look into the future and try to imagine how things would go if you chose *this* college, or *that* career, or *those* weekend activities. If you could see that a certain choice now would cause you unhappiness now or later, you would likely steer clear of that option. You would instead select the option that seems to lead to the most happiness down the road.

A prominent ethical theory takes this method of *individual* decision-making and applies it to *moral* decisions. According to *utilitarianism*, the *morally right* choice in any situation is whichever option will lead to the most happiness overall. There is admittedly one big difference between the individual case and the moral case: when you are deciding just for yourself, it's only *your own* happiness that you consider. But when you are making a *moral* decision, it is the happiness of *everyone concerned* that you should take into account. Utilitarianism

DOI: 10.4324/9781003319962-2

sees morality as an important counterweight to our tendency to care only about ourselves (and perhaps a few other select people). For *moral* purposes, it insists, *each person's* happiness must count *equally*.

We can sum up this simple version of utilitarianism as follows. An action is *morally right* if and only if it leads to the greatest *total happiness* of all the options available to you; it is *morally wrong* to choose anything else. And when tallying up total happiness or "utility," every "unit" of happiness counts the same, regardless of whose happiness it is. In other words, utilitarianism is fundamentally *impartial*.

For utilitarianism, the moral status of an action is a function— indeed, *solely* a function—of its *outcome*, or *consequences*. For this reason, utilitarianism is often viewed as one specific version of a broader category of ethical theories called *consequentialism*. Consequentialist theories all demand that we perform the action with *the best* consequences, impartially considered. But they might have a different view than utilitarianism does on the question of which consequences are best. (For example, a non-utilitarian consequentialist theory might hold that both total happiness *and* equality make consequences better.)

Utilitarianism seems like a highly intuitive and logical ethical theory. But we present a number of puzzles in this chapter which suggest that it is neither as appealing nor as straightforward as it seems. In **#1, George and the Bioweapons**, we look at a person who has to make a decision which we would have thought purely personal, but utilitarianism has its own opinion about what he should (indeed must) do. Entries **2–4** consider some of the odder aspects of making decisions guided solely by total happiness. **The Utility Monster** (#2) presents a "monster" whose happiness prevails in every utility calculation. **Parfit's Harmless Torturers** (#3) argues that a *group* can do something horribly wrong even if every single *individual* in it acts rightly (according to utilitarianism). And **#4, Infinite Utility**, shows how weird things get when you allow *infinite* quantities of utility into the picture.

As **#1** also did, the **World Cup Accident** case in **#5** shows the disastrous effects that a utilitarian calculation of total happiness can have for a lone individual. Philosopher T. M. Scanlon, who created the example, uses it to motivate his strongly anti-utilitarian model of moral decisions when some people will benefit and others will be harmed.

1. GEORGE AND THE BIOWEAPONS

George is a chemist who is having severe trouble finding a suitable job. He is very anxious about this situation, not least because he has a spouse and kids who are relying on him for support, and his health problems are worsening under the stress. He is grateful when an older chemist who is familiar with the difficulties George is having says she may be able to pull some strings and throw a job his way. There's only one catch: the job is in a lab which develops chemical and biological weapons (CBW). If George took the job, his remit would be to create bigger and better versions of such weapons.

Everything in George shrinks from the idea of working in the field of CBW. He is deeply and instinctually opposed to chemical and biological warfare: he considers it beyond the pale to even contemplate unleashing chemical and biological agents on human beings. For George, that is a line that should never be crossed. When he conveys his strong opposition to the older chemist, she replies that she's not a particular fan of CBW either. But, she adds, if George does not get the job she thinks she knows who will. That other chemist, she says, is a real keener—and he's not deterred by any moral qualms about CBW. He will work so enthusiastically at the job that he's likely to make even *more* progress on new CBW weaponry than George would. In fact, she explains, she's suggesting the job to George not *just* out of concern for George, but also in order to keep that fellow from getting the position.

What should George do? Bernard Williams introduces this example not in order to defend a particular answer to this question, but to demonstrate that the *utilitarian* answer to it is inadequate. The utilitarian maintains that the right thing to do in any situation is whatever will lead to the largest possible total of human happiness. Let's assume that developing bigger and better CBW is likely to greatly *diminish* total human happiness. Then the conclusion is simple: that outcome simply must be prevented, to the extent one can. (There is one exception: if the only way to prevent it is to do something that would be even *worse* for overall happiness.) In this case, the other fellow getting the job will move us closer to that bad outcome—unless George intervenes. So from a utilitarian perspective, it is clearly George's duty to step in and prevent the keener from getting the job by taking it himself.

Among the factors that do *not* play a prominent role in the utilitarian's reasoning is the fact that by taking the job George would be devoting his life to something which he deems abhorrent and which runs counter to all he believes in and stands for. On top of having to spend forty hours a week designing ever more destructive chemical weapons, he'd have to find a way to live with himself the rest of the time. It seems it might destroy George as the person he is to follow this path. But utilitarianism, it appears, hardly cares.

In fairness, utilitarianism does consider the harms to George when it dictates which course of action he must follow. (It also considers the benefits, such as his having a job and therefore being able to support his family.) But these are only minor factors in the utilitarian's reasoning, because they are dwarfed by the differing impacts on humanity as a whole of the more vigorous vs. the less vigorous pursuit of next-gen CBW weapons. If one person is made miserable by having to work in a CBW lab, that is after all pretty small beans from the point of view of the universe.

This example effectively brings out a more general moral: that utilitarianism generates what we might call an *unlimited requirement of prevention*. According to utilitarianism,

> Whenever there is some bad state of affairs that you could prevent, it is morally wrong of you not to prevent it—unless you could do even more good from an impartial standpoint by doing something else instead.

In other words, if you are in a position to forestall some bad outcome, you *must* interrupt whatever you are doing to forestall it. (There is one exception, which we will discuss in the next paragraph.) Note that this requirement does not depend on you being the *sole* person who can prevent this bad outcome. If there are many people in a position to prevent it, it is equally incumbent on each of them to drop what they are doing and prevent it. (Once one of them does, of course, the ethical situation changes, since the danger has now receded.)

The only exception to this unlimited requirement of prevention is when whatever you are doing instead is *so* beneficial to human happiness that you are obligated to continue doing it. But this is unlikely in the case of poor George. If he rejects this job, he might eventually end up using his chemistry training to work on dishwashing detergent or some other innocuous thing instead. We can charitably grant that this might modestly advance total human happiness. But from a utilitarian perspective it is far more important that he block the CBW advances which the keener is likely to make. If George's situation is a dilemma, it is not one for the utilitarian.

A non-utilitarian might think the above outlook turns each of us essentially into a servant of the greater good. Rather than living our own life, we must instead be a kind of first responder to potential disasters not of our own making, on call 24 hours a day. And we are expected to play this role even when the response we are called upon to make runs counter to our own values and moral convictions. Williams points out that this stance contravenes the ideal of *integrity*, or living in a way that exemplifies and harmonizes with who you most fundamentally are. He concludes that utilitarianism "makes integrity as a value more or less unintelligible" (1973: 99).

Classic Presentation

Bernard Williams, "A Critique of Utilitarianism," in J. J. C. Smart and Bernard Williams, *Utilitarianism: For and Against* (Cambridge: Cambridge University Press, 1973): Section 3.

Responses and Other Treatments

Frances Myrna Kamm, *Intricate Ethics: Rights, Responsibilities, and Permissible Harm* (Oxford: Oxford University Press, 2007): Ch. 10, particularly Section X.A.

J. E. J. Altham and Ross Harrison, eds., *World, Mind, and Ethics: Essays on the Ethical Philosophy of Bernard Williams*, with "Replies" by Bernard Williams (Cambridge: Cambridge University Press, 1995): particularly p. 211.

Questions for Reflection

1.   What might a plausible *limited* requirement of prevention look like?

2.   Do you think *integrity* in Williams' sense is a value that morality must accommodate? What about the "integrity" of a bad person with bad ends?

2. THE UTILITY MONSTER

Take a moment to think of a truly, undeniably *terrible* ethical view. What comes to mind?

You might be thinking of a noxious ideology, like Nazi anti-semitism, white supremacy, or sexist beliefs about the "proper role" of women. Or maybe you're thinking of everyday jerks, like the narcissist who sees himself as the center of the universe.

One thing terrible views almost always have in common is that they are deeply committed to *inequality*. The sexist man thinks that men matter more than women, just as the narcissist thinks that he matters more than everyone else.

So it's no wonder that utilitarians love to emphasize that their view, in a crucial sense, treats people as equals. For the utilitarian, what matters is *total utility*—the sum of everybody's happiness. Because everyone's utility counts the same towards the total, everybody matters equally. If you're choosing between a big benefit to one person or small benefit to another, you have to give the bigger benefit—no matter the race, sex, or religion of anyone involved. Utilitarians are therefore deeply opposed to saying that anyone's utility matters more than anybody else's. To use a slogan from Derek Parfit:"Each counts for one" (1978: 301).[1]

The slogan does—by universal admission—sound cool. But critics worry that utilitarianism is still "embarrassed" by a subtler way in which it approves of inequalities (Nozick 1974: 41). This problem pops out most dramatically when we imagine a certain kind of imaginary creature.

A *utility monster* is a being who receives "enormously greater gains of utility from any sacrifice of others than these others lose;" the worry is that utilitarianism "seems to require that we all be sacrificed in the monster's maw" (Nozick 1974: 41).

To illustrate: Suppose your friend Sally would enjoy eating a sandwich. Should you take away Sally's sandwich and give it to the utility monster? According to utilitarianism, yes! Whatever enjoyment Sally gets from the sandwich, we're supposed to imagine that the monster gets *vastly more* enjoyment. Think of the utility monster as the world's most efficient utility generator. However much utility you might create by giving a resource to somebody, that will always pale in comparison to the awesome sums of utility you would generate by just giving the goods to the monster instead. So *of course* the sandwich should be snatched from Sally, along with everybody else's sandwiches, and indeed all other goodies of any kind. In fact, there is no end to the sacrifices that we have to make to the utility monster. Think about it. Even if Sally is loving her life, and even if she would hate to be eaten, we can imagine that the utility monster would *really, really* love to eat Sally, and would *really, really* hate it if we kept her away. In this way, the utility monster's utility comes to trump Sally's—along with anybody else's. Thus we should all be flung into the monster's maw.

In this way, utilitarianism can favor even the most unequal *distributions* of utility. Here, the utility monster gets everything; we get nothing. But utilitarianism still in a sense counts the monster *itself* as the equal of anybody else. The monster's utility doesn't get special weight. The monster only gets the goods because it always has, objectively, the most to gain or lose. Think of it like this: If Sally gets 1 utility point from her sandwich, the utility monster gets 2. That's why it gets the sandwich—not because 1 point for the utility monster counts for double, but because its 2 points count for twice as much as Sally's single point. Everyone's utility matters equally, in a sense, but the result is that utility is distributed in a totally unequal way.

Summing things up, utilitarians believe in one kind of equality, which we can call:

> The Principle of Equal Weight
> A certain amount of utility matters the same no matter who enjoys it.

But this leads them to deny, in a spectacular fashion, another attractive kind of equality, which we might call:

> The Principle of Equal Distribution
> It's better, at least in one way, if people's utility levels are closer to being equal.

If we are against a distribution that gives everything to the monster, we can't be utilitarians.

RESPONSES

Not so fast! Before we draw any big conclusions, we have to ask if the monster is really as "embarrassing" as it initially seems.

To start: Does the idea of a utility monster even make sense? For the thought experiment to work, the monster must be capable of enjoying *mind-boggling* amounts of utility—more than the rest of the world combined—and all within the slender confines of a single life. Is that really possible? If not—and there is an upper limit to any being's utility—then the utility monster may turn out to be a harmless bogeyman, made up to scare impressionable ethics students.

This reply has some force. If the monster is supposed to be a kind of higher being, whose pleasures outclass ours just as ours outclass the crude pleasures of lobsters, then utilitarians can respond that such a being is impossible. But that's just one kind of monster. It's easier to imagine a monster who is just like a human, only much longer-lived. Then it seems we can perfectly appreciate the problem. Suppose that humanity, as a collective, stands to enjoy a net total of 10 quintillion years of pleasure. Then we can imagine a choice: Either humanity enjoys that pleasure, or we sacrifice everyone to the utility monster, who then enjoys 100 quintillion years of pleasure. The utilitarian has to say: sacrifice everyone! But this seems, for lack of a better word, monstrous.

What can utilitarians say for themselves?

Strategy #1: try to show that helping the utility monster isn't as monstrous as it seems. Notice that 100 quintillion years is a long, long time. Perhaps we are reticent to side with the monster simply because we can't wrap our minds around the sheer length of the pleasures it will feel? (Some utilitarians will say a similar thing about the sheer intensity of pleasures felt by the "higher being" version of the monster.) But if we're unable to appreciate big numbers, why are we so sure that it's better for the many, many *non-monsters* to enjoy their quintillions of years of pleasure?

Strategy #2: try to show that the monster is a problem for everyone. Consider, for example, the *egalitarian*, who thinks that equal distribution matters. The egalitarian may think that equality sometimes matters more than total utility. But surely it doesn't *always* matter more. If a kid falls and breaks her nose, we shouldn't all break our own noses just to keep things even. But if total utility can sometimes outweigh equality, then why not in the case of the utility monster, where forsaking the monster *massively* decreases the total utility the world could have had?

And a version of that question faces almost everyone in ethical theory. Whether you're a utilitarian, egalitarian, or deontologist, if you think that total utility is even *part* of what matters, you are going to have to grapple with the monster. Sacrificing to the monster is, of course, a sacrifice—something is lost. The puzzle is to explain why the things we stand to lose should matter more than the awesome, monstrous amounts of utility we stand to gain.

Classic Presentation

Robert Nozick, *Anarchy, State, and Utopia* (New York: Basic Books, 1974): 41.

Responses and Other Treatments

Richard Yetter Chappell, "Negative Utility Monsters," *Utilitas* **33** (2021): 417–421.

Further Reading

Derek Parfit, "Innumerate Ethics," *Philosophy & Public Affairs* **7** (1978): 285–301.

Questions for Reflection

1.   In this section, we have been talking about *total utilitarianism*, which—as you'd guess—tells us to maximize total utility. But consider *future average utilitarianism*, which tells us to maximize the average utility of those who exist after our action is complete. Would this view also recommend sacrificing to the monster? What about *timeless average utilitarianism*, which tells us to maximize the average level of utility among people who ever did or will exist?

2.   We have been considering a *positive utility monster*, on whom we can bestow many years of pleasant life. But there could also be a *negative utility monster*, whom we can rescue from many years of horrible torture (Chappell 2021). For example, suppose that we can save the monster from 100 quintillion years of torture by depriving humanity of its future, which would contain 10 quintillion years of pleasure. Do you think we should help the negative utility monster? Can you think of

any reasons for helping the negative utility monster that don't also count in favor of helping the positive utility monster?

3.   In our discussion, we were often talking about "pleasure" and "utility" as though they were the same thing. But you might think that there is more to life than pleasure—knowledge, friendship, achievement, love, and so on. (See Ch. 7, **Well-Being and Value**.) If you believe in these sorts of goods beyond pleasure, is it still plausible that a solitary being could have a better life than the rest of humanity combined? Why or why not?

3. PARFIT'S HARMLESS TORTURERS

Sometimes, a group of people can do something awful—like voting in a tyrant or wrecking their environment—even though no individual in the group makes a decisive difference. When this happens, let's call it a *collective action problem.*

For an ethical theorist, collective action problems are puzzling. On the one hand, they are clearly problems. On the other hand, it's often unclear *who* is the problem. Sometimes, *no* individual seems to be at fault!

To illustrate this puzzling duality, Derek Parfit (1984) came up with a pair of unforgettable thought experiments. Back in:

The Bad Old Days
There were 1,000 victims, each of whom started the day with a mild pain. For each victim, there was a torturer, who had his own switch. When a torturer turned the switch, his victim's pain would be increased by a small amount—too small to be perceptible. But each torturer turned his switch 1,000 times, with the result that every victim spent the day in agony.

Here we have a bad collective action, but it's obvious that we can blame the individuals. Everyone's a torturer!

Contrast that with:

The Harmless Torturers
It's like the Bad Old Days, but with a twist: instead of turning a switch 1,000 times, each torturer presses a button that turns all 1,000 switches one time.

Here we have the same bad result: 1,000 people being tortured. But this time, how could we possibly blame anyone? No *individual* does any *torturing*, since no one makes his victims perceptibly worse off. Individually, they are harmless; together, they are torturers.

That's a shocking paradox. Our ethical theories—applied to certain collective actions—let people get away with torture.

Worse, lots of *real* collective action problems seem a lot like Parfit's torturers. Take air pollution. Together, the world emits so many billions of tons of CO_2 that we are literally raising sea levels.

But when you drive your car, you barely emit a few kilograms.[2] Your emissions seem diffuse and imperceptible—like harmless torture. You might conclude that you don't have to worry about your contribution. But by that reasoning *no one* has to worry, and we will *all* suffer.

RESPONSES

There are two ways out of this problem: (1) show that each Harmless Torturer does something wrong after all; (2) show that real collective action problems aren't like harmless torture.

Let's start with the torturers themselves. Is there a way for us to blame them? A natural thought is that each is responsible for his *share* of the harm that they do *together*—which means each of the 1,000 torturers is responsible for one victim's torture, just like in the Bad Old Days.

But this "Share-of-the-Total View" can't possibly be right, as Parfit (1984: 68) showed with another pair of examples. In:

The First Rescue Mission
100 miners are trapped, and at least four people are needed for a rescue mission. Four volunteers are already on their way. You can either join them as a fifth or go singlehandedly rescue another 10 miners elsewhere.

What should you do? The Share-of-the-Total View says to join the team, since you'll get *credit* for saving 20 lives. (Your "share" is 1/5th of 100.) But then only 100 survive rather than 110. Here, the Share-of-the-Total View overrates participating in collective actions. The view also sometimes *underrates* it. In:

The Second Rescue Mission
The 100 miners are trapped as before, but this time, the rescue mission will require five people. You can either join the big mission as the fifth or go off to single-handedly rescue 50 others, a mission that needs only one person.

Here, the Share-of-the-Total View says you should save the 50 alone, since you would only get credit for saving 20 if you joined the team. But then only 50 survive rather than 100.

So much for sharing. Another way to blame a Harmless Torturer is to say that even imperceptible pains are bad. They still, according to

Parfit's definition, *make a difference* to how their victims feel. It's just a difference that the victim can't reliably detect, like how you can't notice subtle shifts in a violin's pitch. This seems like a fair point. But even if 1,000 tiny pains are bad, how bad could they be? None of the 1,000 victims can even notice the difference! Even if the Harmless Torturers' acts aren't harmless, that doesn't show that they're even remotely comparable to torture, which means that there isn't much blame to go around. (For more on how little pains don't always add up, see **#5, World Cup Accident**.)

A third way to blame the Harmless Torturers is to say, even if their individual actions don't have bad *consequences*, they are still forbidden by a *deontological* principle. A nice idea—but which principle? Any candidate principle will come with its own problems. Consider Immanuel Kant's fundamental principle of morality, the Categorical Imperative: "*act only in accordance with that maxim through which you can at the same time will that it become a universal law*" (4:421). Roughly, this says you should judge an action by how things would turn out if *everybody* did it. That seems to get the right answer for the Harmless Torturers. If *everyone* presses their button, the result is just as bad as the Bad Old Days—so the Harmless Torturers do wrong. But what about the First Rescue Mission, where the solution is for you to save the 10 while the others save the 100? In this case, there's not *any* single course of action that we should all be taking. As a guide to collective action problems, the Categorical Imperative seems incomplete at best.

What does this mean for real world collective action problems—voting, pollution, and so on? Well, if we want to say that the individuals who contribute to these problems are doing something wrong, and we can't say the same about the Harmless Torturers, we had better find some difference between the real-world cases and harmless torture.

There is a lot to say here, but let's at least consider one important difference. The Harmless Torturers each make an imperceptible difference. But an individual voter, for example, obviously *can* make a huge difference in an important election. Even the biggest election can be decided by a single vote—in which case *every single voter* on the winning side makes a difference, since any of them could have flipped the outcome by switching votes. To put it another way, the voters in favor of the good candidate have to reach a threshold corresponding to the number of votes they need to win. Below that threshold, none of the individual votes makes a difference. But each voter can trigger a change if their vote plays an essential role in helping their candidate cross the threshold. Shelly Kagan (2011) calls collective action problems like this *triggering cases*. In such cases, the chances of triggering a good outcome can (at least in principle) give you a strong moral reason to vote for the better candidate. Even if your vote is probably not going to trigger a victory, when the stakes are high enough, and when the chances of triggering are not *too* terribly low, you had better vote!

In the wake of Kagan's work on triggering cases, ethical theorists have explored a bunch of interesting questions. Are all collective action problems, deep down, triggering cases? Can we estimate the chances that someone's vote will trigger a victory in a real-world election? Can we expect any help from deontological principles? Could it be that collective actions are wrong even though no individual contributor acts wrongly?

The answers, for now, remain up in the air. And so the Harmless Torturers remain a source of inspiration—and, for some of us, consternation!

Classic Presentation

Derek Parfit, *Reasons and Persons* (Oxford: Oxford University Press, 1984): Ch. 3.

Responses and Other Treatments

Shelly Kagan, "Do I Make a Difference?" *Philosophy & Public Affairs* **39** (2011): 105–141.

Zach Barnett, "Why You Should Vote to Change the Outcome," *Philosophy & Public Affairs* **48** (2020): 422–446. (Barnett ingeniously argues that the expected value of voting in a big election is much higher than you might think!)

Brian Hedden, "Consequentialism and Collective Action," *Ethics* **130** (2020): 530–554.

Julia Nefsky, "How You Can Help, Without Making a Difference," *Philosophical Studies* **174** (2017): 2743–2767. (Nefsky argues that you have a reason to participate in the production of collective goods even if you won't make a difference to whether those goods are produced.)

Further Reading

Immanuel Kant, *Groundwork of the Metaphysics of Morals*, in his *Practical Philosophy*, Mary Gregor, ed. and trans. (Cambridge: Cambridge University Press, 1996): 37–108. Allen Wood's Introduction at pp. 39–40 provides some useful background.

(There are many translations of Kant's works, but they should all include the standardized page numbers which we have used in the citation above.)

Questions for Reflection

1. Can you revise the Share-of-the-Total View so that it no longer overrates contributing to collective actions? Does your revision help with the problem of underrating contributions to collective action? (Can any version of the view solve this problem?)

2. Why might it be important to contribute to a collective good (or abstain from a collective bad) even when one's action does not make a difference to whether that good is produced? For example, is there any good moral reason to vote when you are unable to change the outcome of the election?

3. Here's a more challenging question. We might be tempted to say that it's wrong for each Harmless Torturer to spread 1,000 pain among 1,000 people, even though we think that's nowhere near as bad as *concentrating* lots of pain on a single individual. But this leads to another kind of trouble. Suppose we pair each torturer with a unique victim—say, T1 gets V1, T2 gets V2, and so on up to T1000 and V1000. Now each torturer must choose between concentrating 900 units of pain in his victim or spreading out 1,000 units of pain evenly among all of the victims. If it's far worse to concentrate pain, each torturer should spread thinly. But then they together cause each victim 1,000 units of pain, whereas if each had concentrated his torture, the victims would have only 900 units of pain. Call this the Hard Version of the Harmless Torturers. What do you think the torturers should do in this case?

4. INFINITE UTILITY

For us mortals, life is short, and while it has its ups and downs, they are only so good and only so bad. Our choices tend to involve merely *finite* utilities. But infinite utilities, to the extent that they are coherent, raise strange and beautiful paradoxes for utilitarianism. They may even teach us something about why utility is so precious in the first place.

Utilitarians say you must do whatever maximizes utility. If sitting on the couch adds no utility to the world, whereas donating to charity adds 5, then donate! If letting the runaway trolley crash into five workers would subtract 50 utility from the world, whereas pushing a large man in front of its course would subtract only 10, then push!

You might not *like* what utilitarians say about these finite cases. But at least the stuff they say is principled.

In infinite cases, however, it is less clear what utilitarians should say. Imagine, for example, that your civilization has discovered infinitely renewable energy. As things stand, there will be infinitely many generations in the future, each of which will enjoy some net positive utility—say, at least 100 utility per person. Now suppose you can activate a bioweapon which will *halve the utility of every future person*. Intuitively, that's wrong. Or is it? Recall that utilitarianism tells us to maximize total utility. But the weapon doesn't reduce the total at all. Either way, the total amount will be the same—specifically, infinity!

This is a serious problem. When all of our options lead to infinite utilities, utilitarianism "loses most of its power to discriminate among actions" (Vallentyne 1993: 212). But *surely* we can discriminate between the future where you activate the bioweapon and the future where you don't! The challenge, for utilitarians, is to modify their view so that it's more discriminating in infinite cases, without giving up on the spirit of the view.

What should utilitarians do?

RESPONSES

One pioneering idea comes from Peter Vallentyne: rather than looking at grand totals of utility across all of eternity, zoom in on the details of the timeline.

Think about the bioweapon case. What makes it wrong to activate the weapon? The heart of the problem is that you are lowering all utilities in the future. This problem disappears, of course, when we are just looking at grand totals. But not when we peer into particular moments. If you activate the weapon, then at each future time, there will be less utility than there would otherwise have been. In other words, the "cumulative utility" of each future time—the sum of all utilities up to that point—will be forever lower if you use the bioweapon.

The idea of cumulative utilities leads naturally to Vallentyne's principle, which we can call:

Forever Better
Action A produces more utility than Action B if doing A leads to more cumulative utility at each future time. (See Vallentyne 1993: 214.)

But as Vallentyne notices, this principle doesn't always go far enough. Imagine that activating a modified bioweapon *briefly* increases cumulative utility: suppose that, in the few minutes before the bad effects kick in, the weapon emits a pleasing whirr and fragrant aroma. Now it's no longer "forever better" to refrain from using the weapon, but surely the utilitarian still wants to recommend against using the weapon. Thankfully, there are clever ways around this problem (see Vallentyne 1993: 215). But there is a deeper problem lurking elsewhere. Sometimes, utilitarians might want to recommend against an action *even though it leads to greater cumulative utility at every future time.* This is where infinite ethics gets interesting!

Consider a thought experiment (inspired by James Cain's "Sphere of Suffering" (1995)). Imagine there are infinitely many people—P1, P2, and so on—who have made it to the infinite afterlife. Now you decide their fates. The first option is to start off everyone in Heaven. If you do this, then each person starts off enjoying themselves in Heaven, but every day, one more person is sent down to Hell to suffer for the rest of eternity. On Day 1, P1 descends; on Day 2, P2 descends; and so on. Your second option is the reverse: everyone starts off suffering in Hell, but on Day 1, P1 ascends to Heaven; on Day 2, P2 ascends; and so on.

Which afterlife would lead to more utility? Or, to put it another way, which afterlife should utilitarians recommend? (It's worth pausing and thinking this through for yourself. To keep things simple, it might help to suppose that a day in Heaven is only finitely good, and a day in Hell is only finitely bad.)

On the one hand, there is a powerful argument for starting people off in Heaven. On any given day, there will only be finitely many people in Hell while infinitely many people remain in Heaven. So the amount of cumulative utility will be forever better if you start everyone off in Heaven. More broadly, every day will involve *infinite happiness*, and only *finite suffering*.

On the other hand, there is *also* a powerful argument for starting everyone off in Hell. Instead of thinking about how much utility there has been up to each *time*, think about how much utility there will be in the life of each *person*. Each person will suffer for as long as they are still in Hell. But each person, no matter how high their number, only has to wait a finite amount of time before they ascend to Heaven—and once they're in, they're happy for the infinite remainder of time. That means each person's *life* has *infinite happiness*, and only *finite suffering*.

So, which should we pick? Starting people in Hell gives each person, over time, infinite happiness, but starting them in Heaven gives the universe, at every time, infinite happiness. What matters more: totals at times, or totals within each life?

In normal finite cases, where we are deciding the finite fates of a certain group of existing people, this distinction never comes up. Maximizing utility across time *just is* maximizing utility across persons. Utilitarians might even be tempted to think of these as just the same idea in different words. But infinite cases reveal that there is a fundamental moral difference here. If we just care about having more utility present in the world at each time, we would start people off in Heaven and thereby *infinitely lower every single person's utility*. And if we just care about raising each individual's utility, we would start people off in Hell and thereby *infinitely lower the amount of utility in the universe at every future time*.

We have a choice. We can focus utilitarianism on times, or on persons. Thanks to the weirdness of infinity—and let's be honest, infinity is weird!—we can see that there are really two types of utilitarians. While they might sound alike when talking about finite choices, in fact their views have radically different implications.

Classic Presentation

Peter Vallentyne, "Utilitarianism and Infinite Utility," *Australasian Journal of Philosophy* **71** (1993): 212–217.

Responses and Other Treatments

Antony Duff, "Pascal's Wager and Infinite Utilities," *Analysis* **46** (1986): 107–109.
(Pascal's Wager, which involves the infinite goodness of a shot at going to
Heaven, is probably the most famous argument involving infinite utility.)
James Cain, "Infinite Utility," *Australasian Journal of Philosophy* **73** (1995): 401–404.
Mark T. Nelson, "Utilitarian Eschatology," *American Philosophical Quarterly* **28**
(1991): 339–346.

Questions for Reflection

1. Do you think that, according to the best version of utilitarian-
    ism, we should start people off in Heaven or in Hell? Why?
2. Can you think of a way to modify Forever Better to deal with
    cases like the modified bioweapon (which briefly boosts future
    utilities, then forever squashes them)?

5. WORLD CUP ACCIDENT

Oh no! While millions of people worldwide are watching the World Cup, there's been an accident in the transmitter room of the Cup's TV broadcaster. An employee, Jones, has been injured by some electrical equipment which has fallen on him. His hand is all smashed up, he can't move, and he is receiving extremely painful electrical shocks from the damaged equipment. He needs to be rescued from the transmitter room. Unfortunately, in order for us to rescue him, we would need to turn off the transmitter—and thereby stop all transmission of the World Cup—for fifteen minutes. The match will be over in an hour. Should we wait?

Philosopher T. M. Scanlon, who created this example, has a clear answer: we should not wait. And he maintains that this is the correct answer regardless of how many people are currently watching the match. While one million, or five million, or even a hundred million people may be frustrated beyond belief to see the Cup match go dark for fifteen minutes, we should nonetheless rescue Jones right now.

Part of Scanlon's point here is to draw a contrast with utilitarianism, since Scanlon thinks a utilitarian analysis would be bound to support the opposite conclusion. As we have seen, utilitarianism evaluates possible actions solely in terms of their outcomes, notably for total human happiness. In this situation we have two choices: rescue Jones now, or wait. Waiting will have at least one bad consequence: Jones will receive extremely painful shocks for an hour. But not waiting will have a million, or five million, bad consequences, because every World Cup fan who will be left in the dark for the next fifteen minutes will be extremely frustrated. Which of these bad outcomes constitutes a greater reduction in total human happiness? Jones' suffering for the next hour is certainly worse than the suffering any *individual* World Cup fan will experience from the match cutting out. But when you add a million, or five million, of those frustrations *together*, you get more *total* unhappiness than Jones will experience from his ordeal.

So it seems correct to say that the utilitarian would tell us to wait—although it will depend on how many people are watching. Jones might have a chance of prevailing if a suitably small number of people were tuned in—if, say, it was a rerun of an 80s sitcom in the middle of the night, rather than the World Cup. But in the circumstances we've described, it's not a close call.

Scanlon wants to show how an alternative, non-utilitarian method of moral reasoning validates the verdict that we should save Jones now, regardless of the number of people watching. Scanlon's own approach to moral theory, called *contractualism*, prescribes reasoning through the case in a very different way from utilitarianism. Rather than asking which of two *actions* we should perform, Scanlon starts from the question which of two *general principles* we should adopt. We are to use the thought experiment that all stakeholders are sitting around a table, seeking general agreement on the principle we will adopt to guide such situations.

One of the candidate principles before us would require us to save a person in a situation like Jones'. "This principle might hold that if one can save a person from serious pain and injury at the cost of inconveniencing others or interfering with their amusement, then one must do so no matter how numerous these others may be" (1998: 235). Scanlon does not spell out the other principle under consideration, but perhaps it says that the enjoyment of a *very large number* of people can take priority over what would in other circumstances be a mandatory rescue.

How are we to choose which of these two principles to adopt? Very significantly, Scanlon does *not* propose that we settle this by majority rule. (That would presumably yield a verdict paralleling that of utilitarianism.) Instead, we are to imagine going around the table and allowing each person to *object*, from his standpoint, to one or the other of these principles. In the case of principle 2, Jones will have a very strong and legitimate objection to it: he will be much worse off if we select principle 2 than if we adopt principle 1. The World Cup fans around the table, by contrast, will all object to principle 1. Each of them will say that *he* will be worse off if we select principle 1, since that principle prescribes interrupting his enjoyment to save Jones. (It's actually not clear that each fan would be worse off *overall* if we adopt principle 1, since they might need rescuing someday too—a possibility we'll return to shortly. But let's suppose they discount the possibility of ending up in a situation like Jones'.)

Given that pattern of objections, which principle ought we select? We should first consider how *strong* each person's objection is. Jones has a *major* objection to principle 2, whereas each World Cup fan has a comparatively *minor* objection to principle 1. Scanlon maintains that we should now choose which principle to adopt in the following way. With respect to each principle, we note the magnitude of the *strongest* objection that was raised to it. If the strongest objection that was made to principle 1 is a fairly weak objection, whereas the strongest objection that was made to principle 2 is quite a powerful objection, then we ought to select principle 1, regardless of *how many* people voiced their (comparatively weak) objection to it. The idea is to choose the principle which is *least unacceptable* to the person to whom it is *most unacceptable*.

Scanlon's method does *not*, as utilitarianism did, aggregate the complaints of all the World Cup fans into a huge mass of unhappiness. Rather, it is as if Jones' objection to principle 2 is measured against the objections of each other individual *on a one-to-one basis*. If we imagine the *pair* of Jones and a single World Cup fan selecting a principle to govern such situations, it would not be reasonable for the fan to insist they adopt principle 2, given Jones' clearly weightier objection to principle 1. For Scanlon, multiplying the number of people around the table does not change this fundamental geometry of comparing one against one. The strongest objection raised will determine which principle to choose, even if that objection is raised by only one person.

Scanlon's contractualism offers an intriguing alternative to utilitarianism. One issue that commentators have pressed, though, is whether the contractualist approach is well equipped to handle cases of risk and uncertainty, where we don't know in advance what the objections of each person may be. (See Chapter 10 for more about uncertainty.) Consider for instance the decision whether or not to mandate vaccination against a dangerous pathogen. Suppose we are confident that the population as a whole will be far better off if we mandate vaccination, but we also know that *someone* (we don't know who) is likely to have an unknown allergic reaction to the vaccine and suffer serious medical consequences. As we sit around the table *now*, nobody thinks *she* will be the person to have complications, so no one objects very strongly to the vaccination program and it is adopted. But if we imagine sitting around the table once all the results of the vaccination program are *known*, the one person who suffered the serious complications would have a retroactive objection stronger than anyone else's, and that objection would suffice to veto the whole program.

Classic Presentation

T. M. Scanlon, *What We Owe to Each Other* (Cambridge: Harvard University Press, 1998): Ch. 5, especially Section 9.

Responses and Other Treatments

T. M. Scanlon, "Contractualism and Utilitarianism," in Amartya Sen and Bernard Williams, eds., *Utilitarianism and Beyond* (Cambridge: Cambridge University Press, 1982): 103–128.

Thomas Nagel, "One-to-One," *London Review of Books* **21** (1999): www.lrb. co.uk/the-paper/v21/n03/thomas-nagel/one-to-one

Derek Parfit, "Justifiability to Each Person," *Ratio* **16** (2003): 368–390.

Further Reading

Johann Frick, "Contractualism and Social Risk," *Philosophy & Public Affairs* **43** (2015): 175–223.

Joe Horton, "Always Aggregate," *Philosophy and Public Affairs* **46** (2018): 160–174.

Alex Voorhoeve, "How Should We Aggregate Competing Claims?" *Ethics* **125** (2014): 64–87.

Questions for Reflection

1. Does Scanlon's example rely on the idea that watching the World Cup is a trivial matter?

2. Scanlon maintains that "serious pain and injury" ground a *weighty* objection to any principle which would allow them to go unaddressed. Are there other things that you think should be granted the same status?

3. In the vaccination case, do you think the contractualist should consider the objections *before* or the objections *after* to be the relevant ones? Would this choice deliver (what you think is) the correct answer about the vaccine program?

NOTES

1 Parfit was not himself a utilitarian, but he often had influential arguments that pushed ethical theory in a utilitarian direction. In the passage we quoted above, Parfit was defending the utilitarian's view that "the numbers count" when deciding which of two groups—one small, one big—to save from equal-sized harms. See **#17, David and the Scarce Drug**, for more on this question.
2 Burning one gallon of gasoline emits under one kilogram (2.2 pounds) of CO_2, per the EPA.

KILLING, LETTING DIE, AND TROLLEY PROBLEMS

Utilitarianism, like consequentialism more generally, has been accused of being far too simple. Morality seems to be about more than producing the goods and avoiding the bads, since it often seems to matter *how* we bring about our ends. It's wrong to kill and use people, for instance, even for the sake of the greatest happiness for the greatest number.

This is the core idea of modern *deontology*. By going beyond the idea that only ends matter, deontologists have sought to do justice to a whole host of commonsense moral judgments that are at best an awkward fit with utilitarianism. To give one famous example: a doctor may not kill her patient for spare parts, even if those parts could be used to save five other patients, who would then go on to live wonderfully happy lives.

But deontologists have to deal with an awkward truth of their own. While it is easy to see that there is something troubling about the doctor's choice, it is almost unbelievably hard to say *what exactly* makes it wrong. The simple, powerful answers tend to invite simple, powerful counterexamples. And the more careful answers can be so complicated that it's hard to see what they're getting at and where they're coming from. Utilitarians may have to worry about oversimplifying—but deontologists have to worry about overcomplicating.

DOI: 10.4324/9781003319962-3

We begin this chapter with the famous *Trolley Problem*, which makes trouble for the simplest and punchiest deontological principle of all: that killing someone is worse than merely letting them die. The first entry focuses on a thought experiment known as the **Bystander at the Switch** (#6), arguably the most famous ethical example in the world. Next, we consider in detail one of the main attempts to solve the Trolley Problem, Judith Jarvis Thomson's "distributive exemption," which she develops using her example of pushing a man off a **Footbridge** (#7)—arguably the most discussed ethical example among 20th-century philosophers.

But the deontologist has more to worry about than "trolleyology." Some ethical theorists argue that even the most basic deontological principles have nothing going for them. It's not just hard to draw the line between wrong and permissible types of killings: the idea that there's *anything* distinctively bad about killings is based on an illusion, according to James Rachels. Rachels' argument focuses on a famous pair of thought experiments, involving drowning a child as opposed to letting a child drown—both of which seem rather nasty (**Drowning and Letting Drown, #8**). Perhaps even more famous is a pair of examples meant to illustrate the difference between intentionally killing someone (as a part of one's plan) and killing someone merely as a side-effect of one's intention; this is the duo of the Terror Bomber, who targets a civilian population that happens to be next to a munitions factory, and the Tactical Bomber, who targets a munitions factory that happens to be next to a civilian population (**The Tactical Bomber and the Terror Bomber, #9**). The same targets are bombed, and yet many deontologists would say that the Terror Bombing is much harder to justify. The puzzle is how to make the charge stick.

Finally, we loop back to the Trolley Problem. If we complicate our principles to deal with the above problems, will they still be worth defending? Or will they become so technical and complex as to be disconnected from our most powerful moral intuitions? This is **The Meta-Trolley Problem** (#10), and it remains to be seen what deontologists will do to solve it.

Taken together, these puzzles and examples show that there will be no clean getaway from utilitarianism. As flexible and subtle as deontology can be, it has a tendency to get *messy*.

6. THE TROLLEY PROBLEM, PART I:
BYSTANDER AT THE SWITCH

No thought experiment in the history of philosophy has made a bigger splash than the Bystander at the Switch—AKA, the "Trolley Problem."

Bystander at the Switch
Imagine a runaway trolley hurtling towards five innocent workers struck on a main track. The driver is out cold (perhaps he fainted under pressure). Now, it is up to you, a Bystander, to act. By pulling a lever, you can turn the trolley on to a side track, saving the five. The only problem: turning the trolley will cause it to strike a sixth worker, stuck on the side track.

Is it wrong to pull the lever? Or may you intervene?

The Bystander at the Switch has in recent years become a runaway meme, with seemingly endless variations used to illustrate all sorts of dilemmas. There has also been something of a backlash, as people ask why ethical theorists would spend their days debating gruesome hypotheticals.

So what's the Trolley Problem about? And does it matter for ethics?

The problem begins with Philippa Foot. In a legendary paper, originally published in 1967, Foot argues that there is more to morality than bringing about good outcomes; it also matters how we bring those outcomes about.

Suppose we have to decide how to use the last remaining dose of a life-saving drug. We could save one patient who needs the whole dose, or we could save five others, who need only one fifth each. In such a case, Foot thinks we not only *may* save the five: we *must*. "We feel bound to let one man die rather than many if that is our only choice" (1967/2002: 24). But what if instead the choice is whether to *kill* the one patient, so that we may use his "spare parts" to save five others who each need different transplants?

Foot thinks it is wrong to harvest the man's organs to save five, but not wrong to let the single patient die. Why? Her answer is that the "negative duty" not to do harm tends to outweigh the "positive duty" to give aid. It's wrong to harvest the patient's organs because that would be killing someone rather than letting five die. But it's fine to give the drug to the five because that isn't killing anyone; it's *letting one die* rather than *letting five die*. In such a clash of positive duties, the bigger duty wins; in a clash between negative and positive duties, the negative duty probably wins. (With some possible exceptions, as in the case of killing one to save a trillion.)

Now comes the first-ever trolley case. Foot thinks her view can also explain her example of the "tram driver." The trolley driver (as he's now known) is at the helm of a vehicle hurtling towards five workers, and his choice is whether to turn towards a side track where the trolley would instead strike just one worker. In this case, Foot thinks you will agree that it is fine to turn the trolley *even though you kill the worker*. But she can explain this. Turning the trolley kills one person; *not* turning kills five people. The driver is killing either way, so he might as well cut down on carnage. Turn that trolley!

Foot's view is beautifully simple. From just two ideas—(1) saving more lives is better, and (2) killing is worse than letting die—she can explain when it's wrong to take lifesaving action.

Might it be too simple? Enter: Judith Jarvis Thomson and her Bystander at the Switch (1986: 96). Recall that the Bystander didn't start up the trolley; if it crashes into the five, the Bystander will not have killed anybody. If the Bystander intervenes, however, he will have *killed* the worker on the side track. Foot's view seems to imply that the Bystander may *not* turn the trolley. Thomson thinks—and most would agree—that turning the trolley would be permissible. (Note: she isn't saying the Bystander *has to* turn the trolley; only that he *may*.)

Why is the Bystander permitted to pull the lever, while the surgeon may not cut up her patient? Both are killers who save five lives. What's the moral difference? The task of answering this question is what Thomson calls *The Trolley Problem*, though "Trolley Problem" can also refer to Bystander at the Switch or any of its endless variations.

RESPONSES

Why might it be wrong to harvest the patient but fine to pull the lever?

One answer is the *Means Principle* (AKA the "Doctrine of Double Effect," our topic in **#9, The Tactical Bomber and the Terror Bomber**).

The Means Principle says it is worse to kill someone as a means to your end than as a foreseen side-effect. Using people as a means is bad! Applied to our cases, the idea is that the surgeon *uses* the patient's organs to save the other five patients, whereas the Bystander does not *use* the body of the one worker to save the five on the other track, and that is why the surgeon acts wrongly, whereas the Bystander doesn't.

Foot objects that the Means Principle doesn't go far enough; sometimes, it's wrong to kill even as a side-effect. She gives the example of a doctor who makes a medicine that will save five lives, but the process lets off lethal fumes that will seep into the vents, killing a patient who can't be moved to safety. The stuck patient doesn't need to die in order to save the five, but killing the patient is still wrong.

Thomson, meanwhile, objects that the Means Principle goes too far; sometimes, it's *not* wrong to kill even as a means. She gives the example of a bystander who turns the trolley towards a side track that loops back around to the main track where the five are stuck. In this case, the trolley *has to* hit the one in order for the five to be safe—and yet, Thomson wonders, how could it matter whether the side track loops back? The case seems to her essentially like the original Bystander at the Switch case, where the side track goes off into the distance.

Plenty more solutions have been offered. Thomson herself made three admirable attempts—before eventually giving up (2008). We'll consider her second solution in Part II (**#7**), and Part III will look at why she and others lost hope (**#10**).

For now, let's look at her first attempt, in "Killing, Letting Die, and the Trolley Problem."

Thomson argues that it's generally worse to introduce a *new* threat than to *redistribute* a threat from one group to another. The Bystander is redistributing the threat of the trolley from the five to the one.[1] The surgeon, however, is introducing a new threat to the sixth patient, not "redistributing" the five's diseases. That said, we do not want to allow just any old redistribution. Suppose you're on a Footbridge overlooking the tracks, and the only way to stop the trolley is to push the large gentleman standing next to you, so that he topples onto the tracks and his body stops the trolley. This "redistributes" the threat from the five to the gentleman, but it is clearly wrong. Thomson's solution is to say that we can generally only intervene to redistribute threats *by doing things to the threats*, not by *doing things to the people about to be threatened* (1986: 92). To "redistribute" the trolley towards the gentleman, you have to put hands on the man. By contrast, the Bystander can redistribute simply by pulling a lever.[2]

Not a bad first stab! But there are some problems with Thomson's solution.

First, it's not very clear. What does it mean to "redistribute" a threat? And what does it mean to say that turning the trolley doesn't "do" anything to the person who is about to get run over? In the words of one harsh critic, "Mrs. Thomson seems to me to have been blundering around in the dark in that paper…"[3]

Second, there appear to be counterexamples. Suppose the switch doesn't turn the trolley: it just moves the tracks. If you hit the switch, you will shift the track with the workers so that it is out of the way of the trolley, but you will also shift the track with the one worker so that he is right in the path of the trolley.[4] This seems awfully similar to the original Bystander at the Switch, but Thomson's theory suggests that shifting the tracks is wrong, since you're doing things to the workers, not to the trolley.

Ethical theorists are still waiting for a knockdown solution to the Trolley Problem. Maybe the true solution is still out there waiting to be discovered—in Part II, we will have another look. Or maybe, as we'll consider in Part III, the problem is flat-out unsolvable.

Classic Presentations

Philippa Foot, "The Problem of Abortion and the Doctrine of the Double Effect," *Oxford Review* **5** (1967): 5–15. Reprinted as Chapter 2 of her *Virtues and Vices: And Other Essays in Moral Philosophy* (Oxford: Clarendon Press, 2002): 19–32.[5]

Judith Jarvis Thomson, "Killing, Letting Die, and the Trolley Problem," *The Monist* **59** (1976): 204–217. Reprinted as Chapter 6 of her *Rights, Restitution, and Risk: Essays in Moral Theory*, William Parent, ed. (Cambridge: Harvard University Press, 1986): 78–93.

Further Reading

Thomas Byrne, "MAKING Metaphysics," *Philosophers' Imprint* **21** (2021): 1–18.

Frances Kamm, "Harming Some to Save Others," *Philosophical Studies* **57** (1989): 227–260.

Judith Jarvis Thomson, "The Trolley Problem," *Yale Law Journal* **94** (1985): 1395–1415. Reprinted as Chapter 7 of her *Rights, Restitution, and Risk: Essays* *in Moral Theory*, William Parent, ed. (Cambridge: Harvard University Press, 1986): 94–116.

Judith Jarvis Thomson, *The Realm of Rights* (Cambridge: Harvard University Press, 1990): Chapter 7. (This is Thomson's third solution, which involves some quite interesting ideas about expected value.)

Judith Jarvis Thomson, "Turning the Trolley," *Philosophy & Public Affairs* **36** (2008): 359–374.

Questions for Reflection

1. Trolley cases are not particularly realistic. Does that matter? Can we come up with more realistic cases to lay out Thomson's Trolley Problem? Do we need to?

2. Does the Trolley Problem have anything to do with the right to life?

3. Is it true that, by turning the trolley, you are killing the one? No doubt, the trolley kills the one—but do you? Now consider a case from Thomas Byrne (2021). Suppose the trolley is heading towards Judy and only you stand in its path. The trolley will kill her if and only if you jump out of the way—and indeed you jump. Do you kill Judy? If not, how is that any different from turning the trolley as the Bystander?

7. THE TROLLEY PROBLEM, PART II: FOOTBRIDGE

We've seen plenty of trolleys by now. Are you starting to sense a problem?

The problem is that it's getting really, really hard to separate out the permissible from the impermissible ways of doing and allowing harm. It would be a massive achievement if you could figure out a way to do this, ideally with a snappy principle. But even the not-so-snappy ones tend to have glaring counterexamples.

To give you a feel for the difficulties here, let's take a closer look at (arguably) Judith Jarvis Thomson's best attempt to solve the Trolley Problem. Along the way, we will learn a bit about what MIT philosopher Caspar Hare (2016: 454) calls "the single most famous and well-worn case from all of twentieth-century normative ethics"— namely, the thought experiment known as Footbridge.

As a reminder: for Thomson, solving the Trolley Problem means explaining why some kinds of killings seem worse than others. In:

Transplant
Five patients are going to die of organ failure unless you, their doctor, secretly kill a sixth patient and redistribute his organs.

Here, killing the sixth patient seems wrong. Next, in:

Bystander at the Switch
Five workers are going to be killed by a runaway trolley unless you, a bystander, pull a lever to redirect the trolley onto a side spur, where it will kill a sixth worker.

Here, killing the sixth worker does *not* seem wrong. (Note: this is just to say that you *may* kill the worker, not that you *should*.)

The two killings have comparable outcomes—five survivors, one death—and yet pulling the lever seems fine, whereas chopping up the patient seems forbidden. What's the difference?

Here is Thomson's second answer, from her 1985 paper "The Trolley Problem." (We considered her first answer in **#6**.)

Killing someone is, in general, a lot worse than merely letting someone die; you typically can't kill anyone even to save five other people. We can call this the *Presumption Against Killing*. It applies to any killing that introduces a new threat to the situation, as when a villain stabs his victim with a kitchen knife. The knife wasn't threatening anyone until the villain got ahold of it.

But sometimes you can get a pass for killing. If you are merely re-distributing a threat, so that it kills a smaller number of people, that can be permissible. Thomson calls this the *Distributive Exemption*. In her view, this is what explains the puzzling permissions in the Trolley Problem. You may pull the lever as the bystander, even though you'd be killing an innocent person, because you would not be killing them with a new threat. The trolley was already threatening five people. You merely "redistributed" the threat onto the one. Similarly, if a bomb is headed towards a huge city, you may deflect the missile so as to "redis-tribute" it to a small town.

The Presumption Against Killing and the Distributive Exemption are the two main ingredients in Thomson's solution. We'll get to the spices and sauces later. Before that, we need details on the Distributive Exemption, which Thomson develops by sharpening it against some skeptical questions.

RESPONSES

First, we might wonder, doesn't *all* killing involve redistributing a threat? In Transplant, the five patients start off threatened by various diseases; if you save them by killing the sixth patient, aren't you just redistributing the threat from the five to the one?

Not quite. You are changing *who is threatened*, but not by *redistribut-ing some particular threat*. You are introducing a *new* threat—namely, the scalpel, or whatever means you use to knock off the poor sixth patient. Thomson's exemption is not meant to apply to such killings, only to killings where some thing or process, which is currently threatening a big group, stops threatening them and threatens a smaller group in-stead. Obviously, Transplant isn't like this.

Next, aren't there plenty of cases where we redistribute a threat but nonetheless act wrongly? Yes, says Thomson, and she illustrates with the now legendary:

Footbridge
Five workers are going to be killed by a runaway trolley unless you, stand-ing atop a footbridge overlooking the tracks, push the large gentleman standing next to you onto the tracks. The fall will break the large man's legs, and the trolley will stop when it runs into him and kills him.[6]

The point of Footbridge is that pushing the man redistributes the threat of the trolley. The trolley starts off threatening the five, then it threatens only the one. Pushing the man does not introduce any new lethal threats. And yet, it seems wrong to push.[7]

Clearly, Thomson thinks, you may not "redistribute" threats by pushing people to their death. Why not, though? Her answer is that you don't qualify for the Exemption if the means by which you redistribute the threat themselves infringe somebody's right. We can call this the Infringement Exception. It applies in cases where you infringe a right in the very process of redistributing the threat. For example, when you push the man onto the tracks, you are infringing his right not to be pushed, but when you pull the lever to redirect the trolley, that doesn't itself infringe anybody's rights.

Wait a minute. When you pull the lever, you're killing the sixth worker on the side track. Doesn't that infringe his right not to be killed?

"Indeed it does," Thomson would be happy to say. She thinks that killing the worker infringes his rights, even though it's permissible to do it (an example of non-absolute rights, as in **#14, Feinberg's Cabin**). Notice, however, that the Infringement Exception is carefully worded. It doesn't say you can't infringe any rights. It says that the means by which you redistribute a threat can't in itself infringe any rights. And pulling the lever doesn't itself infringe any rights. Why not? The test, for Thomson, is to focus only on the stuff that happens up to the point when the threat is successfully redistributed—ignoring all effects further downstream—and then ask if anything so far in that process has infringed any rights. The trolley is redistributed as soon as the lever is pulled, but no rights are infringed until later, when the trolley hits the worker.

That is the essence of Thomson's solution. Killing is forbidden, unless you're redistributing a threat by means that don't themselves infringe any rights.

Is this solution right?

It's certainly complicated. Thomson has, in effect, added an exception (the Distributive Exemption) to the view that killing is worse than letting die—and then added an exception (the Infringement Exception) to the exception. (She even considers an exception to the exception to the exception—perhaps you can redistribute by means that infringe a right if the right's not too stringent.) That's a lot to wrap your head around.

Thanks to its complexity, Thomson's view gets a lot of cases right. But there's a risk of losing the forest for the trees here. Step back a moment and ask yourself, "Why is it wrong to push the guy in Footbridge?" A natural answer is that you're using the man's body without his consent (see **#9, Tactical Bomber and Terror Bomber**). Or perhaps we'd just say that you're killing him (see **#8, Drowning and Letting Drown**). But for Thomson, the problem is that pushing the guy in front of the trolley *in itself* infringes his rights—you're putting hands on him, and you're causing him to have a painful landing.

Well, what if you could just get the guy in front of the trolley some other way? Suppose he's dancing on a parade float that you own, and you push the float onto the tracks? Pushing the float doesn't itself infringe anybody's rights, and yet this seems just as wrong as pushing the man off the Footbridge. It is hard to think of any further exception we could add to Thomson's view to get this case right.

And in the end, we might not want another exception. The more byzantine the principle, the harder it is to see why it matters. While we can't solve the Trolley Problem with crude rules like "Don't kill" and "don't use," at least they have some familiar place in our moral thinking, with clear links to other moral concepts. One cannot say the same for Thomson's intricate exemptions (an idea to which we return in Part III (**#10**).).

Still, we have a lot to learn from Thomson's efforts—perhaps above all we can see how hard it is going to be to truly solve the Trolley Problem.

Classic Presentation

Judith Jarvis Thomson, "The Trolley Problem," *Yale Law Journal* **94** (1985): 1395–1415. Reprinted as Chapter 7 of her *Rights, Restitution, and Risk: Essays in Moral Theory*, William Parent, ed. (Cambridge: Harvard University Press, 1986): 94–116.

Further Reading

Caspar Hare, "Should We Wish Well to All?" *Philosophical Review* **125** (2016): 451–472.

David Edmonds, *Would You Push the Fat Man? The Trolley Problem and What Your Answer Tells Us About Right and Wrong* (Princeton: Princeton University Press, 2014).[8]

Frances Myrna Kamm, *Intricate Ethics: Rights, Responsibilities, and Permissible Harm* (Oxford: Oxford University Press, 2007). (Kamm may be the greatest living "trolleyologist," and this book's first chapter is probably the best introduction to her work. Her "Lazy Susan Case" on p. 24 is a counterexample that aims to show that we can sometimes kill even if we introduce a new threat—which means we need more than a *Distributive* Exemption!)

Questions for Reflection

1. What does it mean, according to Thomson, to redistribute a threat? Try to answer in your own words. It may also help to illustrate with some of your own examples.

2. Thomson has a potential counterexample to her Infringement Exception. Suppose you are on the Footbridge, but rather than pushing the large gentleman, you wobble the rail he's holding, which causes him to topple over and fall in front of the tracks. Thomson thinks you act wrongly. But (here's the problem) you're redistributing the threat of the trolley simply by wobbling the rail, and surely wobbling *in itself* doesn't infringe anybody's rights! (Remember: the test for whether an act "in itself" infringes a right is to ask if any rights would be infringed if we ignored effects downstream of the act.) What do you think Thomson would or should say to fix this problem?

3. Consider Philippa Foot's example of the lethal fumes (from **#6**). You're a doctor who can save five patients only by manufacturing a special medicine, but this process will cause toxic fumes to seep into the hospital's vents, killing an immobile patient in the basement. Would Thomson's view say that it's wrong to save the five by manufacturing the medicine? Why or why not? (Try testing out Thomson's view on other cases, while you're at it!)

8. DROWNING AND LETTING DROWN

Gregory wants his nephew dead. That pesky six-year-old is all that stands between Gregory and a big pot of money. So one night while the kid is taking a bath, Gregory sneaks into the bathroom and drowns him in the bathtub. He makes everything look like an accident and tiptoes out of the room.

Samantha wants *her* nephew dead. Just like Gregory, she stands to gain big time if anything should happen to that six-year-old. So Samantha sneaks into the bathroom one night, preparing to drown the kid. But just as she enters the room, she sees her nephew slip and hit his head, falling face down into the water. She's delighted at this turn of events and stands next to the bathtub, ready to push the kid's head back under if necessary. But it's not necessary: the child drowns all on his own.

James Rachels introduced this famous pair of cases in 1975 in order to show that there is no inherent moral difference between killing and letting die. Gregory kills his nephew, but Samantha doesn't kill hers: she "merely" lets him die, without lifting a finger to help him. If killing were intrinsically morally worse than letting die—"in itself worse," as Rachels puts it—then Gregory's action should be worse than Samantha's. But it's not: Rachels is confident that we find Samantha's conduct "no less reprehensible" than Gregory's.

Why does it matter whether killing is worse than letting die? Here are two ways in which it matters. Rachels himself is concerned in this paper with the (alleged) moral difference between *active* and *passive euthanasia*. *Active* euthanasia involves *killing* the patient, i.e. ending his or her life, for instance by administering a lethal injection. *Passive* euthanasia of a terminally ill patient instead consists in *letting the patient die*, for instance by withdrawing treatment without which the patient will not survive. Rachels believes that the sharp moral distinction often drawn between these two forms of euthanasia—for instance, by the American Medical Association—is unjustified. He takes such views to rest on the assumption that killing is inherently worse than letting die: the very supposition that this pair of cases is meant to expose as incorrect. According to Rachels, these cases show that "the bare difference between killing and letting die does not, in itself, make a moral difference."

So our stance on this general issue may affect—even drive—our views on euthanasia. The issue of killing vs. letting die also matters for a more abstract reason. *Utilitarianism*, or more generally *consequentialism*, shares Rachels' view that killing is not as such worse than letting die. Why? Consequentialist moral theories, of which utilitarianism is the most prominent, base moral assessment only on the *outcomes* of actions. They rank the moral desirability of an action purely in terms of what states of the world it brings about, comparing those with the outcomes of other actions which the person could have performed instead. But the outcomes of a killing and a letting die are the same: the person in question is dead. Moreover, in both cases, the victim could still have been alive if the agent had chosen to act differently. The consequentialist moral comparison seems to play out in identical fashion in the two cases, yielding identical moral verdicts.

However, it turns out to be hard to swallow the idea that there is no moral difference between killing and letting die because the outcomes are the same. Consider the people on this planet who are dying of starvation or curable diseases right now. Are you doing anything to save them and prevent their deaths? If not—and many of us are not taking any action to prevent such deaths—you are *letting those people die.* Whether this is morally acceptable is perhaps a hard question. If indeed there is *something* you could do that would prevent *some* of those deaths—for instance, by giving to a reputable charity—we may wonder whether it is OK to instead do *nothing.* But contrast our inaction with the act of *sending poisoned food* to some of those starving people, thereby killing them. The latter does not seem like a hard case: it is a morally horrific, unspeakable thing to do. It is very difficult to believe that our failure to save starving people is morally equivalent to sending them poisoned food.

It is important for the consequentialist, then, to convince us that we are confused in thinking that killing is morally worse than letting die. Do Rachels' bathtub cases succeed in doing this?

One possible response is that the cases seem morally equivalent only because both Gregory and Samantha wish harm on their nephews and act out of ill will toward them. Perhaps this factor "swamps" any general moral difference between killing someone and letting them die. If so, it would not follow from Rachels' cases that killing and letting die are morally equivalent in *all* cases. For instance, nothing would follow about euthanasia (where the aim is to do what is best for the patient) or "trolley problems" (where the aim is to do what is best overall). There might still be important moral differences between killing and letting die in *those* contexts.

The philosopher Frances Kamm offers another interesting response to these cases. What exactly does it mean, she asks, for one type of action to be morally worse than another? It does not mean that *every* case of the first type must be worse than *every* case of the second type. Rather, she notes that killing and letting die differ in their *definitional features*. For example, in letting die cases the victim by definition faces a threat that is already present independent of the agent, whereas killing by definition involves the introduction of a *new* threat. In similar fashion, it is part of the definition of letting die (but not of killing) that the victim loses life she would only have had because of aid by others. Kamm proposes that definitional features can have moral significance and that "one type of thing is morally superior to another if it has more positive properties *by definition*" (1996: 34, emphasis added). So even if we can cook up an unusual case where a letting die has some of the characteristics of a killing or *vice versa*, it will not have those qualities *by definition*. For Kamm, we should decide on the *definitional* level whether one type of action is better or worse than another.

Classic Presentation

James Rachels, "Active and Passive Euthanasia," *New England Journal of Medicine* **292** (1975): 78–80.

Responses and Other Treatments

Frances Myrna Kamm, *Morality, Mortality Volume II: Rights, Duties, and Status* (New York: Oxford University Press, 1996): Ch. 1.

Judith Jarvis Thomson, "Killing, Letting Die, and the Trolley Problem," *The Monist* **59** (1976): 204–217. Reprinted as Chapter 6 of her *Rights, Restitution, and Risk: Essays in Moral Theory*, William Parent, ed. (Cambridge: Harvard University Press, 1986): 78–93.

Questions for Reflection

1. Suppose Gregory is about to kill his nephew. What kinds of actions may you permissibly take in defense of the nephew? Now suppose Samantha is about to let her nephew die (and no one else can save him). What kinds of actions may you permissibly take to get Samantha to help?

2. Do your answers to question 1. suggest that there is a moral difference between killing and letting die? Why or why not?

9. THE TACTICAL BOMBER AND THE TERROR BOMBER

Consider a bombing mission ordered by a country fighting a just war. (In other words, that country did not start the war, it is fighting for a just cause, etc.) The objective of Country A's mission is to bomb a munitions factory in an enemy city. The broader military aim of the bombing is to diminish the enemy's fighting capacity by removing a source of weapons production. One wrinkle, though: the factory's urban location means that civilians live close to it. Thus any bomb dropped on the munitions factory will foreseeably kill a certain number of civilians as well. But civilian deaths are not the mission's objective or target; destruction of the factory is.

Now consider a second bombing mission, ordered by another country fighting a just war. The objective of Country B's mission is to kill enemy civilians. The broader military aim of the bombing is to diminish the enemy's fighting capacity by striking terror into its civilian population and thereby lowering morale. The urban area targeted for the bombing also contains a munitions factory, so any bomb dropped on the civilians will foreseeably damage or destroy the factory as well. But destruction of the factory is not the mission's objective or target; civilian deaths are.

Is there a moral difference between these two missions?

Let's stipulate that the result of each bombing run is *n* enemy civilian deaths and one heavily damaged enemy factory. The outcomes of the two missions, then, are isomorphic. (This suggests that a utilitarian would not see any moral difference between the two cases, since for a utilitarian moral assessment is sensitive only to outcomes.) The larger context of the two missions is also the same: a just war, being fought for a just cause. The ultimate military aim of each mission is the same: to diminish the enemy's fighting power. However, Country A has chosen different *means* toward that goal than Country B. Mission #1 aims to diminish the enemy's fighting power *by removing a source of weapons production*; Mission #2 aims to do this *by killing civilians*, thereby terrorizing the population and lowering morale. Thus, although the two countries share an ultimate aim, their *plans for achieving that aim* differ.

If you are not a utilitarian, here is one way you might respond to these examples. Depending on the details, Mission #1 is likely morally permissible. It depends on *n*, of course, and on the relation between that number and the military significance of the munitions plant. But if suitable details are filled in, *tactical bombing* of legitimate military targets in wartime can be morally justified, even if such operations sometimes unavoidably harm civilians.

Mission #2, on the other hand, could aptly be characterized as *terror bombing*. Unlike Country A, Country B is *deliberately targeting* civilians: it is killing civilians *on purpose*. The *goal* of this mission is to terrorize the population by killing civilians indiscriminately. But that is just what terrorists do! In Mission #1, the civilian deaths were a regrettable by-product of taking out the factory; but civilian deaths are *the whole point* of Mission #2. The second mission thus differs crucially from the first: terror bombing, or any intentional targeting of non-combatants, cannot be morally justified.

If there is a moral difference between the cases, say along the above lines, what features of the two missions are responsible for these divergent moral assessments? You might assume that these particular examples turn on something specific to the ethics of war. But many non-utilitarian philosophers instead take cases like the above to illustrate a general moral thesis often called *the doctrine of double effect*. As Philippa Foot expresses the idea,

> there are circumstances in which it is morally permissible to bring some-thing about *without* aiming at it although it would not be morally permissible to aim at it; even though the balance of benefit and harm in the consequences remained the same. (2002: 91, emphasis in original)

As applied to Missions #1 and #2, this thesis would say that it may be morally permissible to bring about the deaths of the civilians if one is not *aiming* at their deaths (as in Mission #1), even though it is not permissible to deliberately *aim* at civilian deaths (as in Mission #2). And this can be so even if the balance of benefit and harm resulting from the two missions is the same.

The central idea which the doctrine expresses has been around a long time. St. Thomas Aquinas is usually credited with having first suggested that there is a crucial moral distinction between *intending* a bad consequence, and merely *foreseeing* that consequence as a side effect of an action which is otherwise good. Many philosophers of an anti–utilitarian bent endorse the doctrine even today. Ralph Wedgwood, for instance, proposes that you have greater *agential involvement* in outcomes which you *intentionally* bring about than in outcomes which you merely *foresee* as a by-product of doing something else. So it makes sense that any moral reason against bringing about a particular outcome (such as civilian deaths) has more force against your *intentionally* bringing about that outcome than against your bringing about that outcome *incidentally*.

Other philosophers think the doctrine of double effect is pure nonsense. First, they doubt that there is any consistent way to distinguish between what is *intended* and what is merely *foreseen*. Perhaps the terror bomber could say that he intends, not the *deaths* of the civilians, but merely that they *appear* dead, so long as that suffices to strike terror into the rest of the population and lower morale. Unfortunately (he might continue), there is no good way to make the civilians convincingly *appear* dead other than by actually killing them. It would follow from this little speech that the civilians' deaths are merely a *foreseen side effect* of the terror bomber's causing them to *appear* dead, which would be his "real aim" (Bennett 1995: 210–211). In this way the terror bomber would get himself off the hook.

Moreover, even some staunch opponents of utilitarianism find it objectionable to suppose that "the permissibility of an action can depend on the agent's intention in performing it" (Scanlon 2010: 13). Imagine the military brass going to their president or prime minister to request authorization to bomb such-and-such a location. They give her all the pertinent details (about the civilians and the munitions factory, notably) and ask if it is OK for them to execute the mission. It would be ridiculous for her to respond,

> Well, it all depends on what your intentions would be in dropping the bombs. If you would be intending to destroy the munitions factory and thereby win the war, merely foreseeing, though not intending, the deaths of the [civilians], then yes, you may drop the bombs. On the other hand, if you would be intending to destroy the [civilians] and thereby terrorize the [enemy population] and thereby win the war, merely foreseeing, though not intending, the destruction of the munitions factory, then no, you may not drop the bombs. (Thomson 1991: 293)

Such a reply clearly seems absurd. But it is not obvious *why* exactly this would be an absurd way to respond. Perhaps one has the strong feeling that whether or not it is permissible to bomb that location must depend simply on *the facts of the case*, and, in particular, on whether those facts supply an adequate justification for the bombing. From this perspective, it would be profoundly confused to think that the permissibility of bombing that location varies depending on the intention with which the bombing would be carried out.

Recommended Treatments

Jonathan Bennett, "Morality and Consequences," in Sterling McMurrin, ed., *The Tanner Lectures on Human Values, Volume 2* (Salt Lake City: University of Utah Press, 1981): Lecture III.

Jonathan Bennett, *The Act Itself* (Oxford: Clarendon Press, 1995): Ch. 11.

Philippa Foot, "The Problem of Abortion and the Doctrine of the Double Effect," *Oxford Review* 5 (1967): 5–15. Reprinted as Chapter 2 of her *Virtues and Vices: And Other Essays in Moral Philosophy* (Oxford: Clarendon Press, 2002): 19–32.

Philippa Foot, "Morality, Action, and Outcome," in Ted Honderich, ed., *Morality and Objectivity: A Tribute to J. L. Mackie* (London: Routledge & Kegan Paul): 23–38. Reprinted as Chapter 6 of her *Moral Dilemmas: And Other Topics in Moral Philosophy* (Oxford: Clarendon Press, 2002): 88–104.

T. M. Scanlon, *Moral Dimensions: Permissibility, Meaning, Blame* (Cambridge: Harvard University Press, 2010): Introduction and Ch. 1.

Judith Jarvis Thomson, "Self-Defense," *Philosophy & Public Affairs* 20 (1991): 283–310.

Ralph Wedgwood, "Defending Double Effect," *Ratio* 24 (2011): 384–401.

Thomas Nagel, *The View from Nowhere* (New York: Oxford University Press, 1986): Ch. 9, Sections 4 and 5.

Questions for Reflection

1.   It's easy to see why it would be morally objectionable for harming people to be one of your chosen *aims*. But why should it be objectionable to intentionally harm people as a chosen *means* toward some further, innocent, goal? In that case you're no sadist: you're not attached to harming people *as such*, and you would never do it if it didn't help you achieve this other aim. Why then should it be wrongful to intentionally harm

people even as a means to a greater good? (Thomas Nagel has a suggestive discussion of this in the work cited above.)

2.   Thomson's example seems to show that the doctrine of double effect is not well deployed as an aid to decision and deliberation about actions yet to take place. Does that mean it is also useless for evaluating actions *after* they have taken place, such as Missions #1 and #2? Or can we still say the one which intentionally killed the civilians was morally worse? What does "morally worse" mean in this context?

10. THE TROLLEY PROBLEM, PART III: THE META-TROLLEY PROBLEM

The Trolley Problem asks us to draw a line in the moral sand. To most people, it seems wrong for a surgeon to save five patients by killing a sixth for spare parts, and yet most would *not* say it's wrong for a bystander to pull a lever to redirect a runaway trolley away from five workers and towards a sixth worker on a side track. Why should it be wrong for the surgeon to kill one to save five but fine for a bystander to kill one to save five? What's the difference?

It is notoriously hard to give an answer that does not generate its own host of tricky counterexamples. Plenty have tried. But no one has come up with a principle that has generated anything close to a consensus among ethical theorists.

Although some hold out hope, many have grown skeptical. What if the Trolley Problem rests on some kind of confusion? What if we haven't found a solution because there *is* no solution? Is there any hope for those who persist in trying to solve the Trolley Problem?

We call this the *Meta-Trolley Problem*. A solution to this problem would tell us (1) what bad assumption the Trolley Problem rests on, and (2) what lesson we can learn from all this—if there is indeed anything to learn. "Perhaps there is no moral to this story," as Lisa Simpson wonders after one strange episode. ("Exactly," continues Homer, "it's just a bunch of stuff that happened.")[9]

RESPONSES

Why might the Trolley Problem be unsolvable? The most salient possibility is that it rests on a false assumption. Maybe killing the sixth patient *isn't* wrong, after all; or maybe turning the trolley *is* wrong.

Utilitarians are open to the possibility that you may kill the patient for spare parts; maybe it's even a moral duty. In their view, the right action is whatever promotes the greatest total happiness. So they might say that the Bystander *as well as the surgeon* may kill one to save five.

Now, in the real world, killing a patient would probably end badly. What if the transplants don't work? What if the doctor is caught, and sick patients stop going to the hospital for fear of being harvested for parts? If these are likely possibilities, utilitarians will gladly admit that killing is wrong. But if we are talking about the pristine world of thought experiments, where it's certain that the transplant sticks and the doctor gets away scot-free, killing is a must, for the utilitarian. The ends justify the means, and here the end of killing is very good indeed: more people living happy lives.

That is one way to solve the Meta-Trolley Problem. We can't explain the difference between the surgeon and the Bystander because there *is* no difference, assuming that killing one to save five has the best result in both cases. But for Thomson, utilitarianism is the solution of last resort. She thinks it is *extremely* hard to believe that it's all right to kill a person for spare parts *even given* that it will lead to the greater preponderance of happy life. Thomson would sooner give up on the idea that the Bystander may pull the lever.

And that is how, three decades after her first paper on the Trolley Problem, Thomson (2008) loops back around and rejects her own fundamental assumption about the Bystander at the Switch. Thomson's ultimate view is that killing the sixth worker is like killing the sixth patient. *Both are wrong.* How else are we to explain the failure to draw the line between the surgeon's wrongful killing and the Bystander's permissible killing? (Without becoming utilitarians!)

Thomson's argument for this conclusion turns on a novel principle: we may not kill someone to save five if they *permissibly* withhold their consent (2008: 367). (Consider this in relation to **#22, Jim and the Villagers**.) The sixth worker, we can observe, would not be required to volunteer his or her life for the sake of saving five. And in the thought experiment, we assume, the worker doesn't actually consent to being killed. Thomson concludes that the Bystander may not kill the worker after all.

Thomson's move is quite extreme—most of us want to insist that it's permissible to turn the trolley. Still, if this is what it takes to get out of the Trolley Problem, maybe it's worth it.

But does Thomson's turnabout do the trick? Frances Kamm (2016) argues *no*. She thinks we can construct a new, Thomson-proof Trolley Problem, just as tough as the original, if we switch out the Bystander with Foot's trolley driver.

In Foot's case, as you may remember, the driver can either steer on to the side track, killing one, or let the trolley go ahead, killing five. Thomson thinks the driver may turn the trolley; if he's killing people either way, he might as well minimize deaths. (Indeed, Thomson thinks the driver *must* turn, even if turning would result in his own death!)

Kamm's twist is to consider two cases where the driver is thrown from the trolley. In case one, *Driver at the Switch*, the driver is thrown next to a lever that will redirect the trolley towards a side track where one worker is trapped. In case two, *Driver on the Footbridge*, the driver is thrown onto a bridge, and the only way to stop the trolley is to push a large gentleman off the bridge and onto the tracks, where the trolley will stop upon lethally crashing into him.

As in the original Bystander at the Switch, turning the trolley seems permissible. Pushing the large man, however, seems clearly wrong, even though it prevents the killing of the five. What's the difference?

This problem seems *just as pressing* as the original Trolley Problem. But Thomson's solution doesn't help us at all with this new version. So, Kamm thinks, Thomson's move isn't worth it. One way or another, we are going to have to face up to the fact that turning the trolley seems morally preferable to other ways of killing. Saying that it's wrong when the Bystander does it only kicks the can down the track.

Kamm's own solutions, which face the problem more directly and relentlessly than anybody else's, are the stuff of legend. Marvelously intricate, tested against a dazzling array of thought experiments, Kamm's principles can be hard to wrap one's brain around.[10] But they raise a further worry, according to philosopher Shelly Kagan. Even if Kamm has managed to find the principle that expresses the felt difference between pulling the lever and pushing the fat man (or cutting up the patient), her principle still has to pass a further test: it has to strike us as drawing a moral distinction that matters. If "our intuitions about trolley problems respond to factors that simply do not have any genuine moral significance," those intuitions aren't worth enshrining in a principle (Kagan 2015: 164). A theory that says that killing is only bad on Tuesdays is silly because there is no reason why Tuesdays should be special. The same goes for a theory that says killing is only allowed when it happens *in this very specific Kamm-approved way*—unless there is some deeper reason why *that* way is special. That, at any rate, is Kagan's contention.

The Trolley Problem is surprisingly hard to vanquish. But whether we give up on solving it or stay on track, there is something important to learn. Either killing is a lot easier to justify in principle than we intuitively think—which is what utilitarians believe—or else morality draws some *very* subtle distinctions between the right and wrong ways of doing harm, so subtle that we might wonder how they could possibly matter.

Recommended Treatments

Judith Jarvis Thomson, "Turning the Trolley," *Philosophy & Public Affairs* **36** (2008): 359–374.

Shelly Kagan, "Solving the Trolley Problem," in Frances Myrna Kamm, *The Trolley Problem Mysteries*, Eric Rakowski, ed. (Oxford: Oxford University Press, 2016): 151–165. (Kagan's paper is a commentary included in Kamm's book.)

Frances Myrna Kamm, *Morality, Mortality, Volume II: Rights, Duties, and Status* (New York: Oxford University Press, 1996).

Frances Myrna Kamm, *Intricate Ethics: Rights, Responsibilities, and Permissible Harm* (Oxford: Oxford University Press, 2007).

Frances Myrna Kamm, *The Trolley Problem Mysteries*, Eric Rakowski, ed. (Oxford: Oxford University Press, 2016).

Questions for Reflection

1. Is it ever reasonable to think that an action is wrong even though *intuitively* it still seems right to you?

2. Kagan insists that the distinction between morally right and wrong ways of killing (if there is such a distinction) must itself have independent moral significance. Is he right? Why or why not?

3. Related to the last question, consider the legal distinction between minors and adults. In the United States, we draw the line at age 18. Presumably, 18 is not the uniquely significant milestone, and we are drawing the line somewhat arbitrarily. Is it acceptable to draw somewhat arbitrary lines in the law? If so, then why can't we accept arbitrary lines in morality, too?

NOTES

1 Note that Thomson's first solution, originally published in 1976, deals with a slightly different example. Instead of a Bystander at the Switch, there is a passenger inside the trolley, who takes over after the brakes fail and the driver dies from shock (1986: 81). The iconic switch does not turn up until 1985's "The Trolley Problem," our topic in Part II (**#7**).

2 Of course, Thomson would be the first to admit that lots of other things matter, too. Who started up the trolley? Why are the people on the tracks? And so forth.
3 That critic, by the way, was none other than Judith Jarvis Thomson, in her later paper "The Trolley Problem" (1986: 112, fn. 14).
4 This is a version of Frances Kamm's (1989) "Lazy Susan."
5 Quite a few people, including scholars, get the name of this article wrong. Foot's title is "The Problem of Abortion and the Doctrine of *the* Double Effect" (our emphasis), but try Googling the title without that third "the." You'll find papers, lectures, and even encyclopedia entries all making the same mistake.
6 Thomson calls our gentleman "The Fat Man," and the name has stuck. There's even a book called *Would You Kill the Fat Man?* But as even that book notes, the traditional name "is considered by some to be indecent" (Edmonds 2014: 37), and so philosophers reimagine the "Fat Man" in all sorts of ways: he's a large man, a heavy man, a man with a large and heavy backpack. At MIT, the home of Judy Thomson, people even used to talk about "the sticky man." Maybe this is a bit sensitive. But hey, if the poor guy's being pushed to death, the least we can do is to be polite towards him!
7 By the way, not many ethicists seem to know this about Footbridge. It's often treated as just another case where killing is wrong (Hare 2016: 454fn. 4; Edmonds 2014: 36), when really it was meant as a whetstone for sharpening the Distributive Exemption. (At least, that's its role in "The Trolley Problem." In Thomson's earlier paper, "Killing, Letting Die, and the Trolley Problem," she uses Footbridge to make a subtly different point: you may not redistribute threats by doing things to the people threatened (see **#6**).)
8 *Would You Kill the Fat Man?* arrives at Thomson and Footbridge in Chapter 5, and like many treatments of the topic, it gets some details wrong. (For example, Edmonds (2014: 36) says that the fat man doesn't feature in Thomson's first Trolley Problem article from 1976. But he does! "George can shove the fat man onto the track in the path of the trolley… or he can refrain from doing this…" (p. 208 in the original, p. 82 in the 1986 reprint).) This illustrates one reason why we wrote this entry: despite Footbridge's fame and glory, it is probably the most misunderstood thought experiment in the history of ethics, and Thomson's views are so complicated that they can even confound the experts!
9 *The Simpsons*, Season 2, Episode 22: "Blood Feud."
10 Just to give you a flavor (don't expect to make sense of this without reading the book), here is her "Principle of Permissible Harm" (PPH), from 2007's *Intricate Ethics* (Chapter 5, n. 78):

> (I) In thinking about the greater good (G) that will justify a particular lesser evil* (E) to innocent, nonthreatening people who are not under comparable threat already, for whom continuing life is a good and who have not consented to evil*, it speaks in favor of permissibility of an act if:

(i)   E can be caused by G or its structural equivalent; or

(ii)   E can be caused by means that have G or its structural equivalent as its noncausal flip side or aspect (or by effects of such means); or

(iv)   E need not be a direct effect of what we must do (or that with which it overlaps) in order to achieve the greater good.

... It speaks against the permissibility of an act if:

(v)   the only possibility provided by that act is that E is a cause of G, unless E is an effect of the structural equivalent of G, or of an event that has this as its noncausal flip side or aspect (or of effects of such events) (as in ii); or

(vi)   the only possibility provided by that act is that a cause of G is an event that has E as a side effect and G as a mere causal effect, unless (a) the production of E is mediated by (i) or (ii) for a different G, or (b) E is an indirect effect.

(II) It speaks against acts involving or causing E, if there is no G.

(III) Possibly, it speaks for the permissibility of agents acting if it is reasonable for them to believe that their acts would satisfy (i), (ii), or (iv), even when they do not. Possibly, it speaks against the permissibility of agents acting, if it is reasonable for them to believe that their acts would satisfy (iv) or (v), even when they do not.

She later adds another clause to (I):

(iii): E is caused by components of G (or their structural equivalents) or by means that have such components (or their structural equivalents) as their noncausal flip side or aspect (or by effects of these), and these components or means could lead to G via (a) good/neutral effects; (b) via evils* smaller than the good of the components, if the evils* produce G; or (c) via evils* that sustain components of G. We would then also have to change (vi)(a) in the PPH to allow that (iii) could also mediate the production of E. (2007: Ch. 5, n. 90)

3

PUZZLES ABOUT RIGHTS

We've seen that the Trolley Problem arises when deontologists try to draw a line in the sand between right and wrong actions. The line, alas, ends up looking rather squiggly. But there is an even more fundamental problem for deontologists, which is that the very concepts they use are deeply puzzling—none more so than the concept of a moral *right*, as we'll see in this chapter.

We'll start with the mother of all deontological paradoxes: the one, the only **Paradox of Deontology (#11)**. Deontologists seem to care an awful lot about rights violations. But suppose you can minimize the total number of violations only by committing a violation yourself—killing one innocent to stop a double murder, for example. Deontologists would say that's wrong. But how could it be? If it's bad to violate rights, shouldn't we want fewer violations?

This naturally raises the question of what it even means to have a right. To answer this question, Joel Feinberg introduces the example of **Nowheresville (#12)**, an imaginary land where the inhabitants are *almost* like us, except that they lack the concept of rights. Feinberg invites us to wonder, "What's missing from life in Nowheresville?" His answer is that they lack any concept of legitimately claiming what's yours.

DOI: 10.4324/9781003319962-4

Another upshot of having rights is that people can't just do whatever they want to you. But there are limits to the protection that rights can afford.

We might think that, if you have the right to life, then people can't permissibly deny you what you need to stay alive. **Thomson's Violinist (#13)** is a potential counterexample to this principle, with profound implications for the ethics of abortion.

We might also think that if you have a right against someone, then any action that contravenes that right will be morally wrong. But again, what sounds plausible in the abstract might not seem so true in particular examples. **Feinberg's Cabin (#14)** seems to show that we sometimes may, and even should, contravene other people's minor rights.

Finally, we turn to **The Paradox of Self-Release (#15)**, an ancient puzzle having to do with the special case of rights and oneself. We often talk of owing things to oneself. But that seems to imply a *right* against oneself, which seems impossible. Having a right means being free (you can waive it at will), but for there to be a right *against* you, you would have to be bound. How can you be free and bound at the same time?

So there you have it. Rights are linked to the idea of claiming what is yours, and they protect your body and property from others' interference. Still, it is very tricky to say which actions are made wrong by a right, and why it's wrong to minimize rights violations. On top of that, we seem to have duties to ourselves, which seem to imply rights against ourselves, which seem utterly incoherent.

Deontologists certainly have their work cut out for them!

11. THE PARADOX OF DEONTOLOGY

Deontology has plenty of paradoxes—from the Trolley Problem (**#6, #7, #10**) to Kamm's Intransitivity Paradox (**#27**). But only one has the honor of being *the* Paradox of Deontology, and that's because it threatens the most fundamental idea of deontological ethics.

Let's start with an example (from **#7**). In:

Footbridge
A runaway trolley is headed towards five innocent workers. You're standing alongside a rather large gentleman atop a footbridge overlooking the tracks. Your only way to save the workers is to push the man over, so that he is struck by the trolley. This will stop the trolley before it reaches the five workers, but it will also kill the one man.

Here, we seem to have a counterexample to consequentialism—the view that it's always right to do what has the best outcome. A death, we assume, is a bad thing, and five deaths would be worse than one. So the consequentialist has to say: push the one and save the five! And yet this seems morally wrong. You can't just go around pushing people off bridges!

…or can you?

Take a closer look at the deontologist's view. The deontologist seems to care an awful lot about pushing people off bridges. Indeed, they seem to think a single lethal pushing is worse than even *five* deaths.

Well, suppose that you can minimize the number of *pushings* by doing a little pushing yourself? In:

Triple Footbridge
There are two people in situations just like the original Footbridge. If you do nothing, each will push a large gentleman, thereby saving a total of ten workers. You can stop these two killings, however, if you push the large gentleman standing next to *you*. (Perhaps this will alert the other two large men in time for them to run away.)

Here, we seem to have a counterexample to deontology. Pushing one to save five, we assume, is a bad thing, and two such pushings are worse than one. So, deontologists have to say: push the one to prevent the other two from being pushed! And yet this, too, seems morally wrong. You can't push someone to their death, even to prevent a double-pushing! (Why not, you ask? One possible answer is that people have a *right* not to be pushed to their death.)

What we have here is not just a special feature of Footbridge, but a very general, very puzzling fact about deontological *restrictions*. A restriction is something that can make an action wrong independently of its consequences. Deontologists believe in all sorts of restrictions— for example, restrictions on lying, stealing, and pushing people off bridges. Restrictions are utterly fundamental to deontological ethics, for just about every moral right seems to function as a restriction. The puzzle is that violating a restriction can seem wrong even when it would minimize the total number of violations of that very same restriction. In other words, it can be wrong to lie even to prevent two lies, to steal even to prevent two stealings, and to push someone off a bridge even to prevent two other pushings.

This seems paradoxical. If the deontologist cares so much about some bad action, why wouldn't they want fewer such actions to be done? How can you care about a restriction, yet be against minimizing violations of it?

RESPONSES

Deontologists have tried out quite a few solutions to the Paradox of Deontology. Nothing like a standard solution has emerged yet, but there are some promising possibilities.

There are also, to be honest with you, a few duds. For instance, we might say that it's wrong to push the man in Triple Footbridge because, although you are minimizing the total number of lethal *pushings*, you are maximizing the number of people pushed by *you*. More precisely, the idea here is that the badness of violating a restriction is agent-relative, in the sense that it's bad *from the perspective of the one doing the violating*. But this doesn't help much. We can just tweak the case:

> *Redemption Footbridge*
> You have just pushed two people onto the tracks in front of a runaway trolley, where they are now stuck. Not your finest hour. But there is still time to undo the damage. You can prevent the trolley from killing the two by pushing a third, larger man in front of them, and the trolley will stop when it lethally strikes him.

Here, it's still wrong to push the man even though you would be min-imizing the number of people *you* push to death. By killing the third man, you stop yourself from killing the first two. Agent-relative value won't save us here.

Perhaps the problem is value itself? In a brilliant, baffling paper, Philippa Foot (1985) tries to get out of the Paradox by denying the most fundamental tenet of consequentialism: that there is such a thing as a "good outcome." It's fine to say your dog is a "good boy," and of course you can say "good news!" when you win a bet. But conse-quentialists can't say that it's right to do what has the best outcome, because there is no objectively correct ranking of outcomes from morally worst to morally best. This rather conveniently implies that it's not a "bad outcome" if restrictions are violated—which means there's no pressure to say that we should minimize restrictions. The Paradox of Deontology never gets off the ground.

But this seems like massive overkill. Isn't there *something* to the idea of a good outcome? How else are we supposed to explain why it can be okay to violate restrictions when the effects are extremely good and the restriction relatively mild—for example, inflicting a tiny harm to save someone's life? (See **#14, Feinberg's Cabin**.) Foot's solution is rather costly.

Worse, it might not even solve the paradox! Think about it. Even if Foot banishes the idea of moral goodness, there is still the plain fact that violating a restriction can minimize violations. Since violations are verboten, it is still natural to wonder why *minimizing* them should be wrong. Shouldn't we want less wrongness? Banning the "g" word doesn't really make the problem go away, because it doesn't tell us why restrictions are the way they are.

A true solution to the Paradox of Deontology is going to have to say something deeper about the nature of restrictions, something that illuminates the apparent fact that it's wrong to violate a restriction even if there are more total violations as a result.

The word "result" may be a clue. *Violating* a restriction has to be different, somehow, from merely acting in a way that *results* in a viola-tion. Maybe that should have been obvious from the start. Deontology isn't supposed to be about consequences, after all.

But that's just to say what deontology *isn't*. We're still left won-dering what it *is*. If not consequences, what makes a violation of a restriction wrong?

Classic Presentations

Samuel Scheffler, *The Rejection of Consequentialism: A Philosophical Investigation of the Considerations Underlying Rival Moral Conceptions* (Oxford: Oxford University Press, 1994). Revised Edition. (This edition contains a reply to some of Foot's arguments.)

Shelly Kagan, *The Limits of Morality* (Oxford: Oxford University Press, 1989).

Frances Myrna Kamm, *Morality, Mortality, Volume II: Rights, Duties, and Status* (New York: Oxford University Press, 1996).

Responses and Other Treatments

Philippa Foot, "Utilitarianism and the Virtues," *Mind* **94** (1985): 196–209.

Ulrike Heuer, "The Paradox of Deontology, Revisited," in Mark Timmons, ed., *Oxford Studies in Normative Ethics, Volume 1* (Oxford: Oxford University Press, 2011): 236–267.

Judith Jarvis Thomson, "The Trolley Problem," *Yale Law Journal* **94** (1985): 1395–1415. Reprinted as Chapter 7 of her *Rights, Restitution, and Risk: Essays in Moral Theory*, William Parent, ed. (Cambridge: Harvard University Press, 1986): 94–116. (There's an example like Redemption Footbridge, about which Thomson raises an intriguing question related to time-relativity.)

Further Reading

Philip Pettit, "Consequentialism and Respect for Persons," *Ethics* **100** (1989): 116–126.

Daniel Muñoz, "The Rejection of Consequentializing," *Journal of Philosophy* **118** (2021): 79–96.

Questions for Reflection

1.   On the standard story, if pushing has agent-relative badness, we can explain why it's wrong to push in Triple Footbridge, but we can't explain why it's wrong to push in Redemption Footbridge. According to some ethical theorists, the solution to this problem is to say that pushing (and other violations) are also bad in a way that is time-relative. A violation now matters more than a violation in the past. Do you think the badness of a violation could be time-relative? Can you think of any problems for this kind of proposal?

2.   Some ethicists think even the old-school consequentialist can explain why it's wrong to push someone in Footbridge and its variations. (The "old school" doesn't believe in agent-relative or time-relative value.) Can you think of a version of old-school consequentialism that entails that it's wrong to push the man in Triple Footbridge?

3.   What kinds of things could deontologists point to as the source of restrictions, if not consequences of actions? Here is one concept that might get you going. Philip Pettit (1989) argues that the core of consequentialism is the idea that we should respond to value by promoting it—creating happiness, preventing deaths, and so on. The core of non-consequentialism (what we're calling "deontology"), as Pettit sees it, is that there's another way to respond to value: honoring it.

12. NOWHERESVILLE

"Welcome to Nowheresville! I know you're considering relocating, so let me tell you a bit about what we have around here. The citizens of Nowheresville are quite remarkable: they are benevolent and compassionate. They value and care about each person's well-being and about the public good. They are motivated to do things which are beneficial to others, rather than things which benefit only themselves. Sounds good, huh?"

"Yes; but there's something important you haven't told me yet. Are there *moral duties* or *requirements* or *obligations* in Nowheresville? Do its citizens think in such terms? You've told me how they 'spontaneously' act, and that's all well and good; but I wouldn't want to live with people who don't have the concept of being under a *moral obligation*. There needs to be something to *constrain* people's 'natural' inclinations, even if those are on the whole well-intentioned, for those motivations can misfire. Morality needs to serve as a *check* on my neighbors' actions and choices—otherwise I'd be too afraid to move in."

"Ah yes! Good question. Yes, I can assure you that the citizens of Nowheresville most definitely have a concept of moral requirement or obligation, of what is *morally mandatory* even if for some reason they did not feel like doing it. They believe in obeying not just the laws of Nowheresville, but the *moral* law. They understand that morality issues not merely *counsels* or *recommendations*, but *demands*. And in fact they are more conscientious about *complying* with those demands than people in your society. For instance, they consider themselves under a duty to contribute to charity, and they do so at a greater rate than your fellow citizens do."

"OK, that eases my mind a bit. But there's still something crucial you haven't told me. What do they take this moral law to *be*? In other words, what morality do the Nowheresvillians adhere to? From what you say about their benevolence and concern for everyone's well-being, I'm guessing they're utilitarians. They probably think they are morally required to do whatever brings about maximum well-being impartially considered. But if that's their view, I don't want to move there. It is terrifying that it could be considered totally moral to kill or torture me, as long as that would sufficiently enhance other people's well-being. I don't want to live in Omelas, or in that lottery town from the Shirley Jackson story.[1] I want there to be some *firm limits* on what people can do to me, even in the service of overall well-being."

"Ah, I understand your concern. Despite what you might have inferred from my initial description, though, the residents of Nowheresville are *not* utilitarians. First of all, they care about *personal desert*, not just well-being. So *what a person deserves* enters into their moral decisions. You don't need to worry that your child's teacher will give your kid whatever grade would make everyone most happy. Instead, the teacher will give your child the grade she *deserves*. Happy yet?"

"No, I'm not. It's fine and dandy to pay attention to desert, but desert doesn't rise to the level of a *moral requirement*. It's not *morally wrong* to fail to give someone a tip for excellent service, even if they deserve it. I admit it's not morally great, but it's not morally *forbidden*. After all, it's a tip, or gratuity: by definition, something *optional*. When I said I wanted firm limits on how I can be treated, I meant that I want to be protected by a *moral requirement* not to harm me in certain ways. Only a moral requirement can give me the kind of protection I seek; simply taking desert into account isn't good enough."

"Well, in that case I'd better tell you about the *second* respect in which the citizens of Nowheresville are not utilitarians. They do care about promoting overall well-being, as you noted; but they maintain that there are important *constraints* on doing so. In particular, they consider it *always morally wrong* to harm individual people in certain ways, *even if* that would lead to greater total happiness. As they see it, everyone in Nowheresville is under a moral obligation not to kill or torture anyone else, no matter how worthy the cause. So the morality of Nowheresvillians is deontological, not utilitarian. Their moral code leaves room for the promotion of well-being, but only when none of those constraints would be violated. So you won't find an Omelas here.

Now would you like to move to Nowheresville?"

* * *

Joel Feinberg, who invented Nowheresville, still answers "no." For despite all that's been said, there is one important thing which *wasn't* said: nobody said the residents of Nowheresville have any *rights*. For Feinberg, this means something very important is missing from

Nowheresville. Despite its attractive qualities, Nowheresville is a "world without rights" (249); and this means we would miss out on a great deal if we moved there. Rights, says Feinberg,

> are especially sturdy objects to "stand upon," a most useful sort of moral furniture... Having rights enables us to "stand up like men," to look others in the eye, and to feel in some fundamental way the equal of anyone. (252)

As Feinberg sees it, having rights confers on you a desirable *status*, one which puts you on an equal plane with everybody else regardless of your economic or social standing.

What exactly does that valuable status consist in? Having a right, Feinberg says, means being able to *claim* things from others *as* your right. "[The] characteristic use [of rights,] and that for which they are distinctively well suited, is to be claimed, demanded, affirmed, insisted upon" (252). If I have rights, I can insist on them; if I have a right *to* something, I can *lay claim* to it as my *due*. A creditor can *demand* repayment from a debtor—which is a very different thing than merely *asking* her for the money, or *reminding* her that she owes you money. Feinberg also links rights to *respect* and *human dignity*: "the activity of claiming... makes for self-respect and respect for others, [and] gives a sense to the notion of personal dignity" (257).

If Nowheresville lacks rights, it also lacks all of these good things, according to Feinberg. But while we certainly wouldn't want to be without self-respect, dignity, equality, and status, it is not easy to identify what exactly Nowheresville (as described above) fails to provide. After all, every resident of Nowheresville is under a *moral obligation* not to kill or torture me: that certainly seems to confer on me a distinctive and valuable status. Moreover, every resident of Nowheresville is disposed to *respect* that moral obligation. These facts seem sufficient to place "firm limits" on how I can be used or harmed in Nowheresville, even in the service of admirable ends.

In fact, some theorists—notably Judith Jarvis Thomson—would say that the existence of such "firm limits" actually *constitutes* my having a right. According to Thomson, a right is nothing more than a behavioral constraint on others' actions. So if others are morally required not to do X, Y, or Z to me—which they are in Nowheresville—I thereby *have* rights. On this view, Feinberg's description of Nowheresville as "a world without rights" (249) involves a confusion. For contrary to his intention, Feinberg has actually written rights into the picture!

Classic Presentation

Joel Feinberg, "The Nature and Value of Rights," *Journal of Value Inquiry* **4** (1970): 243–257.

Responses and Other Treatments

Jan Narveson, commentary on "The Nature and Value of Rights," *Journal of Value Inquiry* **4** (1970): 258–260.

Judith Jarvis Thomson, *The Realm of Rights* (Cambridge: Harvard University Press, 1990): esp. Ch. 2.

Thomas Nagel, "The Value of Inviolability," in Paul Bloomfield, ed., *Morality and Self-Interest* (Oxford: Oxford University Press, 2007): 102–114.

Questions for Reflection

1. What connection(s), if any, do you see between having rights and being able "to look others in the eye"? Between having rights and "personal dignity"? (These are questions that you should think about for a while by yourself, or with a friend. You might find a few distinct connections, including some that Feinberg never spells out.)

2. We speak of "having" rights or claims. But for Feinberg the fundamental thing is the *act* of claiming what you have a right to. In his view, to say you "have a right" to a certain thing just means you're in a position to claim it. (If you *lack* a right to that thing, you are in *no* position to lay claim to it.) But if claiming is just an act, why can't they do it in Nowheresville? Isn't claiming just a matter of telling, or reminding, people what they are morally required to do, and don't the folks in Nowheresville understand moral requirements?

3. Do you—unlike Thomson—see a difference between people being morally *obligated* not to treat you in certain ways and your having a moral *right* not to be treated in those ways? If so, what is that difference, and why is it important?

13. THOMSON'S VIOLINIST

Is the typical abortion morally permissible?

Many think *no*, because the human fetus is a person, and persons have the right to life, which means they may not be killed. No doubt, the mother has rights over her body, too, which are worth caring about. But body rights do not seem as awesome and weighty as the right to life.

This argument has many critics, who often focus their attacks on the first premise: that fetuses are people. But the status of the fetus is a fraught issue, difficult to debate. Often the fracas bottoms out in some deep philosophical or theological disagreement—is the fetus a clump of cells or ensouled flesh? If we have to settle such questions before we can debate the ethics of abortion, we might not get far.

Enter Judith Jarvis Thomson. In her classic "A Defense of Abortion," Thomson argues that abortion is not wrong *even if fetuses are people*. The argument against abortion has a second weak spot, she thinks. Sometimes, it's permissible to kill a person, even one who clearly has a right to life.

That might sound a bit heartless. But consider this now-legendary thought experiment, which Thomson uses to illustrate her point:

> You wake up in the morning and find yourself back to back in bed with an unconscious violinist. A famous unconscious violinist. He has been found to have a fatal kidney ailment, and the Society of Music Lovers has canvassed all the available medical records and found that you alone have the right blood type to help. They have therefore kidnapped you, and last night the violinist's circulatory system was plugged into yours, so that your kidneys can be used to extract poisons from his blood as well as your own. The director of the hospital now tells you, "Look, we're sorry the Society of Music Lovers did this to you—we would never have permitted it if we had known. But still, they did it, and the violinist is now plugged into you. To unplug you would be to kill him. But never mind, it's only for nine months. By then he will have recovered from his ailment, and can safely be unplugged from you. (1986: 2–3)

Unlike a fetus, the violinist is *undoubtedly* a person. But is it undoubtedly true that you must let him use your kidneys for nine months?

Thomson has her doubts. It would be "very nice of you if you did it, a great kindness" (1986: 3). Staying plugged in would be like the act of a Good Samaritan (1986: 15), someone who goes beyond the call of duty. But giving free use of your kidneys is not a duty. You would be within your rights to say, "Sorry, but it's my body, so it's my choice." That is especially true if we imagine a more extreme version of the case in which the violinist's use of your kidneys would kill you, in which case killing the violinist first by unplugging seems like perfectly permissible self-defense.

What does all this show?

For Thomson, the moral is that there is something problematic in our idea of the "right to life." She isn't a total skeptic; she agrees that, in some sense, innocent persons have such a right. Cold-blooded murder violates it. But not all killings are murders. Killing the violinist to save your life is self-defense. And even in the less extreme case, where you survive being plugged in, it would not be a murderous wrong to kill the violinist by unplugging him from your kidneys.

In other words, it matters what *kind* of killing we are talking about. Some killings—Thomson calls them "unjust" killings—violate the right to life. Other killings, like the more and less extreme ways of killing of the violinist, are "just" and do not violate the right to life. The big gap in the argument against abortion is that it doesn't do anything to show that killing the fetus is unjust. So, the defender of abortion can say that abortion is compatible with a fetal right to life.

The right to life, however real and robust, does not entail the right to use another person's organs against their will—but the fetus must use the mother's organs to survive. That, for Thomson, is the key to defending abortion.

RESPONSES

Thomson's violinist analogy has sparked hundreds if not thousands of responses. The main complaints fall into three categories.

First, we might insist that unplugging the violinist is actually *wrong*. Perhaps we owe stringent duties to aid the violinist? (See **#16**, **Singer's Pond**.) Thomson herself does not think that the right to life includes a right to be saved at great expense—or even for free! She imagines a case where she is sick in bed and will die without help from Henry Fonda (which was a dated reference already in 1971). If Henry will just wipe the sweat from her "fevered brow," she will survive. But that does not give her the right to have poor

Henry Fonda flown in from the West Coast to save her, and even if by chance he is in the room, that shouldn't make his right not to help "disappear."

Many ethicists will probably not want to disagree with Thomson's judgment about the violinist, though, since unplugging him is an exercise of your body rights.

The second kind of complaint is the most popular: deny the analogy between aborting a fetus and unplugging the violinist. Unplugging the violinist is the removal of aid; abortion often crushes bones and cuts flesh. The violinist is a stranger; the fetus is family. You did nothing to cause yourself to be plugged into the violinist; the mother's pregnancy might be the result of her choice to have (consensual) sex. These factors, and others, might lead us to say that abortion is wrong even if unplugging from the violinist isn't.

Finally, there is what David Boonin calls the "weirdness objection" (2002, Ch. 4). It is hard to imagine *really* being kidnapped by a Society of Music Lovers, and *really* being hooked up to a famous violinist. Isn't this sort of thought experiment just a bit, you know, weird? What can we actually learn from such far-fetched hypotheticals?

Perhaps one might reply, borrowing a line from Derek Parfit, that we should ignore scenarios if they are so weird that we cannot form clear moral thoughts about them. But we do have clear moral thoughts, says Thomson, about the violinist. Clearly, you may unplug! The weirdness does not seem to get in the way of that particular judgment. So why not squeeze as much ethical insight out of that judgment as we can?

Classic Presentation

Judith Jarvis Thomson, "A Defense of Abortion," *Philosophy & Public Affairs* **1** (1971): 47–66. Reprinted as Chapter 1 of her *Rights, Restitution, and Risk*, William Parent, ed. (Cambridge: Harvard University Press, 1986): 1–19.

Further Reading

David Boonin, *A Defense of Abortion* (Cambridge: Cambridge University Press, 2002).

Kate Greasely, *Arguing About Abortion: Personhood, Morality, and the Law* (Oxford: Oxford University Press, 2017).

Questions for Reflection

1. How serious is the weirdness objection? Can you imagine a less weird version of the thought experiment? Would it be any better for Thomson's purposes?

2. What is the main disanalogy, in your view, between the violinist case and cases of pregnancy? Does this difference ultimately make a moral difference? If so, can you repair the analogy by coming up with a new version of the violinist case?

3. Can you think of any snappy way to spell out which kinds of killings are unjust? (Remember: "unjust" is Thomson's catch-all term for the kinds of killings that are supposed to violate, rather than bypass, the right to life.) If there is no snappy way to do this, should that make us doubt the right to life?

14. FEINBERG'S CABIN

You may have gotten the sense from **Nowheresville (#12)** that *rights* are a pretty cool thing to have. When you have a right, it is *not OK* for people to do certain things to you; they are *not allowed* to do those things. Plus, when you have a right you can *stand on* that right, *insist* on your rights, and *claim* things as a matter of right. Pretty nifty stuff.

What *exactly* follows from your having a right, though? Let's zoom in and see if we can get clearer about that. It might be useful to take as our example a right less freighted and ambiguous than the right to life (see **#13, Thomson's Violinist**). How about *property* rights? We of course have *legal* property rights: it is a criminal act—legally not allowed—for someone to take your property. But we also have corresponding *moral* rights over our property, and these are the ones that interest us. Do you own a car, for instance? Then you have certain rights concerning that car. Because you own that car, it's not OK for other people to get in and drive it away—at least not without your permission. (Notice that this *would* be OK if it were an abandoned car, owned by nobody.) If somebody gets in your car and drives it away without your permission, we would say they have done something *morally wrong*.

Let's introduce a piece of terminology. Let's say that *A infringes* a right of *B*'s if *A* does something that *B* has a right that *A* not do. We've agreed that you have a right that people not get in your car and drive off with it. So if someone does that, they have infringed one of your rights.

But does it follow that they have done something *morally wrong*? Infringing a right is clearly *bad* in some respect. But that's not a guarantee of wrongness. When we pronounce an action morally wrong, we are judging it to be unjustified "all things considered." By definition, such an assessment takes into account *all* the relevant pros and cons. An act could be bad in some respects but really really good in others; so we can't be sure that an act which has one bad feature is overall unjustified.

So there is a real question here: is it always morally wrong to infringe a right? If so, rights are *absolute*. Theorists of rights may be very tempted by this idea. The whole point of rights, they might say, is that rights take precedence over other moral concerns, such as maximizing utility. Individual rights are supposed to be *constraints* on what you may do even in the service of laudable aims (Nozick). Rights are *trumps* (Dworkin): they outrank even the highest "card" of a non-trump suit. They serve to decisively *rule out* courses of action which would violate someone's rights. Only understanding rights as absolute gives them the right sort of moral force.

Consider, however, the following case, dreamed up by Joel Feinberg:

> Suppose that you are on a backpacking trip in the high mountain country when an unanticipated blizzard strikes the area with such ferocity that your life is imperiled. Fortunately, you stumble onto an unoccupied cabin, locked and boarded up for the winter, clearly somebody else's private property. You smash in a window, enter, and huddle in a corner for three days until the storm abates. During this period you help yourself to your unknown benefactor's food supply and burn his wooden furniture in the fireplace to keep warm. (1978: 102)

Have you *acted wrongly* by sheltering in this cabin to save your life? Were your actions unjustified all things considered? Or were they acceptable all things considered? Feinberg thinks it clear that under the circumstances your actions were *not* morally wrong. If your life is in peril in this way, you are justified in breaking into an empty cottage, sheltering there, and doing what you need to do to keep yourself alive.

But this has an interesting implication for the nature of rights. Ask yourself: doesn't the cabin owner have a right that people not enter his cabin and burn his furniture? The correct answer seems to be: "Sure he does, just like you have a right that people not get in your car and drive off with it." *If* the cabin owner indeed has a right that people not enter his cabin and burn his furniture, then you have just infringed that right. But you have not acted wrongly. So rights are not absolute.

Rights theorists might find this conclusion alarming. Luckily, there is an alternative interpretation which would avoid this implication. Perhaps we *misdescribed* the cabin owner's right. Perhaps he has a right of the following form instead:

> that A not enter B's cabin and burn B's furniture
> *unless this is necessary to save A's life.*

Note that your action did not infringe *that* right. Perhaps that is why it was OK for you to do it.

Feinberg raises an important objection to the above reply, however. While we agreed that you acted permissibly, it also seems clear that *you owe the cabin owner compensation* for what you did to his cabin and furniture. It would be unacceptable for you to waltz down the mountain after the storm thinking, "Thank God it was permissible for me to break into that cabin and burn that guy's furniture. I don't owe him anything now, since I didn't do anything wrong." No: while it *was* OK all things considered to break into the cabin and so on, you are now morally bound to try to make restitution to the cabin owner for the damage you caused to his property.

Suppose we agree that you owe him compensation. *Why* do you owe him compensation? What is the *explanation* of that fact? Feinberg thinks there is an easy answer to that question: you owe him compensation *because you infringed his right!* If you infringed a right of the cabin owner's, that would certainly make sense of your being obligated to offer him compensation for having done so. But it seems mysterious why this would be required if we "shrink" the cabin owner's right in the way mooted above, such that you did not in fact infringe it. "If the other had no right that was infringed in the first place," Feinberg says, "one could hardly have a duty to compensate him" (102). Thus, we seem to have good reason to reject the second interpretation. If we reject it, however, we are thrown back on the conclusion that rights are *not* absolute.

Classic Presentation

Joel Feinberg, "Voluntary Euthanasia and the Inalienable Right to Life," *Philosophy & Public Affairs* **7** (1978): 93–123.

Responses and Other Treatments

Robert Nozick, *Anarchy, State, and Utopia* (New York: Basic Books, 1974): Ch. 3.

Ronald Dworkin, *Taking Rights Seriously* (Cambridge: Harvard University Press, 1977): Introduction (esp. xi–xv) and Ch. 7.

Judith Jarvis Thomson, "Rights and Compensation," *Noûs* **14** (1980): 3–15. Reprinted as Chapter 5 of her *Rights, Restitution, and Risk*, William Parent, ed. (Cambridge: Harvard University Press, 1986): 66–77.

Judith Jarvis Thomson, "Self-Defense and Rights," *The Lindley Lecture* (1976). Reprinted as Chapter 3 of her *Rights, Restitution, and Risk*, William Parent, ed. (Cambridge: Harvard University Press, 1986): 33–48.

Questions for Reflection

1. Could it be that *some* rights—perhaps property rights—are not absolute, but other rights are? Or do you think there would be exceptions like the cabin case to *any* supposed absolute right?
2. If rights are not absolute, can they still be used to argue that utilitarianism is incorrect? Why or why not?
3. Can you think of any alternative explanation for why you seem to owe the cabin owner compensation, other than that you infringed one of his rights?

15. THE PARADOX OF SELF-RELEASE

"Help me," pleads your friend Sam, "I'm in debt! I've promised somebody $100 by tomorrow, and they don't want to give me any extra time." You mull over your friend's predicament, considering whether to help her out with a loan. It then occurs to you to ask a follow-up question: to whom does Sam owe the money?

"Oh, right," she says. "I forgot to tell you. I owe it to myself."

Suddenly, your friend's "debt" doesn't seem so binding. In fact, it seems *impossible* for Sam to have a binding obligation to herself—not just in this example, but in principle.

For imagine that Sam does owe some obligation to herself. Then, as the person to whom it's owed, she can waive it away at will. But that means she can release *herself* from the obligation. How can she be "bound," in any meaningful sense, if she can get out whenever she wants? That's like saying that somebody is "trapped" in a room when they have the key to the door. So Sam can't be bound. But then, if her obligation isn't binding, how could it be in any sense an obligation? Isn't the whole point of obligations—as opposed to, say, kindly tips or friendly suggestions—to tell you that you're bound to do something no matter what you want?

This is the *Paradox of Self-Release*. It has been used to argue not just against the impossibility of silly obligations like Sam's, but *any* true obligation to oneself—duties not to harm oneself, not to debase oneself, not to let one's talents go to waste.

The Paradox, in its most general form, goes as follows.

1. If you owe something to someone, then they can release you from that obligation at will.
2. You cannot release yourself from an obligation at will.

So: You cannot have an obligation to yourself.

To the extent that we believe in obligations to self, the conclusion will seem unacceptable, and we will have a Paradox on our hands.

Although obligations to oneself are (at best) a medium-sized topic in ethical theory these days, it's rather amazing that the Paradox of Self-Release has come up in so many classic texts. Hobbes, Kant, and Rousseau all discuss it. Even Aristotle has an early version.

But has anyone got a solution?

RESPONSES

Marcus Singer (1959), who gives the best modern version of the Paradox, thinks it's a knockout blow. There simply *are* no obligations to, or rights against, oneself.

But what then do we make of all the familiar examples of such obligations? Can't we make promises to ourselves, and don't we owe it to ourselves not to be servile or self-loathing? Sure, Singer would say, we *talk* in these terms. It's just not literal speech. We "owe it to ourselves" to take care of our health only in the sense that it's a smart thing we should do, and we "make promises to ourselves" only in the sense that we make firm resolutions. Resolutions aren't literally promises, and reasons of self-care aren't literally obligations.

Is it so clear that this is just figurative? When we say "You owe it to yourself," we at least sometimes seem to mean it. "A moral theory should explain rather than discount inconvenient moral discourse," in the words of Anita Allen (2011: 859). That would mean attacking one of the premises of the Paradox. But which?

Kantian ethicists tend to attack (1), the idea that you can release people from their obligations to you. But this is a delicate task. We have to preserve *some* deep connection between obligations and powers of release. When you sign consent forms, cut deals, and dissolve contracts, you are releasing people from their obligations to you. For example, by saying "Come on in," you might waive someone's obligation to stay out of your apartment, and by signing a consent form at the dentist's office, you might release them from a duty not to drill your teeth. Kantians can't be denying this, right?

Thankfully, they're mostly not. The majority of Kantians will gladly admit that there are some "juridical" obligations that come with powers of release. They just insist on there also being some "non-juridical" obligations, from which no one can be released. When we're in the realm of rights and promises, we're talking about juridical obligations, which can be externally enforced by demands and punishment. But obligations to oneself aren't like this. They are non-juridical and non-enforceable: they just tell us to do the right thing for the right reason. (Notoriously, while you can force someone to do what they promised, you can't force them to do it for the right reason!)

The trouble for Kantians is that it's not clear why "non-juridical obligations" count as obligations. You don't literally *owe* yourself anything, in any clear and interesting sense.

This objection is even more potent against what we'll call the Aristotelian Switcheroo. When discussing suicide in the *Nicomachean Ethics*, Aristotle says it cannot be an "injustice to oneself," since you're a willing party to your own actions, and "no one willingly suffers injustice" (1138a). But he doesn't want to say that suicide is just. Hence the Switcheroo: instead of an injustice to oneself, he says it's an injustice to someone else—in this case, the state, who would very much like to have you around a while longer. This is not a plausible swap. Killing yourself isn't just a wrong to your local mayor; it wrongs yourself. (And other Aristotelian Switcheroos, though not actually Aristotle's fault, are similarly dubious—like when people say you only have to develop your talents so that you can better fulfill your duties to others.)

If we want a robust defense of obligations to self, we are going to have to take on (2), the premise that you can't release yourself from your obligations. Here, the worry is that obligations have to be binding, and if you can wriggle out at will, an obligation isn't binding after all.

One reply to this is that we still be bound by obligations to ourselves as long as our powers of self-release are *limited*. For example, Yuliya Kanygina (2022) argues that we can't release people (self-included) from their obligations to us unless we are choosing to do so autonomously. If we are "drunk or confused," for instance, we may not be in a position to autonomously sign off on actions that seriously affect us (2022: 570). So the bar for self-release is reasonably high, and so it is not so easy to get out of an obligation to oneself. They still require us to pull ourselves together; a careless and confused choice to sign up for dangerous medical experiments, for example, counts as a wrong to oneself.

Another reply is to say that obligations could be "binding," in the relevant sense, even if it were trivially easy to wriggle out of them. G. A. Cohen was the first to make this point in response to Hobbes' version of the Paradox. Consider the sovereign who makes a law that binds everyone, but who can change the law to make exceptions for himself at will. Is the sovereign bound? Hobbes says no, but Cohen says yes. Since the law is valid, it *should* bind the sovereign—but only until he changes the law! By analogy, we might say that an obligation to oneself binds oneself *until* one decides to waive it (Muñoz 2020). This obligation isn't going to strike fear into anyone's heart, assuming it's really so easy to wriggle out of. But that just makes it a rather unusual obligation. It doesn't make it incoherent.

Suffice it to say, ethical theorists are still figuring out what to make of the Paradox of Self-Release, even after all these centuries. But at least we can all agree that your friend Sam has probably gotten something mixed up, and you probably shouldn't fork over that $100.

Classic Presentation

Aristotle, *Nicomachean Ethics*, Terence H. Irwin, ed. and trans. (Indianapolis: Hackett Publishing, 2019). Third Edition. See the discussion of "Injustice to oneself" in Book V.

(There are many translations of this classic text, but they should all include the standardized page numbers we have used in the citation above.)

Marcus Singer, "On Duties to Oneself," *Ethics* **69** (1959): 202–205.

Responses and Other Treatments

Anita Allen, "An Ethical Duty to Protect One's Own Information Privacy?" *Alabama Law Review* **64** (2011): 845–866.

G. A. Cohen, "Reason, Humanity, and the Moral Law," in Christine M. Korsgaard, *The Sources of Normativity* (Cambridge: Cambridge University Press, 1996): 167–188.

Daniel Muñoz, "The Paradox of Duties to Oneself," *Australasian Journal of Philosophy* **98** (2020): 691–702.

Paul Schofield, *Duty to Self: Moral, Political, and Legal Self-Relation* (New York: Oxford University Press, 2021).

Yuliya Kanygina, "Duties to Oneself and Their Alleged Incoherence," *Australasian Journal of Philosophy* **100** (2022): 565–579.

Further Reading

Michael Cholbi, "On Marcus Singer's 'On Duties to Oneself'," *Ethics* **125** (2015): 851–853.

Daniel Muñoz, "Obligations to Oneself," in Edward N. Zalta, ed., *The Stanford Encyclopedia of Philosophy* (Summer Edition, 2022): https://plato.stanford.edu/archives/sum2022/entries/self-obligations

Janis Schaab, "On the Supposed Incoherence of Obligations to Oneself," *Australasian Journal of Philosophy* **99** (2021): 175–189.

Questions for Reflection

1.   Paul Schofield (2021) has a highly original solution to the Paradox of Self-Release. He thinks obligations to oneself over time can be binding, since you can't release yourself from obligations to yourself in the *future*. Just as you can't release yourself from obligations to others in the present, since you don't occupy their perspective, you can't release yourself from obligations to yourself in the future, since you can't *now* occupy the perspective you'll have *later*. You aren't now suffering from the lung cancer that smoking will cause, so you can't consent from your future perspective to smoking now. What do you make of this solution? Does it make duties to oneself too binding, not binding enough, or just right?

2.   In what sense does an obligation have to be "binding" in order to be a genuine obligation?

3.   Can you think of any examples of self-harm or self-disrespect that are *not* examples of violating an obligation to oneself?

NOTE

1   Ursula K. LeGuin, "The Ones Who Walk Away from Omelas," in Robert Silverberg, ed., *New Dimensions* **3** (1973); Shirley Jackson, "The Lottery," *The New Yorker*, June 18, 1948.

4

PARTIALITY

We naturally look out on the world from our own perspective, not from a God's-eye view. But morality often coaxes us to take up a more objective standpoint. Utilitarianism, for instance, in effect asks us to make decisions as if we weren't one of the people involved: we should simply ascend as it were to God's perspective and count the likely units of happiness associated with each of the options our agent faces. Utilitarianism's strong commitment to an especially straightforward form of impartiality is one of its signature features and, many think, one of its great strengths. The idea that *morally speaking* everyone counts equally is deeply appealing, especially in a world in which it seems so many people do *not* count equally.

Although these theories understand it differently, impartiality is also a hallmark of deontological and rights-based views. Here the equal moral status of every person is expressed not by considering everyone's happiness equally, but by granting everyone equal moral *rights*. You don't have any more rights than anyone else, and you are morally bound to honor other people's rights even if that's inconvenient for you, or even if you really *hate* that person. Morality is again inviting us to view the situation more impartially than we probably would have otherwise.

The strong association between morality and an impartial standpoint raises questions of its own, however. Is it really always forbidden

DOI: 10.4324/9781003319962-5

to favor yourself, or those you love? That's pretty harsh! The worry here is not just that it's *unrealistic* to ask us to act from God's perspective—although no doubt it is—but that such special concern often seems *morally appropriate*. The puzzles in this chapter invite you to consider when and to what extent *partiality* rather than impartiality is morally acceptable—or perhaps even morally required.

One person to whom you are definitely partial is *yourself*. You act to advance *your* goals and secure *your* happiness to an extent you couldn't possibly match for every person who is your moral equal (i.e., everyone). This doesn't give you *carte blanche*, of course: morality sometimes asks each of us to *sacrifice* some of our goals or happiness when something morally important is at stake. **#16, Singer's Pond**, probes the limits of this plausible idea. How much sacrifice can morality ask for?

If we are morally permitted to favor *ourselves*, perhaps we are also permitted to favor certain *other people*. **David and the Scarce Drug (The Numbers Problem), #17**, asks how far we can push that thought. Philosopher John Taurek seeks to push it as far as it can go—possibly farther than it can go—in order to reach a surprising conclusion. If you have a choice between saving five strangers and saving one stranger, Taurek maintains that you are *not obligated* to save the five. It would *not be wrong* to choose to save the one and thereby leave the five to die. It is easier to be shocked by this claim than it is to identify what is wrong with Taurek's argument.

The remaining entries in this chapter all concern partiality toward people with whom you are or have been in a close relationship. **#18** on *The Third Man* visits the cinema to present a moral quandary involving friendship, loyalty, and betrayal. **The Archbishop and the Valet (#19)** portrays a stark conflict between an uncompromising utilitarianism and the moral force of claims rooted in special relationships. **One Thought Too Many (#20)** seeks to question the moral ideal of impartiality itself. As a loved one, you might feel that even to consider the impartial permissibility of a loving action is "one thought too many."

16. SINGER'S POND

Imagine that you're on your way to class, walking past a shallow pond, when suddenly you hear some splashes and gurgles in the water. It's a small child—drowning!—and there is no one else around who could help. Thinking fast, you reckon that you can easily wade into the pond and yank the child to safety. Then again, looking down, you realize that saving the child would mean getting your shoes muddy. What should you do?

For Peter Singer, this is a no-brainer. You should forget the shoes and save the child—in fact, you are morally *obligated* to save the child. Why? Simple: because you have the chance to prevent a big harm without sacrificing anything of comparable moral significance. The death of a child matters. Your shoes, in comparison, do not. Whenever you can make this kind of moral trade—a relatively small sacrifice to avoid a relatively big harm—Singer's reasoning says that you have to make the sacrifice.

This all sounds reasonable, maybe even undeniable. What kind of monster is in favor of letting kids drown? And yet, if we take Singer's reasoning seriously, we do not get to save the child and call it a day. We may have to rethink our most fundamental values, and even our very way of life.

For most people living in affluent countries, life is stuffed with luxuries: fancy coffee, trendy clothes, shiny cars, gourmet gastronomy. No doubt *some* of what you spend goes towards essentials. But much of it does not. Be honest: how much money have *you* spent in the last week on things you didn't really need?

Now think about what it must be like to live in a desperately poor country; Singer's example was East Bengal, now Bangladesh, during a devastating famine.

> As I write this, in November 1971, people are dying in East Bengal from lack of food, shelter, and medical care. The suffering and death that are occurring there now are not inevitable, not unavoidable in any fatalistic sense of the term. Constant poverty, a cyclone, and a civil war have turned at least nine million people into destitute refugees; nevertheless, it is not beyond the capacity of the richer nations to give enough assistance to reduce any further suffering to very small proportions. (Singer 1972: 229)

Why are people suffering, Singer asks? Not because they have to. "The decisions and actions of human beings can prevent this kind of suffering," he thinks (229). We *can* stop the suffering, but we *choose* not to stop it. We could prevent a great harm without sacrificing anything of comparable significance, and yet we do not. That, Singer thinks, is deeply immoral. We (at least, we who live in affluent countries) spend our money on lattes and other luxuries when we could instead be preventing serious harm—specifically, the needless suffering of people in poor countries who lack food, shelter, and medical care.

Wait a minute. How can *we* help someone in a distant country? It's not as though you can just save up some money by forgoing lattes then hop on a plane to Bangladesh.

True—but we don't actually have to trot around the globe to help the global poor. The world is now extraordinarily interconnected: a global village, as Singer puts it. An effective charity "can direct our aid to a refugee in Bengal almost as effectively as we could get it to someone in our own block" (232). All we need to do is donate. By forgoing luxuries for a year, you could save up money to donate to highly effective charities, and that money could be used to save lives. And this is not just a good deed. It is a moral imperative, just like saving the drowning child.

So here is what Singer's argument ultimately looks like:

1. Suffering and death are bad.
2. If we can prevent something bad without sacrificing anything of comparable moral significance, then we are morally obligated to do so.
3. We *can*, by donating money, prevent suffering and death without sacrificing anything of comparable moral significance.

So: We are morally obligated to prevent suffering and death by donating our money.

What if Singer is right? What if we do have to donate our money to charities that help the global poor, just as we would have to sacrifice our shoes to save the drowning child? Then our current lifestyles are seriously immoral. We have to start donating *lots* of our money—maybe even *most* of it—until the point when the sacrifices are so painful that they are comparable in moral significance to the harms they could prevent. (So you don't have to be *totally* selfless. If you are down to your last $20, even Singer would probably tell you to keep it!)

There is, however, some wiggle room in the argument, thanks to Singer's phrase "comparable moral significance." Singer himself thinks "significance" is all about the size of benefits and costs (measured in terms of utility): you have to keep making sacrifices until the next one hurts you as much as it helps others. That means donating until you are on the brink of poverty! But Singer doesn't expect you to agree with him about what counts as "significant." He wants you to fill in *your own* moral judgments. Maybe you think giving up your standard of living *is* morally significant. But, presumably, if you are spending tens of thousands of dollars on autographed Justin Bieber memorabilia, you will have a hard time convincing anyone, even yourself, that your purchase is as significant as the lives that you could save by donating the money to an effective charity.

RESPONSES

One response to Singer is that he is not extreme enough. Peter Unger argues that donating our wealth is only part of what morality demands. If we have to beg, borrow, or even steal to raise money for vital foreign aid, we must do so. When people are suffering from extraordinary harms that only we can prevent, we may have to take extraordinary measures.

That said, most others find Singer's conclusions too extreme already. How do they resist Singer's argument? It will be hard to dispute premise (1), since suffering and death are clearly horrible. That leaves two options.

We might push back on premise (2), which says that you have to prevent bad things when it isn't too costly. (Compare this with the *unlimited requirement of prevention* in **#1, George and the Bioweapons**.) But this is not going to be easy; we would have to argue that people can favor their own concerns over the greater good of others. If we are not careful here, we may end up allowing too much selfishness. We don't want to end up with a view that lets you walk past the drowning child rather than muddy your shoes.

Finally, there is premise (3), which says that donating in fact isn't too costly relative to the huge benefits. To argue against premise (3), we could try to show that the costs of donating are surprisingly high— there may be moral significance in, for example, saving money for your kid's college fund. Or we could argue that the benefits of aid are less certain than Singer supposes. As Leif Wenar puts it, "Poverty is no pond." The problems of global poverty are more complex than a kid in the water, and the solution is not as simple as pulling someone above the surface; there are many real-world examples of aid projects backfiring or sputtering out.

But just because a problem is hard, that doesn't mean we can ignore it. No wonder, then, that Singer's Pond remains one of the most widely discussed thought experiments in all of ethics.

Classic Presentation

Peter Singer, "Famine, Affluence, and Morality," *Philosophy & Public Affairs* **1** (1972): 229–243.

Responses and Other Treatments

Critiques of Premise (2):
Travis Timmerman, "Sometimes There Is Nothing Wrong with Letting a Child Drown," *Analysis* **75** (2015): 204–212.
Susan Wolf, "Moral Saints," *The Journal of Philosophy* **79** (1982): 419–439.
Critique of Premise (3):
Leif Wenar, "Poverty Is No Pond: Challenges for the Affluent," in Patricia Illingworth, Thomas Pogge, and Leif Wenar, eds., *Giving Well: The Ethics of Philanthropy* (Oxford: Oxford University Press, 2011): 104–130.

Further Reading

Garrett Cullity, *The Moral Demands of Affluence* (Oxford: Oxford University Press, 2004).
Peter Singer, *The Life You Can Save: Acting Now to End World Poverty* (New York: Random House, 2009).
Peter Unger, *Living High and Letting Die: Our Illusion of Innocence* (Oxford: Oxford University Press, 1996).

Questions for Reflection

1.   Try to think of a moral difference between saving the drowning child and donating to charity—a difference that might lead someone to say that it's permissible not to donate, even though

it's obligatory to save the drowning child. (For example: "I am the only person who can save the child, but others can donate to charity instead of me.") Can you modify the pond case so that this difference is no longer a factor? In the modified case, would it be permissible not to save the child?

2. Suppose someone says, "If you think it's obligatory to save the drowning child, but not obligatory to donate to charity, then you can't be valuing everyone's life equally. You must think there's more value in the lives of those who happen to be near to you." Is this right?

3. Suppose Susie has fallen into the well. There are 100 of us, and we need to buy a $100 ladder if we are to rescue her. You suggest that everybody chip in $1. Unfortunately, you are the *only* one willing to chip in; the rest of us refuse to give even a single dime. Do you have to buy the ladder and save Susie yourself? Or is it enough that you offered to pay your share?

17. DAVID AND THE SCARCE DRUG (THE NUMBERS PROBLEM)

Some paradoxes arise from exotic examples, carefully constructed to bring out subtle tensions in our thinking. Not this one. The Numbers Problem is about a moral choice so basic—and so seemingly straightforward—that we only recently noticed that something might be going on with it. The choice is that of whether to save the many or the few. The Problem is that we might not be obligated to save the many.

As you might expect, most ethical theorists just assume that saving the many is obligatory. Consider a thought experiment from Philippa Foot:

> We are about to give a patient who needs it to save his life a massive dose of a certain drug in short supply. There arrive, however, five other patients each of whom could be saved by one-fifth of that dose... We feel bound to let one man die rather than many if that is our only choice. (1967: 9/2002: 24)

Saving the five would increase total utility, and we don't have any special reason to save the one (they aren't about to cure cancer, they aren't your mom, you aren't their bodyguard, etc.). For Foot, it's just obvious that we should save the many here. Virtually every ethical theorist in history would agree.

Thankfully, Elizabeth Anscombe (1967/2006) is not "virtually every ethical theorist." In a short-but-sweet reply to Foot, Anscombe argues that it would *not* be wrong to save the one, since we wouldn't thereby be *wronging* anybody. After all, we don't owe it to anyone among the five to save him or her rather than the one. So who can complain if we go ahead and save the one?

This argument is pretty good, except for the premises and inferences. If you think the numbers should count, you can just insist that the five *are* owed assistance, in virtue of their many-ness. Or you could reject the inference from "no one was wronged" to "it wasn't wrong." Anscombe's argument, however intriguing and original, isn't very persuasive.

This is where John Taurek comes in. Unlike Anscombe, Taurek was a one-hit wonder. His one paper is called "Should the Numbers Count?" His answer is *no*. Some parts of the paper, undeniably, indulge in trash talk (utilitarian reasoning is "contemptible" and "foolish" (1977: 300)); some arguments are air balls ("Five individuals each losing his life does not add up to anyone's experiencing a loss five times greater than the loss suffered by any one of the five"—try that one on a utilitarian! (307)).

But Taurek's main argument has some real persuasive potential. He wants to show other theorists "the difficulty of reconciling" the duty to save the many with "other convictions they are inclined to hold with even greater tenacity"—in particular, convictions about partiality, both towards oneself and towards friends (294).

Imagine that you own the scarce drug, and you must choose whether to use it to save five strangers or *yourself.* You are "the one." Here, utilitarians would still say you have to save the five, but most ethical theorists would say that's too extreme. You're not obligated to give up your own life even to save five others. Sacrificing yourself would be supererogatory, not obligatory. So far, so good.

Next, what if the one isn't you, but your friend David? Well, given that David would be allowed to save *himself* if the choice were up to him, why shouldn't it be permissible for *you* to empathize with David, and to use your drug to do as he would? If he would be allowed to save himself with his own drug, you should be allowed to save him with yours. Again, many would agree with Taurek that you may save your friend.

But friendship is not such a morally transformative thing. If you really had an obligation to save the five, then surely you would not be permitted to shirk that obligation just because you wanted to play favorites with a friend of yours. If you had promised the drug to Elise (who also needs a whole dose to live), you would not be permitted to give it to David instead, merely on the grounds that you are friends with David and not with Elise. So, Taurek concludes, it is not the fact of your *friendship* with David that explains why you may save him. Nor is the fact of your *selfhood* that explains why you may save yourself. The real explanation is that you *don't have a duty to save the many rather than the few.*

The Numbers Problem is the problem of how to avoid this bizarre conclusion—or learn to live with it.

RESPONSES

Taurek's argument has three steps:

1. You may save yourself rather than five.
2. So, you may save a friend rather than five.
3. So, you may save even a stranger rather than five.

As we've seen, utilitarians might reject (1), but that's not terribly surprising. They aren't the target of his argument.

A more interesting response is to press Taurek on what "friendship" means. Sure, if we're talking about intimate, lifelong relationships, then we might indeed have obligations towards our "friends." Maybe it would even be fine to break a promise to help a friend, all things considered. So we can't infer from (2) the permissibility of saving a friend to (3) the permissibility of saving anyone.

But Taurek is careful here. When he says "friend," he means a friendly acquaintance—not your BFF, but someone you merely "know and like." (Think of your barista or your bus driver.) His point is that *this* kind of friendship isn't a source of moral duties, so if you can save even *this* kind of friend, you can save anyone. That seems fair enough.

At last we arrive at the all-time classic response. It is due to Derek Parfit, whose reply to Taurek is called "Innumerate Ethics" (more trash talk…).

Parfit's point is this. If friends are just people we "know and like," we can't infer from (1) the permissibility of saving ourselves to (2) the permissibility of saving a friend. We can only save ourselves because we have special "agent-relative permissions"—that is, permissions to be partial towards ourselves. These permissions, naturally, should also let us favor some intimate loved ones. But not just anyone. We cannot favor strangers in the same way that we favor ourselves, and we cannot favor those we merely know and like. So while it's supererogatory to sacrifice oneself to save five, it's obligatory to forsake one's "friend," in Taurek's sense of friendship.

At the time, Parfit's reply was just *devastating*. Agent-relative permissions were a hot new thing, and Taurek didn't even mention them.

But in hindsight, this doesn't look like such a clean kill. The entire topic of supererogation, including "agent-relative permissions," is now teeming with paradoxes. (See Chapter 6.) Parfit's first book (1984) would introduce some legendary objections to agent-relativity. And Parfit's last book (2011) would give up on permissions (opting instead for reasons).

If we are, for whatever reason, wary of agent-relative permissions, but still on board with (1) the permissibility of saving oneself rather than five, we can't just leave David in the dust. We have to face "the difficulty of reconciling" our beliefs about partiality with our beliefs about counting the numbers.

Classic Presentations

John M. Taurek, "Should the Numbers Count?" *Philosophy & Public Affairs* **6** (1977): 293–316.

Background Reading

G. E. M. Anscombe, "Who Is Wronged? Philippa Foot on Double Effect: One Point," *Oxford Review* **5** (1967): 16–17. Reprinted as Chapter 19 of her *Human Life, Action and Ethics: Essays by G. E. M. Anscombe*, Mary Geach and Luke Gormally, eds. (Exeter: Imprint Academic, 2006): 249–252.

Philippa Foot, "The Problem of Abortion and the Doctrine of the Double Effect," *Oxford Review* **5** (1967): 5–15. Reprinted as Chapter 2 of her *Virtues and Vices: And Other Essays in Moral Philosophy* (Oxford: Clarendon Press, 2002): 19–32.

Responses and Other Treatments

Derek Parfit, "Innumerate Ethics," *Philosophy and Public Affairs* **7** (1978): 285–301.

Frances Myrna Kamm, *Morality, Mortality Volume I: Death and Whom to Save From It* (New York: Oxford University Press, 1993): Chs. 5 and 6.

Further Reading

Daniel Muñoz, "The Many, the Few, and the Nature of Value," *Ergo* **9** (2021): 70–87.

David Edmonds, *Parfit: A Philosopher and His Mission to Save Morality* (Princeton: Princeton University Press, 2023): 137–138.

Questions for Reflection

1.   One reason why Taurek's paper has become so notorious is that he doesn't think it's *better* to save many than to save few—not even if it's a billion versus one! Does this view follow from the three-step "David" argument? How would we have to change the argument to derive the view? Do the changes make the argument more persuasive—or less?

2.   Anscombe, unlike Taurek, thinks that you might have a *reason* to save five rather than one. Could Anscombe hold on to this view while also accepting Taurek's three-step argument?

3.   Can a version of Taurek's argument be used to show that you may save one stranger from a small harm rather than saving another stranger from a big harm? Why or why not?

18. *THE THIRD MAN*

In the classic 1949 film, Joseph Cotten plays Holly Martins, a guileless American who writes potboiler Westerns. Holly has just arrived in the shadowy and mysterious world of postwar Vienna. The city is tenuously governed by four powers; the black market flourishes amidst the rubble. Holly has been invited to Vienna by his oldest friend, who has offered him a job. Holly knows no one in Vienna except this friend—Harry Lime—and he doesn't understand a word of German.

Holly doesn't know it yet, but he has entered a moral maze whose twists and turns will threaten to swallow him up. At the start of the film, Holly's moral categories are roughly those of the dime-store Westerns he churns out: good guys, bad guys, damsels in distress, renegade sheriffs, and so on. But he is decidedly out of his depth in Vienna. Holly has now been plunged into a world of moral complexity and ambiguity for which those simple concepts will prove inadequate. He will need a keen moral compass to pick a difficult path through the treacherous shoals of friendship, loyalty, justice, and betrayal. The central question of the film is whether he does so successfully.

The situation soon proves to be very complicated indeed. Holly is told on arrival in Vienna that Harry Lime has been killed. Holly falls in love with the beautiful Anna, Harry's girl, but she can think only of Harry. Then Harry is revealed to be a truly bad guy: he and his cronies were running a penicillin racket in which they stole medicine from hospitals and diluted it for sale on the black market, to the great detriment of the children who were treated with it.[1] What's more, once Holly starts seeking information about Harry's suspicious death, an innocent informant is suddenly killed.

The culminating complexity comes when the charismatic Harry, played by Orson Welles, turns out to be very much *alive*. (He had faked his own death to get the police off his trail.) He is unapologetic about his crimes and even about tipping off the Russians to Anna's false papers (which, ironically, he had procured for her). At the top of the ferris wheel in Vienna's Prater Park, Harry says to Holly:

> Look down there. Would you feel any pity if one of those *dots* stopped moving forever? If I offered you £20,000 for every dot that stopped—would you really, old man, tell me to keep my money?

As they leave the ride Harry makes Holly an offer.

> [There's] nobody left in Vienna I can really trust—and we have always done everything together. When you make up your mind, send me a message... I'll meet you any place, any time. And when we do meet, old man, it is you I want to see, not the police. Remember that, won't you?

All of this places Holly in a moral bind. He could ensure that Harry is caught and brought to justice by setting up a decoy rendezvous with Harry, knowing that the police will be lying in wait. But Harry is Holly's oldest friend. Harry is also, however, a callous criminal who views people as dots, has in effect had Anna deported behind the Iron Curtain, and is totally prepared to kill to save his skin. (He even seems ambiguously to threaten Holly.) Should Holly betray Harry?

Two characters on either side of Holly think this question is simpler than Holly does. Major Calloway, the British policeman tracking Harry, is impatient with Holly's reluctance. The best outcome overall is clearly that this dangerous criminal be captured and gotten off the streets. Why should anyone hesitate to contribute to bringing this about? When Calloway tells Holly that "It won't make any difference in the long run: I'll get him," Holly replies "Well, I won't have helped." Calloway sardonically answers, "That will be a fine boast to make."

Calloway's impartial, consequentialist moral outlook may be fine for a policeman who represents the public interest and is not connected to any of the particular people involved. But he seems to expect Holly—who *is* deeply entangled with these people—to have the same view of the situation as he does.

Anna occupies the opposite moral pole. Her outlook is crystal clear: she loved Harry and is still on his side. After she finds out about his crimes, she no longer wants to see him or hear him; but "he's still a part of me. I couldn't do a thing to harm him." She responds angrily when Holly proposes that he could get her out of Vienna by helping the police. "If you want to sell your services, I'm not willing to be the price... I loved him. You loved him... Look at yourself. They have names for faces like that." She recoils from what she sees as Holly's treachery. Throughout the film, her preoccupation is Harry's well-being.

In the end Holly does betray and then kill his friend, in a famous scene in the sewers of Vienna. The very last scene of the film takes place at Harry's (second) interment; Holly and Anna are the only mourners. After the burial Holly waits for Anna at the end of an avenue of trees. In a long take, Anna slowly approaches, walking steadily. When she arrives at the end of the avenue she just keeps on walking, past Holly and out of the frame. She doesn't give Holly so much as a backward glance. It is one of the most devastating rejections in cinema: Anna's icy revulsion at Holly is almost palpable.

The Third Man offers up a complicated mix of moral considerations and presents us with several different views on how they add up. How do justice, friendship, loyalty, and betrayal balance out in the case of Harry Lime? The film's view may seem to be that Holly does the right thing by betraying and killing Harry. But the film also gives Anna the last word: her disgust for Holly at the end of the film should make us question that assessment. The film ultimately leaves us to sort through these questions ourselves.

Classic Presentation

The Third Man, dir. Carol Reed, 1949.

Responses and Other Treatments

Julia Driver, "Justice, Mercy, and Friendship in *The Third Man*," in Ward E. Jones and Samantha Vice, eds., *Ethics at the Cinema* (Oxford: Oxford University Press, 2011): 267–284.

Dean Cocking and Jeanette Kennett, "Friendship and Moral Danger," *Journal of Philosophy* **97** (2000): 278–296.

Questions for Reflection

1.   Anna refuses to benefit from any plot to entrap Harry. Is this stance irrational? What if she simply never found out what was behind her ticket out of Vienna?
2.   Does Harry's moral character cancel all duties of loyalty or friendship which Holly might otherwise have had toward Harry?
3.   Do you see value in the kind of steadfast loyalty which Anna maintains *vis-à-vis* Harry? If so, is this compatible with thinking that Anna's moral position is mistaken?

19. THE ARCHBISHOP AND THE VALET

It's happened again. (See **#6** and **#7, The Trolley Problem Parts I and II**; **#16, Singer's Pond** and **#17, David and the Scarce Drug**; **#26, The All or Nothing Problem**; and others.) There is a mortal threat—a runaway trolley, an imminent drowning, a fiery conflagration—and you are once again called upon to rescue someone if you can and so choose. This time it's a fire, threatening to engulf a house. In France. At the end of the 17th century. In Cambrai, a city in northern France, if you must know.

There are, at present, two people at home, both now mortally threatened by the fire. One is François Fénelon (1651–1715), Archbishop of Cambrai and tutor to Louis XIV's grandson, second in line to the throne. The other is Fénelon's valet. You can save only one. What should you do?

William Godwin, the English political philosopher who presented this thought experiment in 1798, has a clear answer for you: you should save the Archbishop. Archbishop Fénelon would later write *The Adventures of Telemachus*, a full-throated attack on absolute monarchy by divine right. It was a runaway bestseller across Europe and helped spur the downfall of the institution it critiqued. Knowing this—remember he is writing a hundred years later—Godwin states that the Archbishop is "a being of more worth and importance" than his valet (60). After all, Fénelon ended up making very significant contributions to human happiness. And in situations of this kind, Godwin says, "that life ought to be preferred which will be most conducive to the general good" (60). That criterion would definitely favor Fénelon.

Notice how very prescriptive Godwin's answer is here: your *only* acceptable choice is to rescue the Archbishop. Godwin does not specifically pronounce on whether it would be acceptable to choose to rescue *neither*,[2] although his discussion strongly suggests that he would not be a fan. But he is very clear that if you *do* go in for rescuing, you *must* choose the Archbishop. It would be *morally wrong* to run into the house and rescue the valet, if you could just as easily have reached the Archbishop instead. It would also be morally wrong to flip a coin, or to choose randomly, which would give each person an equal chance of being saved. These options are off the table: instead, you are *required* to save the Archbishop and not the valet. Why? Because the Archbishop's survival "will be most conducive to the general good" (60).

Let's now add just one more detail to the example, though: *the valet is your father.*

Now, you might think, things look very different. Instead of both people being strangers to you, now one of them is your intimate. Now there is someone you love inside that burning house—someone who's known you literally your whole life, who helped raise you, and who is partly responsible for your existing at all. You might well think this alters the moral calculus considerably. While a "God's-eye view" might be the right perspective to take on a situation when you have no connection to either party, surely your special relation to your father makes a moral difference in this version of the scenario.

Godwin denies this. *If* his instruction to save the Archbishop was correct in the original scenario, it is equally correct now. Adding this detail about the cast of characters, he says,

> would not alter the truth of the proposition. The life of Fenelon would still be more valuable than that of the valet; and justice, pure, unadulterated justice, would still have preferred that which was most valuable. Justice would have taught me to save the life of Fenelon at the expense of the other. What magic is there in the pronoun "my," that should justify us in overturning the decisions of impartial truth? (60)

Godwin holds that "my" is powerless against "impartial truth." The correct thing to do, *for anyone*, is to rescue the Archbishop; this verdict cannot vary across rescuers according to their connection with the people involved.

Godwin's view is certainly uncompromising.

> Justice requires that I should put myself in the place of an impartial spectator of human concerns, and divest myself of retrospect to my own predilections. (xv)

Such a strict impartialism appears extreme almost to the point of ridiculousness. Brian Barry claims that "for anti-utilitarians, if Godwin had not existed he would have to have been invented" (225); Bernard Williams speaks of Godwin's "ferociously rational refusal to respect any consideration that an ordinary human being would find compelling" (107). Godwin's denial of any moral significance to love and personal relationships seems to justify these digs.

But there is another aspect of Godwin's view worth attending to. The reason Godwin gives for why you must (allegedly) save the Archbishop is "his importance to the general weal" (61). This invites at least two questions, even in the version of the example in which the valet is not your father. First, we might ask whether it is *fair* to both potential rescuees to use the above principle of choice. If we adopt as our guiding criterion the prospect of future contributions to the general happiness, the poor valet has virtually *no* chance of being saved. But shouldn't each of these people have some claim to be saved, simply as human beings? Second—and related to the question we have just raised—we might wonder whether Godwin's criterion would prescribe leaving *both* people to burn, if there were something *else* sufficiently contributory to the general happiness also in the house. Imagine for instance that on the study table lay a confidential manuscript by Edward Jenner explaining how to use cowpox virus to inoculate against smallpox.[3] Surely the loss of this document before it could be published would set back the general happiness even more than the loss of the Archbishop. If things other than people can make contributions to the general weal, then we may not be required to save a *person* at all.

Classic Presentation

William Godwin, *Enquiry Concerning Political Justice and Its Influence on Morals and Happiness* (London: J. Watson, 1842). Fourth Edition. Book II, Chapter II.

Responses and Other Treatments

Marcia Baron, "Impartiality and Friendship," *Ethics* **101** (1991): 836–857.
Brian Barry, *Justice as Impartiality* (Oxford: Clarendon Press, 1995): Ch. 9.
Peter Singer, Leslie Cannold, and Helga Kuhse, "William Godwin and the Defense of Impartialist Ethics," *Utilitas* **7** (1995): 67–86.
Bernard Williams, *Ethics and the Limits of Philosophy* (London: Fontana, 1985).

Questions for Reflection

1.   In the version of the case in which both people are strangers to you, what do you think about the idea of flipping a coin to determine whom you would save? What do you see as the pros and cons of this proposal?

2.   Suppose you disagree with Godwin's verdict that you *must* save the Archbishop in preference to your father. Do you disagree because you think it is *permissible* for you to save your father, or because you think it is *obligatory* that you save your father? What reasons could you give in support of your position?

20. ONE THOUGHT TOO MANY

A man is on a boat at sea in the midst of a terrible storm. Looking ahead, he sees two people struggling to stay afloat, thrown from their vessel in a boat crash, each at equal risk of drowning. To one side, there is a total stranger; to the other, there is the man's wife. The man has time to save only one person. What should he do?

Normally, morality says we have to treat people equally. But not in this sort of case, thinks Charles Fried:

> surely it would be absurd to insist that... he must treat both equally, perhaps by flipping a coin. (1980: 227)

Most ethical theorists would heartily agree.

But why *isn't* the man required to treat the two equally? Why would morality let him just save his wife? Fried takes this line of questioning very seriously. He continues:

> One answer is that where the potential rescuer occupies no office such as that of captain of a ship, public health official or the like, the occurrence of the accident may itself stand as a sufficient randomizing event to meet the dictates of fairness, so he may prefer his friend, or loved one. Where the rescuer does occupy an official position, the argument that he must overlook personal ties is not unacceptable. (1980: 227)

In other words, there's no need to flip a coin, since the entire predicament is itself a random event, and the wife just got lucky that her loved one happened to be the potential savior nearby.

Maybe there's something to Fried's take. But it has long since been overshadowed by an insight that it inspired in the critic Bernard Williams, one of the great iconoclasts of ethical theory.

To Williams, the problem isn't that Fried is giving the wrong answer. He's fretting over the wrong question. There shouldn't be any mystery as to why the man may show a preference for his wife. Of course he may! The puzzling thing is why ethical theorists like Fried would see any need to justify such a preference. Why put the "onus of proof" (1981: 17) on those who think the man may save his wife, rather than on those who think he must give her a 50% chance of a watery death?

The moral of the story, Williams suggests, could be that "some situations lie beyond justifications" (1981: 18). But what does this mean?

Presumably, Williams is not saying that the man's choice to save his wife is unjustifiable. Then it would be *wrong*, which is the view that Fried rightly dismissed as "absurd."

Williams' meaning becomes clearer as he continues on:

> surely this is a justification on behalf of the rescuer, that the person he chose to rescue was his wife? (1981: 18)

Williams' answer is a yes—with an asterisk. He continues:

> It depends on how much weight is carried by "justification": the consideration that it was his wife is certainly, for instance, an explanation which should silence comment. But something more ambitious than this is usually intended, essentially involving the idea that moral principle can legitimate his preference, yielding the conclusion that in situations of this kind it is at least all right (morally permissible) to save one's wife... But this construction provides the agent with one thought too many: it might have been hoped by some (for instance, by his wife) that his motivating thought, fully spelled out, would be the thought that it was his wife, not that it was his wife and that in situations of this kind it is permissible to save one's wife. (1981: 18)

This idea of "one thought too many" has utterly fascinated ethical theorists, even if we can't seem to agree on what it means. Is Williams warning against cool rationality in the heat of the moment? Is he saying that morality is irrelevant when the life of a loved one is on the line? That we should expect a kind of devotion that transcends morality from those who love us?

Whatever Williams meant, his quip has made Fried's thought experiment one of the most well-known of the last century, a source of insights for ethical theorists interested in love, reasons, and impartial morality.

RESPONSES

What did Williams mean, though?

His view seems to be something like this. When the man saves his wife, "It's my wife!" is a perfectly good reason to act ("an explanation which should silence comment"). But many ethical theorists would insist that this is only part of the real reason; the rest has to involve a moral principle. Rather than just "It's my wife," the complete reason should be: "First: it's my wife. Second: morality allows one to save one's wife in a situation like this." It is that second thought that Williams sees as otiose—or worse, insulting! (Imagine the wife's reaction. "You see I'm about to die, and you *still* need to think more before making your move?")

So what makes "it's morally permissible" a problematic thought? According to what Susan Wolf calls the "Standard View" of Williams:

> the thought of moral permissibility *would* be one thought too many *if* it is understood to occur at the moment of action... however... there seems nothing wrong with a person wondering, in a cool and reflective moment, under what conditions one may give preference to one's loved ones and under what conditions one may not. (2012: 74)

Williams is not troubled, on this view, by the thought of morality itself, but only by the man's motive in the moment. As John Deigh puts it, it is "inappropriate" for the husband to bring in "impartiality at the ground level, the level of deciding what to do in concrete situations"—though impartial morality could well be a fine "ideal" when thinking in the abstract about one's moral principles (1991: 860). In the philosophy room, where time is not exactly of the essence, it's fine to dwell on the dictates of morality. In an emergency, just save your spouse!

But some "non-standard" readers, like Wolf and Marcia Baron, interpret Williams as making a deeper point. He is not just saying which thoughts should run through your head in a "concrete situation." Even when thinking abstractly, there is no need to "check in" with morality before you could be moved to save your spouse. Why would you need to check? Suppose morality told you to let your spouse die—would you?

Wolf thinks the real problem with having "one thought too many" is that it reveals a kind of obsessive attitude towards morality: an unconditional and absolute commitment. She and Williams see room in life for other commitments, such as to one's projects and loved ones. "Life has to have substance if anything is to have sense," says Williams (1981: 18). But the substance of life consists in attachments to people, not just to principles.

Classic Presentations

Charles Fried, *An Anatomy of Values* (Cambridge: Harvard University Press, 1980).
Bernard Williams, "Persons, Character, and Morality," in his *Moral Luck: Philosophical Papers 1973–1980* (Cambridge: Cambridge University Press, 1981): 1–19.

Responses and Other Treatments

"Standard" interpretations of Williams:
John Deigh, "Impartiality: A Closing Note," *Ethics* **101** (1991): 858–864.
Nicholas Smyth, "Integration and Authority: Rescuing the 'One Thought Too Many' Problem," *Canadian Journal of Philosophy* **48** (2018): 812–830.
"Non-standard" interpretations of Williams:
Marcia Baron, "Rethinking 'One Thought Too Many'," in Mark Timmons, ed., *Oxford Studies in Normative Ethics, Volume 7* (Oxford: Oxford University Press, 2017): 31–50.
Susan Wolf, "'One Thought Too Many': Love, Morality, and the Ordering of Commitment," in Ulrike Heuer and Gerald Lang, eds., *Luck, Value, and Commitment: Themes from the Ethics of Bernard Williams* (Oxford: Oxford University Press, 2012): 71–92.

Further Reading

Harry Frankfurt, *The Reasons of Love* (Princeton: Princeton University Press: 2004). (See especially pp. 36–37 in relation to the first question for reflection.)

Questions for Reflection

1. Suppose the man's wife is named Judy, and she finds out that her husband saves her on the basis of two thoughts: "First: Judy needs me. Second: Judy is my wife." Might Judy think of the second thought as one thought too many? Might Williams agree?

2. Williams, on the "non-standard" reading, thinks that we shouldn't be unconditionally and absolutely committed to morality; we may instead act from our attachments to people we care about. Does that mean that we may do immoral things to save our loved ones? (Imagine a runaway trolley headed towards a family member—may you push two strangers in front of it, if that's the only way to stop the trolley?) If not, what *does* it mean?

NOTES

1 Graham Greene, who wrote the screenplay, may have been inspired by various actual cases of fake or diluted penicillin being sold on the black market after the war. See www.bmj.com/content/bmj/355/bmj.i6494.full.pdf and https://bshm.org.uk/the-third-man-was-true-penicillin-in-post-war-austria/.

2 See **#26, The All or Nothing Problem**, for attention to that question.

3 Edward Jenner performed the first ever vaccination (against smallpox) in 1796, but he did not publish his treatise "On the Origin of the Vaccine Inoculation" until 1801. So a manuscript explaining his findings might well have been lying on a desk in 1798, when Godwin published the Archbishop/valet example. Let us imagine that it was the only copy.

5

MORAL DILEMMAS

Morally freighted decisions can be complex. In previous chapters we've talked about a variety of factors which all seem morally relevant, such as consequences, rights, and special ties to particular persons. As we've also seen, those factors can conflict: different aspects of a situation can point in opposite moral directions. In **#14, Feinberg's Cabin**, for instance, the property rights of the cabin's owner give you a reason *not* to break in, whereas the threat to your survival gives you a strong reason *to* break in. In this particular case, the resolution of the moral conflict seemed clear. All things considered, it is *not* morally wrong for you to break in; under the circumstances, this is morally permissible. Why? Because while there is admittedly a moral case *against* breaking in, the moral case *for* being permitted to break in is stronger. More specifically, it's because the owner's property rights pale in importance compared with your urgent need. (They do not vanish altogether, however, as is shown by your duty to compensate him or her after the fact.)

Not all cases of moral conflict are as easy to resolve, however. Sometimes the factors pulling in opposite moral directions are each very powerful, and it is not clear whether one of them morally outweighs the other(s). In such cases we may doubt whether there *is* a satisfactory resolution of the conflict. Could it be that in light of the strong

DOI: 10.4324/9781003319962-6

reasons in play there is *nothing* we could do that would be morally OK?

If there are such cases, they constitute *moral dilemmas*—the theme of this chapter. Ethicists dispute whether any genuinely irresolvable moral dilemmas actually exist. Some maintain that even in the worst of circumstances there is always a *least bad* option, and it is at least morally permissible to do *that*. Others think there can be conflicts so tragic that *no* option is morally acceptable. The cases that follow will give you a chance to form your own opinion. You may think that *none* of them is really a dilemma; or that some of them are.

The (potential) dilemmas in this chapter come in a variety of flavors, although several of them have a feature in common: they are generated by *someone else's* wrongdoing. In **#21, Kant's Murderer at the Door**, you receive a most unwelcome visit; in **#22, Jim and the Villagers**, Jim must choose how to respond to an imminent execution of innocent civilians; in **#23**, Sophie and her children have just arrived in Auschwitz, and she is faced with **Sophie's Choice**. The alleged dilemma in **#24, The Gentle Murder Paradox**, is of a different kind. Here no one is *faced* with a dilemma; the problem is rather that we can use some seemingly irresistible moral logic to derive flatly inconsistent claims. We can even do this in plain-vanilla cases which don't feature any moral conflict!

As you'll see, these entries illustrate that there are really two distinct reasons why you might seem to confront a moral dilemma. Either you are an unlucky actor in a tragic moral conflict, or you are the unwitting perpetrator of a mistake of moral logic.

21. KANT'S MURDERER AT THE DOOR

As far as moral principles go, "Don't lie" is about as universal and be-loved as it gets. We agree that it's wrong for sellers to hawk a "miracle cure" they know to be worthless goop, and wrong for criminals to render false testimony in order to escape justice.

But is it *always* wrong to lie? What if lying is the only way to avoid something bad? A common example of this is the white lie, told to spare a friend's hurt feelings. ("Don't worry, you look great in polka dots!") White lies seem like no big deal—mini-sins, at worst, and probably forgivable ones at that.

The philosopher Immanuel Kant, however, takes lies—all lies—extremely seriously. For Kant, it is wrong to lie to avoid hurting a friend's feelings, or indeed even to save their life. Kant's extremism emerges from a thought experiment known as the "murderer at the door."

Imagine that your friend, on the run from a murderer, is taking shelter in your house. Along comes a knock at the door—it's the mur-derer! Hate in his eyes, he asks you where your friend is. Now you have a few options. You could tell the truth, dooming your friend. You could also say nothing, which would suggest that you have something to hide; again, doom. The most plausible way to save your friend is to lie, to insist that your friend is somewhere else, throwing the murderer off the scent.

Do you think it's morally wrong to lie in this case? Probably not. If anything, it seems like you have a moral *duty* to tell the lie and save your friend.[1]

But Kant thinks you have the exact opposite duty. Your duty is not to lie—even though a lie would save a life! Even though the person demanding the truth is an evildoer, who will use that truth to do a really evil thing!

What was Kant thinking? Is there anything to be said in favor of telling the truth to the murderer at the door?

Let's think about it. One possibility is that you have a duty to the murderer not to deceive him. Kant, surprisingly, doubts it. We do owe it to people in general to be truthful towards them. But here, the mur-derer is unjustly compelling you to say where your friend is. He's put you in a pinch, and the situation is all his fault. That means you don't owe him the truth anymore. Think of it like self-defense. Usually, you have a duty to people not to use force against them. But that duty goes out the window if they unjustly attack you.

Another possibility is that you have a duty to yourself not to lie. "To thine own self be true." Misrepresenting your own thoughts is, perhaps, a sign that you do not ultimately *respect* or *value* your own thoughts as such, that you don't think it matters what you really think. (Compare the liar to a sloppy book critic, whose work clearly sends the message, "I don't care what this book really says.") Kant, however, does not go this route. He does not say that lying to the murderer is wrong merely or even mainly because of a duty you owe to yourself. (Though he does agree that your lie would earn you reproach for "*worthlessness*" (8:426).)

So what is the nature of the duty not to lie? If it's not a duty owed to the murderer, or to oneself, then to whom is it owed?

Kant's answer is that you owe the duty to *everyone*. He explains:

> Truthfulness in statements that one cannot avoid is a human being's duty to everyone, however great the disadvantage to him or to another that may result from it; and although I indeed do no wrong to him who unjustly compels me to make the statement if I falsify it, I nevertheless do wrong in the most essential part of duty *in general* by such falsification... I bring it about, as far as I can, that statements (declarations) in general are not believed, and so too that all rights which are based on contracts come to nothing. (8:426)

In other words: when I lie, I undercut the social trust that so many rights depend on. I make it hard to believe *anything that anyone says*, like the trolls and bots who make it harder for us to trust what we read online.

RESPONSES

A natural question, in response to Kant's view, is: *huh?*

Why is Kant such a stickler about lying? In his defense, he does make an intriguing argument. Suppose you lie, saying that your friend is out on the town. Then before you can tell your friend that she's safe, she leaves her hiding place to go out on the town—where she encounters the murderer! If she is then murdered, Kant would say that *you are responsible*. After all, there was a chance that if you'd told the truth, "neighbors might have come and apprehended the murderer while he was searching the house for his enemy and the deed would have been prevented" (8:427). So, the murder happens as a result of your lie, and you are on the hook. This shows that you are not altogether innocent when you lie, even in the lucky case where the murder is thwarted.

There is something to this. Liars do often "own" the consequences of their lies. If you sell useless goop as a cure for heart disease, and people die because they used your goop instead of real medicine, those deaths are on you. But this lie seems quite unlike your lie to the murderer. When you lie about the goop, you're conning someone for a quick buck. When you lie about your friend's whereabouts, you're doing your best to save her life! Most ethicists would say that makes a world of difference.

Today, hardly anyone is tempted by Kant's take on the murderer at the door. Partly, that is because it is doubtful that single lie, told in an emergency, is going to obliterate our broader systems of social trust. And partly it is because lying does not seem absolutely wrong. Rather than being wrong no matter what, lying is only wrong in general, with plenty of exceptions.

Even most Kantians think Kant went too far. In "The Murderer at the Door: What Kant Should Have Said," Michael Cholbi gives a Kantian argument in favor of lying to the murderer. It goes like this. If the murderer is coming for you, and lying is the only way to save yourself, you have to lie. Kant, after all, believes in a duty of self-preservation. But Kant also believes in a "symmetry" between self and other: what you have to do for yourself, you have to do for anybody else. So, you have to lie to save your friend from the murderer at the door.

Still, in ethical theory, the most extreme ideas are often the most interesting and challenging. Don't expect Kant's thought experiment to go away anytime soon!

Classic Presentation

Immanuel Kant, "On the Supposed Right to Lie from Philanthropy," in his *Practical Philosophy*, Mary Gregor, ed. and trans. (Cambridge: Cambridge University Press, 1996): 605–616.
(There are many translations of Kant's works, but they should all include the standardized page numbers which we have used in the citations above.)

Responses and Other Treatments

Immanuel Kant, *Lectures on Ethics*, Peter Heath and J. B. Schneewind, eds., Peter Heath, trans. (Cambridge: Cambridge University Press, 1997): 27:444–27:449, particularly 27:448 (in the standardized Kant page numbers). (Here, Kant seems less extreme.)

Christine Korsgaard, "The Right to Lie: Kant on Dealing with Evil," *Philosophy & Public Affairs* **15** (1986): 325–349.

Tamar Schapiro, "Kantian Rigorism and Mitigating Circumstances," *Ethics* **117** (2006): 32–57.

Michael Cholbi, "The Murderer at the Door: What Kant Should Have Said," *Philosophy and Phenomenological Research* **79** (2009): 17–46.

Seana Shiffrin, *Speech Matters: On Lying, Morality, and the Law* (Princeton: Princeton University Press, 2015): Ch. 1.

Questions for Reflection

1. Do you think anyone is wronged if you lie to the murderer at the door? Who—you yourself, the murderer, or everyone?

2. Suppose that the murderer at the door isn't just a random murderer, but a representative of the government. Often the example is used of a Nazi officer hunting for Jewish people. If the Nazi asks you if you are helping hide a Jewish family, and you indeed are, would it be wrong to lie? Does the fact that the Nazi purports to represent the government change anything?

3. Kant thinks that the duty to be truthful is "unconditional." Others think that the duty depends on context. Whom are you talking to? How much trouble would result from telling the truth? Are you being pressured to give answers? And so on. Do you think these factors make a difference to the duty to be truthful? Can you think of any other factors that might matter?

22. JIM AND THE VILLAGERS

Jim is traveling in a country plagued by political instability and rival militias, especially in remote areas far from the capital. After viewing the remains of an awe-inspiring ancient temple, Jim is walking through a village in search of a cool beverage. He is brought up short by a strange scene playing itself out just off the main street. A man in military-style fatigues is facing a large group of what seem to be locals lined up against the wall of a building. He is holding a gun, and Jim notices that several other armed men discreetly encircle the group. One of the locals gives Jim a terrified glance.

Jim feels he cannot simply walk on by. He butts in. The camo-clad man is not happy about the intrusion, but he reluctantly lowers his gun while he tells Jim that someone in this village ratted out a group of his men to a rival militia, with the result that his men were killed as they slept. He now intends to demonstrate to the villagers in the most forceful way possible that they should keep their mouths shut. The deaths of these twenty random inhabitants, he says, will surely send that message.

"On the other hand, though," says Mr. Camo, now warming to his subject, "here you are, a visitor from a faraway land. In honor of your visit, I will be pleased to offer *you* the opportunity to kill just one of these men. If you do, I will allow the rest of these vermin to escape with their lives—for now. But if you do not wish to avail yourself of this opportunity, I'll just proceed with my business. If you please?"

Jim is horrified. The locals look at him with pleading eyes. Mr. Camo raises his gun. What should Jim do?

★ ★ ★

Jim seems to be faced with an awful dilemma. He can't just kill an innocent man! But if he doesn't, all twenty are sure to be shot as soon as his back is turned. (He can see that there is no way for the locals to escape.) What is the right thing to do in a situation of this kind?

Bernard Williams offers this example as part of his critique of utilitarianism. Utilitarianism cares only about outcomes; and in this case, a very bad outcome is about to ensue if Jim does not intervene to prevent it. (See **#1, George and the Bioweapons**, and the "unlimited requirement of prevention" discussed there.) But even if we are not utilitarians, we can see a big difference in outcomes for these twenty men depending on Jim's choice. If Jim chooses to execute just one of the twenty, nineteen will live. (Since this is a thought experiment, we can stipulate that Mr. Camo is sincere in his "offer" and that he really will let the others go.) If, on the other hand, Jim refuses to have anything to do with Mr. Camo's murderous reprisals, all twenty will be killed. The first outcome—one dead—is significantly less bad than the second—twenty dead.

On the other hand, what Jim would himself *do* if he shot an innocent local would be far *worse*. That's a terrible thing to do! These locals have clearly done nothing to deserve execution. For him to shoot one of these innocent men would be no better than a stone-cold murder. If he walks away, at least he hasn't murdered anyone—and he hasn't been complicit in the militia's brutal revenge.

Jim is experiencing a clash of perspectives. From a perspective that simply looks down on the world and evaluates what it sees—philosophers call this an *agent-neutral* perspective—it is far worse for twenty innocent men to be killed than for one innocent man to be killed. (If a hurricane hit this village, we would certainly rather learn that it killed one inhabitant than twenty.) But from Jim's own personal perspective as an agent—that is, from the *agent-relative* standpoint—it is far worse *to kill* than *not to kill*. As Thomas Nagel puts it, "what *happens* will be better... But [you] will have *done* something worse" (180; second emphasis added). We may feel that such clashes between the agent-neutral and the agent-relative perspectives preclude any clear moral resolution.

Christine Korsgaard suggests that we can break through the apparent deadlock here by framing the issue in a different way. For we risk forgetting that there is another perspective here which is highly relevant: the standpoint of the villagers themselves. Korsgaard urges that we pay attention to those "pleading eyes" which we noted in passing. What do the *villagers* want Jim to do? If the villagers themselves want Jim to select one of them to kill—even more so, if one of them *volunteers* to be killed to spare the others[2]—that changes the moral parameters of the situation significantly. Korsgaard proposes that rather than leaving Jim to work out the clash between the agent-neutral and the agent-relative on his own, he and the potential victims should *talk to each other*.

Classic Presentation

Bernard Williams, "A Critique of Utilitarianism," in J. J. C. Smart and Bernard Williams, *Utilitarianism: For and Against* (Cambridge: Cambridge University Press, 1973): Section 3.

Responses and Other Treatments

Thomas Nagel, *The View from Nowhere* (New York: Oxford University Press, 1986): Ch. 9, Sections 4 and 5.
Christine Korsgaard, "The Reasons We Can Share: An Attack on the Distinction Between Agent-Relative and Agent-Neutral Values," *Social Philosophy and Policy* **10** (1993): 24–51.

Questions for Reflection

1. Jim is well aware that the overall outcome will be better if he chooses one of the men to kill. Should this lead him to set aside his concerns about the wrongness of his potential action and his seeming complicity with evil?
2. Suppose Jim *was* able to talk to the villagers, and they all said they wanted him to select one man to kill. However, each one of them said Jim should choose someone *else*: none of them was willing to be the sacrificial lamb. Would this alter the moral situation for Jim? If so, how?

23. *SOPHIE'S CHOICE*

In the novel by William Styron and the film starring Meryl Streep, Sophie and her children have just arrived at Auschwitz. Sophie, Eva, and the older Jan are standing in line waiting for "selection." Being sent off to the left means the labor camp; off to the right means the gas chambers. The SS officer on the rail platform leers at the beautiful Sophie and openly tells her he'd like to have her in his bed. He asks if she is a Communist or a Jew; she says she isn't. Then, seeing a chance to possibly help her children, she speaks to the officer in terms she hopes might influence him. She tells him her children are "fully Aryan" and their blood is "pure."

The SS man appears to think about this. He says that normally all young children are immediately sent to the right. But for this very beautiful prisoner, he is prepared to extend a special favor. Sophie may choose just *one* of her children to go to the gas chambers. In that case the other child will be allowed to stay with her (and be assigned to the labor camp). If Sophie refuses to choose, however, the SS will simply take both children.

In response, Sophie, anguished, begs him not to make her choose. She says she *cannot* possibly choose. She holds her daughter tighter in her arms and pushes her son behind her legs to hide him. But then SS soldiers move in and start to grab the children. Sophie tries to resist, but at the last possible second she cries out, "Take my daughter!" Eva's face immediately registers her mother's betrayal, and as she is carted off by the SS men she screams in terror. Jan and Sophie can only watch as Eva disappears.

Sophie has been put in an absolutely horrific position. She has no good options. If she refuses to choose, both children will be killed. Sophie would give anything to avert that outcome. But if she *does* choose, she thereby delivers one of her children to their death. And they know it, too—even little Eva. Moreover, Sophie then becomes a *participant*, an active party, in the SS officer's cruel scheme: a kind of accessory or accomplice, albeit unwilling, to her child's murder. On the other hand, if she refuses to cooperate, *both* children will be marched to the crematorium. That would be too high a price to pay for non-participation.

The SS man is asking Sophie to do the unthinkable: save one of her children by dooming the other. Sophie's choice looks like a genuine *moral dilemma*: a situation in which no matter what you do you will have committed a grave moral wrong for which there is no adequate justification. Normally, pointing to serious moral objections to all other alternatives suffices to justify an action. But here, arguably, it does not: in a true moral dilemma, there are *conclusive* moral reasons against *every* option. Sophie experiences forsaking her daughter as unforgivable, as violating an unconditional commandment to protect your child in all circumstances.

The novel and film show how her choice haunted Sophie for the rest of her unhappy life. She could never rid herself of guilt for what she did, and she took that guilt to her grave. Philosopher Patricia Greenspan characterizes Sophie's predicament as follows:

> She knows she is responsible for doing something wrong, something she could have avoided—even though she could not have avoided doing wrong. The same would be true if she had chosen differently, and allowed both children to be killed. It would be strangely insensitive for a mother in her position not to experience guilt at either choice. (120)

While we may see Sophie as blameless, we nonetheless understand her tremendous guilt at what she did.

Some philosophers dispute whether there really are any moral dilemmas in this strict sense. Can wrongdoing, they say, really be *unavoidable*? What if you chose the *least bad* of your options? (In the case of Sophie we are to understand that saving her son *was* the least bad option: since he was older, he seemed more likely to survive the camp. However, we never find out if he did.) They would urge that if you've done the best you could given the circumstances, then it is unfair to charge you with a *moral violation*, or to say you acted *morally wrongly*. For given your options (they would say), you made the right moral decision.

These critics perhaps see moral judgment as essentially *comparative*. On this picture, moral assessment always turns on how a given action ranks *in comparison to the alternatives*. For example, Earl Conee writes: "the existence of an absolute obligation always depends on the moral qualities of the act's alternatives as well as on its own merits" (135). When the alternatives all suck, that doesn't make right action impossible—it means you need to find the thing that is *least bad*. If you do that, you have compensated as best you could for any badness inherent in the situation.

Other theorists, however, maintain that certain wrongs cannot be compensated for. For example, sending your daughter to her death cannot be compensated for by saving your son. Nor can that action be justified by the small difference in their respective probabilities of survival. Your daughter and your son are not like a dime and two nickels: exchangeable for each other and of equal value. Rather, each child possesses a unique and non-fungible value the loss of which cannot be traded for a different gain. Your obligation as a parent to protect each of your children is therefore absolute: your obligation to one can neither override nor be cancelled by your obligation to the other. For this reason, philosopher Lisa Tessman suggests that certain moral requirements "are *non-negotiable* and remain binding even if they become impossible to satisfy" (2017: 22, emphasis added). Sophie's choice might well be an example.

Classic Presentations

William Styron, *Sophie's Choice* (New York: Random House, 1979).
Sophie's Choice, dir. Alan Pakula, 1982.

Responses and Other Treatments

Patricia Greenspan, "Moral Dilemmas and Guilt," *Philosophical Studies* **43** (1983): 117–125.
Lisa Tessman, *When Doing the Right Thing Is Impossible* (New York: Oxford University Press, 2017).
Earl Conee, "Why Moral Dilemmas Are Impossible," *American Philosophical Quarterly* **26** (1989): 133–141.
Lisa Tessman, *Moral Failure: On the Impossible Demands of Morality* (New York: Oxford University Press, 2014): Ch. 4.
Philippa Foot, *Moral Dilemmas: And Other Topics in Moral Philosophy* (Oxford: Clarendon Press, 2002): particularly Chs. 3 and 11.
Thomas E. Hill Jr., "Moral Dilemmas, Gaps, and Residues: A Kantian Perspective," in his *Human Welfare and Moral Worth: Kantian Perspectives* (Oxford: Oxford University Press, 2002): 362–402.
Rosalind Hursthouse, "Discussing Dilemmas," in her *Virtue and Action: Selected Papers* (Oxford: Oxford University Press, 2023): 162–172.

Questions for Reflection

1. Do you see the older child's greater probability of surviving the camp as a *tie-breaker* between Sophie's obligations to each of her children? (For more on tie-breaking, see **#33, Sweetening**.)

2. Consider the following claim:

    Given the circumstances, Sophie's obligation was merely to do *one or the other* of saving her daughter and saving her son. She fulfilled that obligation. Therefore she did not act wrongly.

    What do you think of this analysis of Sophie's situation? What are its implications for the possibility of genuine moral dilemmas?

3. Genuine moral dilemmas seem to threaten the well-known principle that *ought* implies *can*, according to which it only makes sense to say that someone *ought* to do something if they *can* do that thing. Why does this principle seem plausible? How is it connected to the possibility of moral dilemmas?

24. THE GENTLE MURDER PARADOX

Ethical theory teems with "ifs." Most are perfectly innocent, like:

- If you make a promise, you have to keep it.
- If you're drunk, you shouldn't drive.

But some "ifs" let you get away with murder. At least, that seems to follow from the *Gentle Murder Paradox*. We owe this paradox to James Forrester, a deontic logician—the kind of logician who studies moral terms like "permissible" and "ought."

Here's the situation. Imagine you're deciding between three options:

- Don't murder James.
- Murder James brutally.
- Murder James gently.

What ought you to do?

Let's go out on a limb here and say you are *not* supposed to murder poor James; he's an innocent guy, wouldn't hurt a fly. So, the right thing to do is not to murder. That said, clearly gentle murder is preferable to the brutal kind. (If we follow Forrester in defining "gently X-ing" to mean "X-ing in the least painful way.") So it seems that, *if* you're going to murder James, you ought to do it gently. Now let's add a twist: you are no angel. In fact, you're going to murder James!

From these assumptions, we can show something totally absurd. We can argue:

(1)   You're going to murder.
(2)   If you're going to murder, you ought to murder gently.

So: You ought to murder gently.

Clearly this can't follow. Gentle murder isn't what you ought to do. We started out assuming that you shouldn't murder anybody! And it can't be both that you ought to murder gently and that you ought not to murder. An obligation to murder gently implies an obligation to murder!

Clearly, the argument is fishy. And yet, it *looks* like a valid way of arguing. Consider:

(1)   You're drunk.
(2)   If you're drunk, you ought not to drive.

So: You ought not to drive.
    Seems like bulletproof reasoning. Same for:

(1)   You made a promise.
(2)   If you make a promise, you ought to keep it.

So: You ought to keep your promise.
    In general, it's safe to make the inference from "A" and "If A, then B" to "B." This form of reasoning is known as *modus ponens*. As you might guess from the Latin name, it's been around for a long time, and for a long time it's been a law of the logic for "if." And yet here it seems disastrous. From the fact that you *will* commit a murder, we infer that you *should* commit a murder—albeit a gentle one.

MURDER AND ROBBERY

Gentle murder may be "the deepest paradox of deontic logic" (Castañeda 1986: 155)—but it's not the only contender!

    Consider the *Robber Paradox*. Robbers should make amends to their victims, but they can only do so if they really did wrong. So, the thing they ought to do (making amends) involves their having done wrong. It seems to follow that they ought to have done wrong! After all, if you ought to do A, and A involves B, you ought to do B. If you ought to be nice to dogs, you ought to be nice to poodles. If you ought to respect all living things, you ought to respect insurance agents. And so on.

    Dan Bonevac (1998: 39) puts the Robber Paradox as follows.

(1)   You are a robber. $r.$
(2)   If you are a robber, you ought to make amends. $r \rightarrow O(m).$
(3)   Repenting involves having done wrong. $m \prec w.$

So: You ought to have done wrong. $O(w).$

To the right, you can see the sentences written in the language of deontic logic. The lower-case letters are sentences; $O(m)$ means m ought to be the case; "→" means "if, then;" and "$m \prec w$" means m strictly implies w—that is to say, there's no possible way for m to be true while w is false. That's what we meant when we said repenting "involves" having done wrong.

As Bonevac points out, the Gentle Murder Paradox can be seen as a special case of the Robber Paradox:

(1)	You're going to murder.	m.
(2)	If you're going to murder, you ought to murder gently.	$m \rightarrow O(g)$.
(3)	Murdering gently involves murdering.	$g \prec m$.
So:	You ought to murder.	$O(m)$.

Notice that the form of argument is the same; the twist is that murder plays the role of both the robbery and the wrongdoing. That said, the Gentle Murder Paradox seems puzzling enough even without the third premise, which we use to derive an obligation to murder. The first two premises alone seem to entail an obligation to murder gently—that's bad enough!

RESPONSES

Some paradoxes can feel like tricks. Not the Gentle Murder Paradox, which forces us to rethink the basics of moral logic, particularly "ifs," "oughts," and adverbs.

We get a paradox from just three premises:

(1)	You're going to murder.	m.
(2)	If you're going to murder, you ought to murder gently.	$m \rightarrow O(g)$.
(3)	Murdering gently involves murdering.	$g \prec m$.
So:	You ought to murder.	$O(m)$.

Do you see any weak links?

We can't reject (1); murder is bad, but hardly inconceivable. Nor can we deny (3); gentle murder is still murder. And there's no way we can accept the murderous conclusion.

Walter Sinnott-Armstrong would warn against premise (2). Not that he prefers brutality. It's more that he wants to change the emphasis of the obligation: instead of a duty to *murder* gently, you want a duty to murder *gently*. So he replaces (2) with something more like:

2.*   If you're going to murder, it ought to be gentle.

$$\exists x M(x) \rightarrow O(G(x)).$$

Where " $\exists x M(x)$" means "there is an x that is a murder," and "$G(x)$" means "it is gentle." The crucial thing is that the murder part isn't obligatory, only the gentleness. "You ought to be gentle" doesn't imply "you ought to murder." It's all in the adverbs!

Sinnott-Armstrong blocks this paradox—but maybe not in all forms. (Notice that there aren't any adverbs in the Robber Paradox.)

The other option is to reject an inference. Forrester himself locates the error in the final bit of reasoning. Even if gentle murder (g) involves murder (m), Forrester says we can't infer a duty to murder from a duty to murder gently (from $O(g)$ to $O(m)$). But this seems like a drastic move: he's saying you don't have to do the things involved in doing our duty. Even worse, he still has to say you should *murder gently*, when you shouldn't be murdering at all!

Maybe the deep paradox happens earlier, in the move from "m" and "$m \rightarrow O(g)$" to "$O(g)$." This inference is called *factual detachment*, because we're "detaching" the obligation on the right-hand side of the arrow given the truth of the fact on the left-hand side. Clearly, there's something wrong about this: not murdering is still the best option. And yet, there's also something right about factual detachment: for the committed murderer, gentle murder is the best option left!

Taking a step back, the obligation to murder gently seems to apply only when we imagine the choice taking place from a restricted set of options: gentle murder and brutal murder. Obviously, gentle murder is not so obligatory once we add in the option not to murder. To solve the paradox, we need a way to understand our moral "ifs" so that they tell us what to choose from a restricted menu of options, but *not* from our *actual* menu. Gentle murder is *only* a duty if we suppose that the *only* alternative is brutality.

We're left with some big questions. Why care what we should choose from a restricted menu of options, when our actual menu includes better things? And what does this restriction business have to do with ifs? Finding the right answers would make deontic logic a lot less paradoxical.

Classic Presentation

James Forrester, "Gentle Murder, or the Adverbial Samaritan," *Journal of Philosophy* **81** (1985): 193–197.

Responses and Other Treatments

Daniel Bonevac, "Against Conditional Obligation," *Noûs* **32** (1998): 37–53.

Hector-Neri Castañeda, "Obligations, Aspectual Actions, and Circumstances," *Philosophical Papers* **15** (1986): 155–170.

Walter Sinnott-Armstrong, "A Solution to Forrester's Paradox of Gentle Murder," *Journal of Philosophy* **82** (1985): 162–168.

Further Reading

Daniel Muñoz and Theron Pummer, "Supererogation and Conditional Obligation," *Philosophical Studies* **179** (2021): 1429–1443.

Questions for Reflection

1.   Forrester considers rewriting (2) as "$O(m \rightarrow g)$," which means "it ought to be the case that *if* you murder, you murder gently." Does this make sense, and if so, does it help with the paradox?

2.   Can you come up with any other special versions of the Robber Paradox? (What does it mean, exactly, to say that one paradox is a special version of the other?)

NOTES

1   Could it be true *both* that it's wrong to lie *and* that you have a duty to save your friend? That would be a genuine moral dilemma.

2   Ernest Gordon, who was a prisoner of war in the camp which inspired the film *Bridge Over the River Kwai*, tells of an episode in which a guard who had distributed shovels to the prisoners claimed at the end of the workday that one of the shovels was missing. The guard waved his gun around and said he would shoot the whole detail if the thief didn't confess. A prisoner quickly stepped forward and said, "I took it," and the guard killed him in front of all his mates. A later recount revealed that no shovel was missing. Ernest Gordon, *To End All Wars* (Grand Rapids, MI: Zondervan, 2002): 101–102. First published in 1963 under the title *Through the Valley of the Kwai*.

6

SUPEREROGATION

So far we have been exploring the debate between utilitarians and deontologists. One question keeps coming up: May you harm one to help others? As it turns out, this is only half of the problem. There is another equally urgent question that we also need to consider: Must you harm *yourself* to help others?

Forget for a moment about stealing, lying, and shoving unwilling gentlemen in front of trolleys. Think about all the things *you* could be doing *at your own expense* for the greater good (and feel free to use your own preferred take on what's good). Some examples might include donating cash or bone marrow, doing favors, and—if you'll allow a thought experiment—throwing yourself in front of a runaway trolley in order to save a great many lives. In these cases, you aren't harming any third parties. You're just sacrificing your own interests for the sake of the greater good of others. Utilitarians would rejoice (you're creating more happiness). Deontologists would not object (you aren't violating any rights).

So, don't you have to do it?

Most of us would say: "Not necessarily!" Helping others is often *supererogatory*, or "beyond the call of duty." The official definition is that a supererogatory act is *optional*, yet *better* than some permissible alternative. Donating bone marrow to strangers, for instance, is

DOI: 10.4324/9781003319962-7

optional—certainly not something you're required to do. It's also morally better than other things you may permissibly do, like going to the movies.

This chapter is about some of the main puzzles involved in, and entailed by, the idea of supererogation. First and foremost is the classic **Paradox of Supererogation** (#25), which is really just a simple question. If supererogatory acts are really so good, why aren't they obligatory? More recently, Joe Horton has come up with a new puzzle: sometimes it seems wrong to go halfway towards supererogating. Think of someone who rushes into a burning building, saves a kid's life, and pointlessly leaves another kid behind in the flames. This seems clearly wrong, whereas doing nothing would have been permissible—and yet it seems perverse to say that you ought to do nothing rather than save the one child. This is **The All or Nothing Problem** (#26). Horton's problem has some echoes of Frances Kamm's earlier **Intransitivity Paradox** (#27), which beautifully brings out the potential for a clash between duty and supererogation.

Finally, we consider what happens when a would-be supererogator decides instead to put some strings on their offer to help. For example, rather than supererogating to help someone in desperate need, you might offer them (what certainly looks like) an exploitative deal—they get help, but they have to work in your sweatshop (or pay you all their money, or something like that). This seems like wrongful exploitation, and yet it's a mutually beneficial and consensual transaction. How then could it be *worse* than the status quo of no transaction? This is the question we take up in **#28, What's Wrong with Exploitation?**—our last stop on our tour of the many paradoxes of supererogation.

25. THE PARADOX OF SUPEREROGATION

Ethical theorists are always going on about duties—things that would be wrong not to do. But plenty of good deeds seem to lie beyond the call of duty. Philosophers call this sort of thing "supererogation," meaning "going above and beyond."

Consider Eli, a (real) philosopher who (really) donated her spare kidney to a stranger. Her decision almost certainly saved that person from years of suffering. If you have chronic kidney failure, and nobody gives you a kidney, your only hope is dialysis: a painful process that requires going to the hospital and having blood drawn from your arm, cleaned in a machine, and sent back into your bloodstream through another tube. A single session takes four hours; a typical week requires three sessions. This goes on for the rest of the patient's life, unless one can receive a transplant. And since buying a kidney is illegal (virtually everywhere in the world), that means the only hope is to wait for someone like Eli to step up and donate.

Clearly, Eli's choice was an admirable one. We think she deserves praise and that more people should try to emulate her. But was she just doing her duty? Was she morally obligated to make that sacrifice for the greater good?

Many ethicists would say *no*. Not because they think Eli did the wrong thing. Donations are a fairly safe procedure. She prevented a big harm at the cost of a small harm to herself, which is a positive thing, not a negative.

Instead, they would call Eli's action supererogatory. When it comes to her own body, she is the one who should get to choose. So, on this view, she may choose *not* to donate her kidney, even when donating would be for the greater good. The same goes for smaller local kindnesses, like favors for friends or thoughtful gifts to family members. These actions are, for the "supererogationist," better than a permissible alternative, but not obligatory to do.

This might strike you as a suspicious combination. In general, it's your duty to do good things: telling the truth, keeping promises, respecting rights. But donations and favors seem like good things, too. So why aren't they just duties? Why would morality let you get away with mediocrity?

Philosophers call this the *Paradox of Supererogation*. There is a deep tension between the two sides of supererogation, its goodness and its optionality. The very fact that supererogatory acts are so very *good* makes it hard to see why they should nevertheless be *optional*.

With this particular puzzle, the stakes are enormous. If we can't solve the Paradox, and supererogation doesn't exist, we aren't just going to have to revise our theories. We have to rethink our lives.

Consider how you feel about people who do the wrong thing all the time: scammers who make a living stealing from the elderly, corrupt officials who spend all day exploiting the public, abusers who mistreat their loved ones. What these people do is just *monstrous*, and anyone who does this sort of thing ought to feel terrible about themselves.

But if supererogation isn't possible, we are probably monsters, too. How many of us can say that, with every day of our lives, we are doing the *very best* things we could be doing? Anyone who spends their spare cash on lattes—or their spare time on video games—could probably find something nobler to do. If so, then buying lattes and playing games is not just ethically "meh" but morally wrong. We are quite literally violating our duties when we do anything less than what is best. That is to say, we are doing the wrong thing virtually all of the time.

If that sounds too extreme to you, then you are going to want to find a way out of the Paradox of Supererogation. But what could the solution be?

RESPONSES

The Paradox of Supererogation breaks down into two steps. First: supererogation is supposed to be better than the moral minimum. Second: one has a duty to do the better thing. From this it follows that any would-be supererogatory act will not truly be optional; one has a duty, not just a permission, to do the best one can.

So, in responding to the Paradox, there are three options.

First, you could give up on the idea that supererogation is better than the minimum. Perhaps we should praise supererogatory acts, but really, they are not better to do. One version of this view says that supererogation is not better than the alternative because it violates one's duties to oneself. This seems too harsh. Do we really think Eli has a duty to herself not to donate her kidney, and that this duty matters as much as the possibility of saving someone from years of dialysis?

A better option, for the fan of supererogation, is to break the link between "best" and "must." Donating the kidney *is* better, on this view, but that doesn't automatically mean that keeping it is wrong. It is a bit tricky to say why not, however; it can't just be that we have no duties to help others, since we often do, when we can save someone from a massive harm at a puny cost. (See **Singer's Pond, #16.**)

Finally, one could deny the supererogatory, embracing the idea that we are all in a sense moral monsters whenever we do less than best. This seems hard to believe. But maybe it is less extreme than it sounds. Although refusing to do best is wrong, on this view, that doesn't mean that we should go around *enforcing* every last duty, the way we enforce the prohibitions on murder and theft. Sometimes enforcing a certain duty can backfire, especially when everybody is violating that duty left and right. Still, even if this view doesn't call for the enforcement of morality, it does still demand quite a lot of everybody—not just a few good deeds here or there, but the *maximally wonderful deed, every single time.* Any conscientious person who tries to answer the call of duty would probably end up with "moral exhaustion," as Michael Schur would call it. Try being maximally wonderful, even just for a day, and see how you feel at the end!

The concept of supererogation, if we can make sense of it, might give us a break from the hassle of being perfectly ethical. But it would still encourage us to strive whenever we can.

Classic Presentation

Joseph Raz, "Permissions and Supererogation," *American Philosophical Quarterly* **12** (1975): 161–168.

Responses and Other Treatments

Jonathan Dancy, *Moral Reasons* (Oxford: Blackwell, 1993): particularly Ch. 8.

Thomas Hurka and Esther Shubert, "Permissions to Do Less Than Best: A Moving Band," in Mark Timmons, ed., *Oxford Studies in Normative Ethics, Volume 2* (Oxford: Oxford University Press, 2012): 1–27.

Daniel Muñoz, "Three Paradoxes of Supererogation," *Noûs* **55** (2021): 699–715.

See Also

Michael Schur, *How to Be Perfect: The Correct Answer to Every Moral Question* (New York: Simon & Schuster, 2022).

Questions for Reflection

1.   Does supererogation seem to you like an incoherent concept? If yes, what's the incoherence? If no, why do you think supererogation *seems* coherent to some people?

2.   Is it really so extreme to deny the possibility of supererogatory acts?

26. THE ALL OR NOTHING PROBLEM

Some paradoxes start with a *bang*. Joe Horton starts his with a building:

> Suppose that two children are about to be crushed by a collapsing building. You have three options: do nothing, save one child by allowing your arms to be crushed, or save both children by allowing your arms to be crushed. (2017: 94)

(How does saving the kids hurt your arms? Perhaps you save them prying open an escape route—depending on where you stick your arms into the twisting metal, you can either open a big route through which both kids escape, or a small one through which only one child can fit. Or you could save neither child and keep your arms.)

What should you do here? What would be permissible, and what would be wrong?

First off, it seems:

Permissible to Save None
You may choose to do nothing.

We aren't saying that you *should* do nothing. It would be heroic to sacrifice your arms to save a life or two. But that sort of heroism goes above and beyond the call of duty. It is, as ethicists say, "supererogatory" rather than obligatory.

Second, it seems:

Wrong to Save Only One
You may not choose to save only one child.

Think about it. If you're going to give up your arms to save one child, why not save both? There's no additional cost. How could you justify not saving the additional child? Given that you're losing your arms anyway, it's as if you are passing on a chance to save that child's life for free. That's wrong! (Compare it to the act of walking past **Singer's Pond** in **#16**.)

Now we're in trouble. Saving only one child is wrong; saving zero is permissible. In general one should choose permissible actions over wrong actions, right? We can call this principle:

Worse to Do Wrong
If A is permissible and B is wrong, then you should do A rather than B.

Another way to put this might be to say that wrong acts are always worse things to do than permissible acts.

But is it really *worse* to save only the one child than to save zero children? Should you save *nobody* rather than somebody? It doesn't seem that you should. If anything, morality would advise saving somebody rather than nobody; there is no sense in letting the morally perfect be the enemy of the morally good.

At a minimum, though, it seems clearly true that:

> No Worse to Save One
> It's not the case that you should do nothing rather than save only one child.

This is Horton's *All or Nothing Problem*. If your only permissible options, in the building case, are saving all and saving none, then you should save none rather than only some—which seems outrageous!

RESPONSES

Horton's problem is a fascinating discovery, one of the few truly new paradoxes in ethical theory. The problem is that we have four inconsistent claims that seem perfectly true. Something has to give—but what?

First, we might insist that it is actually *wrong* to do nothing and keep your arms. Most ethicists who think this are "Maximizers," who think we always have to do the morally best thing we can do—a very demanding kind of morality. Maximizing has a lot going for it as a philosophical view. But as a way out of the All or Nothing Problem, it is more of a surrender than a solution. We'd be giving up on the possibility of supererogation!

A second option is to say that it's permissible to save only one child. This is not a very demanding morality—quite the opposite. The view is that you may save the one even though you would be gratuitously letting the second child die. This is just very hard to square with the idea that it's wrong to let people die for no good reason, since there is no good reason why you should save only one rather than both.

Third, we might say that you should indeed do nothing rather than save the one child. But how could saving a life be *worse* than not saving any lives? One possibility is that saving one is worse simply because it is wrong. Another is that saving the one child expresses disrespect to the second whom you forsake. It's as if you're saying, "I wouldn't lift a finger to save you." Not the most heart-warming message one could send to a dying child! Still, as disrespectful as that is, it is worth remembering that the other child's life hangs in the balance. Would morality prefer that you save *zero* lives rather than one, so as to avoid disrespecting the second child? Does disrespect matter that much? We could ask the same question about wrongness. Should morality prefer that you save zero lives rather than one, so that your action doesn't count as wrong?

Finally, we could keep all of the intuitions and deny the principle that says they're inconsistent. Maybe saving one is wrong; saving zero is permissible; and yet it isn't the case that you should save zero rather than one. A mind-boggling combination! But isn't it always Worse to Do Wrong?

Certainly, it's often true, as Horton himself points out. You shouldn't be rude (wrong!) rather than nice (supererogatory!). You shouldn't spend your night going on a murder spree (wrong!) instead of staying at home watching cooking shows (permissible!).

Still, some ethicists do reject Worse to Do Wrong and see Horton's case as a counterexample. For these ethicists, the key to the All or Nothing Problem is that "wrong" doesn't mean "(very) bad." It means "can't be justified over every alternative." You can justify saving zero over the alternatives, even though they are morally very good, because they are so much more costly. You can't justify saving one over saving two, however, because saving two is better *and no more costly to you*. So, saving one is wrong, while saving zero is fine. But it can still be true that saving one is just as good as (or even better than) saving zero.

As of now, the dust has yet to settle on the All or Nothing Problem. Ethical theorists are still debating solutions and trying to interpret what the problem really means. That's pretty exciting, when you think about it. In a field with so many ancient paradoxes, it's a treat to be there for the discovery of a genuinely new one!

Classic Presentation

Joe Horton, "The All or Nothing Problem," *Journal of Philosophy* **30** (2017): 94–104.

Responses

Christian Barry and Seth Lazar, "Supererogation and Optimisation," *Australasian Journal of Philosophy* **102** (2024): 21–36.

Daniel Muñoz, "Three Paradoxes of Supererogation," *Noûs* **55** (2021): 699–715.

Theron Pummer, "All or Nothing, but If Not All, Next Best or Nothing," *Journal of Philosophy* **116** (2019): 278–291.

Tina Rulli, "Conditional Obligations," *Social Theory and Practice* **46** (2020): 365–390.

Further Reading

Derek Parfit, "Future Generations: Further Problems," *Philosophy & Public Affairs* **11** (1982): 113–172. (On p. 131 Parfit analyzes an example like Horton's.)

Questions for Reflection

1. Suppose someone responds to the All or Nothing Problem in the following way: "The Problem disappears once we get clear on the *time of action*. Saving the one child isn't wrong from the start; it only *becomes* wrong once one has paid the costs of life-saving." Do you see any problems with this response?

2. Horton's own solution involves a quite different principle: "Optimific Altruism." Here is the basic idea. Whether you may save zero, and whether you should save zero rather than one, depends on your *willingness to pay the costs of altruism*. If you aren't willing, then you can cite the cost to justify saving zero; so, saving zero is permissible, and you should save zero rather than one. But if you are willing to pay the cost, then you can't cite it as a justification for not saving both kids; so, saving one and saving zero are *both* wrong, and you should save one rather than zero. What do you think of this solution? Which of the four claims in the All or Nothing Problem is Horton rejecting?

27. KAMM'S INTRANSITIVITY PARADOX

When thinking about supererogation, philosophers can't help but reach for the metaphor of distance. We talk of acts lying "beyond" the call of duty, and when a saint or hero supererogates, we say they "go the second mile."

Suppose, for example, that a distant relative of yours has a failing kidney. Showing up at the hospital might be the minimum that morality requires—Mile #1. Donating your spare kidney, meanwhile, would probably be supererogatory—Mile #2. To go the first mile is to do your duty; to go the second is to go beyond.

The "second mile" metaphor seems natural and obvious. It is hard to imagine anyone wringing a paradox out of such an unassuming thought.

That didn't stop Frances Kamm (1985).

Here's what she noticed. When you "go the second mile," the implication is that you go the first mile, *then* you go the second. It's not as if you hit a fork in the road: the first mile on your left, the second mile on your right.

The big bad assumption here, smuggled in by the metaphor, is that you can only supererogate *after* taking care of your duties. Sometimes, things do work like that: first you show up at the hospital—that's the minimum—and, second, you can take the extra step of donating your kidney. Kamm's insight was that supererogation doesn't have to work like this. Sometimes, rather than two miles in a row, there really is a fork.

Consider Kamm's *Lunch Case*. You're on your way to meet your friend for lunch, as you've promised to do, when suddenly a nearby stranger suffers a catastrophic organ failure, and they will die unless you step up to donate your spare kidney. In this case, keeping your lunch promise is a duty, whereas donating the kidney is supererogatory. But you cannot do your duty *and* supererogate. You have to choose. Keeping the promise means abandoning the stranger. Saving the stranger means breaking the promise.

We have to be careful here. When Kamm says you have a duty to keep the promise, she doesn't mean that you *have to* keep the promise. You don't! You could permissibly give the kidney instead. The promise confers a "duty" only in the sense that, other things being equal, you have to keep your promises. It would be wrong to break the promise for a bad reason, or for no reason.

Of course, as just about any ethicist will tell you—anyone except Kant—you may sometimes break a promise in order to fulfill an even more compelling duty.[1] Kamm's discovery was that you may *also* break a promise for the sake of something that *isn't* a duty. You may sometimes violate a duty in order to do a supererogatory act. Or, as Kamm puts it, supererogation may take precedence over doing your duty.[2] You're not doing the supererogatory act *after* your duty. You're doing it *instead of* your duty.

Suppose you agree with all this. You've given up on "second mile" thinking and achieved a new level of ethical subtlety. But subtlety has a price. You now have to contend with a new puzzle: *Kamm's Intransitivity Paradox*.

Here's the problem. In the Lunch Case, donating the kidney is supererogatory, so you don't have to do it. And that's not just because you have a promise to attend to. Even in a choice between doing nothing and donating, you wouldn't have to give. Let's express this by saying that *doing nothing may take precedence over donating*. Now, as we've seen, donating may in turn take precedence over keeping the promise. But keeping the promise is a duty: if your only options were to keep the promise and to lounge around, it would be morally wrong to lounge around. Doing nothing, therefore, may *not* take precedence over keeping the promise.

But this violates a seemingly undeniable principle, which we might call *Transitivity for Precedence*, which says:

Transitivity for Precedence
If A may take precedence over B, and B may take precedence over C, then A may take precedence over C.

This idea will probably strike you as obviously true. After all, precedence isn't random. If A may take precedence over B, A must be at least as important as B. And if A is at least as important as B, which is at least as important as C, then surely A is at least as important as C.

Here's an analogy. If Alice can see over Bert's head, and Bert can see over Carole's head, it just seems *obvious* that Alice should be able to see over Carole's head. That's because who can see over whom depends on who has more of a certain kind of underlying quantity: height.

Similarly, precedence depends on which actions have more of an un-derlying moral quantity: importance. The paradox here is to explain how Transitivity of Precedence could fail, where similar principles—like the *Transitivity for Seeing Over Heads*—hold true.

RESPONSES

So what do we make of Kamm's paradox?

Well, if we want to hang on to Transitivity for Precedence, we are going to have to rethink which options may take precedence over which. There are three ways to do this.

First, we could say that doing nothing may take precedence over keeping the promise. But that's extreme. It means that keeping your promise isn't really a duty. Second, we could say that doing nothing may *not* take precedence over donating the kidney. But that's extreme, too. It means that donating the kidney isn't really supererogatory. Fi-nally, we could deny that donating the kidney may take precedence over keeping the promise. This isn't exactly extreme. But it is *strange*—as if a lunch mattered more than a life. According to Kamm: "I would be a moral idiot (though not immoral) if I felt that I had to keep my lunch appointment" instead of donating the kidney (1985: 120). Harsh, but she's got a point!

If we don't like those solutions, we have to face the music. Prece-dence will have to be intransitive.

How could it be? If the more important thing always takes prece-dence, then Transitivity for Precedence will seem inevitable. Or rather, it will seem that way if we think of importance, like height, as being measured with a single fixed number. But Kamm points out that prec-edence could depend on multiple factors. A natural thought is that precedence depends on duty as well as on the agent's prerogative to do what's in their interests. But this view alone may not help much. You have a strong duty to keep your promise, but you also seem to have a prerogative to do nothing—otherwise, you'd have to give your kidney rather than do nothing!

We need another puzzle piece. Maybe we should add, again follow-ing Kamm, that the "reasons" behind precedence are context-sensitive. More concretely, we could say that you have a prerogative to do noth-ing *rather than give the kidney*, but no prerogative to do nothing *rather than keep the promise.* This seems true. But why? The most obvious answer is that there's something special about promises that nullifies the force of your prerogative. But this won't help with nearby cases. For example: suppose you can either do nothing, costlessly save Alice's finger, or give your kidney to save Bert's life. There's no promise in sight, and yet we have the same puzzling intransitivity. Doing nothing takes precedence over saving Bert, which takes precedence over helping Alice, and yet doing nothing may *not* take precedence over helping Alice. You can't just let her suffer!

Thanks to Kamm's Paradox, we now have a deeper appreciation for the subtleties of supererogation. But tracing out the details, without getting bogged down in paradoxes, is surprisingly delicate work.

Classic Presentation

Frances Myrna Kamm, "Supererogation and Obligation," *Journal of Philosophy* **82** (1985): 118–138.

Responses and Other Treatments

Alfred Archer, "Moral Obligation, Self-Interest, and the Transitivity Problem," *Utilitas* **28** (2016): 441–464.

Dale Dorsey, "The Supererogatory and How to Accommodate It," *Utilitas* **25** (2013): 355–382. (Dorsey's paper revived interest in the Paradox, introducing several relevant examples and inspiring responses by Archer and Portmore.)

Frances Myrna Kamm, *Morality, Mortality, Volume II: Rights, Duties, and Status* (New York: Oxford University Press, 1996): Ch. 12. (This is an updated version of her classic paper.)

Daniel Muñoz, "Three Paradoxes of Supererogation," *Noûs* **55** (2021): 699–715.

Daniel Muñoz and Theron Pummer, "Supererogation and Conditional Obligation," *Philosophical Studies* **179** (2021): 1429–1443.

Derek Parfit, "Future Generations: Further Problems," *Philosophy & Public Affairs* **11** (1982): 113–172. (On p. 131 Parfit discusses a similar intransitivity in the context of what we would now call **The Non-Identity Problem (#49)**, and he introduces a case that is similar to the Building Case from **#26, The All or Nothing Problem**.)

Douglas Portmore, "Transitivity, Moral Latitude, and Supererogation," *Utilitas* **29** (2017): 286–298.

Questions for Reflection

1. The Lunch Case is not exactly realistic. (If someone stops you on the way to lunch asking for your kidney, they are probably not a real doctor.) Can you think of a more realistic version? More generally, can you think of real-world cases where someone has to choose between supererogation and doing a duty?

2. Here's a bonus puzzle (see Kamm 1985: 120; Muñoz and Pummer 2022). In the Lunch Case, you have exactly two permissible options: donating your kidney and keeping your promise. It seems plausible that, when you have only two permissible options, if you're not going to do one, then you have to do the other. But suppose you're not going to keep the promise. Does that mean you have to donate the kidney? (You may find it helpful to connect this puzzle to **#24, The Gentle Murder Paradox** and **#26, The All or Nothing Problem**.)

3. An advanced question: Is the Lunch Case, as analyzed by Kamm, the only kind of case that violates the Transitivity of Precedence? See if you can think of other views that lead to intransitivities in other cases. (Hint: consider the **All or Nothing Problem** (**#26**) and the **Non-Identity Problem** (**#49**).)

28. WHAT'S WRONG WITH EXPLOITATION?

In life, when it rains, it pours. The same tends to be true in ethical theory. When an act is wrong—like a theft or murder—it often results in downstream harms or injustices, and it likely springs from cruel or callous intentions. What's bad in one way tends to be bad in lots of ways.

But some wrongs are bad in only one way, while being fine or even downright good in others—less of a downpour, more of a sunshower.

One notoriously puzzling example of this is wrongful *exploitation*. Of course, when someone exploits a vulnerable person, often everything about the transaction is irredeemably bad. Think of a human trafficker coercing young women, or a drug cartel profiting from addicts' suffering.

But sometimes exploitation seems like the *only* thing bad about a transaction, and as a result, it's hard to see how the transaction could be wrong. Consider an example from the political philosopher Nicholas Vrousalis:

> *Pit*
> Alice finds Bob in a pit. She can get him out easily at little to no cost to herself, and to Bob's relief she offers to save him—but on one condition. Bob has to either pay a million dollars, or sign a contract promising that he'll work in Alice's sweatshop. Poor Bob, pitifully stuck, mulls over his predicament and decides that, as much as he would hate working in a sweatshop, he had better sign that contract in order to save his own life. (2018: 2)

This is, as Vrousalis puts it, "paradigmatic of wrongful exploitation" (2018: 2). Bob is vulnerable, and Alice is taking advantage of him for her own benefit. And yet, it's not so easy to see how her action could be wrong, given that it's quite good in two relevant ways.

First, Alice's action is *better for Bob* than the status quo. While the victims of trafficking might wish that their traffickers never existed, Bob should be glad that Alice happens to be in the area. (Assuming, of course, that she's not the reason why he's down there!) Without Alice on the scene, we can suppose, Bob would be doomed to die. Thanks to her offer, at least Bob has a chance at something better than death, even if the sweatshop job isn't as good as a free rescue. Alice's offer is therefore mutually beneficial in a clear sense.

Second, Bob *consents* to the transaction. Unlike the victim of trafficking, Bob is not being coerced into working for anyone; Alice isn't holding a gun to his head. And unlike the reluctant addict, Bob is fully in control of his choices; he is not suffering from withdrawal or otherwise less than fully rational. On the contrary, we can suppose that he's making a fully rational decision to make the best of a bad situation.

In a nutshell, then, the problem is that exploitation is "sometimes mutually consensual and beneficial" (Vrousalis 2018: 1). So how could it be wrong?

Perhaps it's just a plain old failure to help? If Alice can easily save Bob from death, then presumably she had better do it. (See **#16, Singer's Pond**.) And so it would be indecently exploitative to put strings on aid that Alice has no right to withhold.

But we can put a twist on the case. In:

Pit 2

Bob is trapped, just like before, but this time, rescuing Bob would be quite dangerous for Alice. Bob again signs the sweatshop contract to save his life, and Alice saves him.

Here, Alice presumably *does* have the right to withhold aid. Saving Bob at great personal risk is paradigmatic of supererogation—that is to say, it's a good deed beyond the call of duty. (See **#25, The Paradox of Supererogation**.) So we can't say that the problem with exploitation is that Alice must help for free.

Maybe the problem isn't what she does to Bob, but what she does to society at large? Sometimes a win-win deal has "negative externalities"—that is, bad effects on third parties. We can imagine a case like this. Bob's work at the sweatshop might cause noxious pollution nearby, or what have you. But we can also imagine that this *doesn't* happen. There might even be significant "positive externalities"— relief for Bob's loved ones, lower prices on garments for Alice's customers, and so forth.

The puzzling thing about exploitation is that it seems wrong *even if* we imagine away any negative externalities, and *even if* the transacting parties give their consent and reap real benefits.

RESPONSES

We are in a pickle. What's wrong with exploitation when it's a consensual win–win?

One answer, of course, is that there's *nothing* wrong with it. Given the upsides of exploitation, it can't be more wrong than the permissible status quo of doing nothing.[3] But then what do we say about real world sweatshops (and other such examples)? Are they permissible? Some say no, on the grounds that sweatshop contracts are not really consensual or not really win–wins. But some say—with caveats—sweatshops are fine! If they *really are* mutually advantageous, and they *really are* consensual, then who can complain?

Well, what about those who are exploited? Can't they complain of unfairness? Maybe. But on the other hand, they signed a contract. Since they agreed to the terms, one might say that they've waived their right to complain that the terms are unfair. (Is this right? Or are some actions so bad that they are indignities even when done to consenting parties?)

Some philosophers say that exploitation is wrong because it doesn't go far enough to help the vulnerable party. They say that, despite appearances, it is *not* permissible to withhold aid, even when giving aid is costly. You don't have to be a consequentialist to think this (though it certainly helps). Joe Horton (2019), for instance, would say that Alice may not sit by watching poor Bob die when she could, *at no cost to herself*, propose to Bob a kind of deal that that will allow her to be just as well off as she is now. Suppose the cost of rescuing Bob is $10,000 for Alice. But Alice could offer Bob a deal whereby she saves his life and he repays her by working for her until she makes $10,000 in profit. In that case, Horton would say, she has no right to do nothing instead of offering such a deal: the deal costs her nothing in the end, and it *massively* helps Bob.

There is something attractive about this. Still, we might wonder if Alice really is obliged to make a dangerous rescue merely because she'll be compensated by Bob's labor. (Suppose you'll be compensated for donating bone marrow. Does that undercut your right not to give it?)

The really puzzling possibility would be for exploitation to be wrong *despite* being consensual and mutually beneficial when compared to a *perfectly permissible* status quo of doing nothing. For this to make any sense, there would have to be some subtle wrong-maker hidden in the exploiter's actions, something that is not erased merely by the presence of consent and the balm of mutual benefit. Perhaps this is unfairness, disrespect, or some other deontological dimension of badness (Sample 2003; Faraci 2019; Muñoz 2021). But what's the problem, exactly?

To get a flavor for the problems here, think about how often fairness and respect *are* sensitive to consent. If we collaborate 50/50 on a project, it would be unfair and disrespectful of you to take 75% of the profits. But suppose I'm just feeling generous, and I give you the extra 25% (half of my half). If the gift is truly consensual, what's wrong with your taking it? Consent seems to erase the sting of unfairness and the stain of disrespect—which is precisely why it's so hard to see why the sting and stain should still be there when someone consents to an exploitative transaction.

Perhaps the deontologist can make some progress here by getting clearer on how they think consent works in cases of desperation and duress—particularly when the duress doesn't come from the exploiter himself, but rather from some aspect of the victim's situation, like a deep pit or the "silent compulsion of economic relations" (Marx 1867/1992: 899). Or maybe the answer will come from thinking about the nature of fairness. Maybe you'll be the one to find the answer. Just don't charge us a million bucks for it.

Classic Presentation

Alan Wertheimer, *Exploitation* (Princeton: Princeton University Press, 1996). (See pp. 289–293.)

Richard Arneson, "Exploitation and Outcome," *Philosophy, Politics, and Economics* **12** (2013): 392–412. (See pp. 393–394.)

Further Reading

Karl Marx, *Capital: A Critique of Political Economy, Volume 1*, Ben Fowkes, trans. (London: Penguin Books in association with New Left Review, 1992). Originally published in 1867.

Joe Horton, "The Exploitation Problem," *Journal of Political Philosophy* **27** (2019): 469–479. (In this remarkably clear and short article, Horton links the issue of exploitation to his own **All or Nothing Problem** (#26); also note that his examples differ slightly from those in this entry.)

Daniel Muñoz, "Exploitation and Effective Altruism," *Philosophy, Politics, and Economics* **20** (2021): 409–423. (A reply to Horton.)

Tyler Doggett, "Letting Others Do Wrong," *Noûs* **56** (2022): 40–56.

Ruth Sample, *Exploitation, What It Is and Why It Is Wrong* (Lanham: Rowman and Littlefield, 2003). (In her book and later papers, Sample gives some great overviews and argues that exploitation involves disrespecting the value of persons.)

Nicholas Vrousalis, "Exploitation: A Primer," *Philosophy Compass* **13** (2018): 1–14.

Matt Zwolinski, Benjamin Ferguson, and Alan Wertheimer, "Exploitation," in Edward N. Zalta and Uri Nodelman, eds., *The Stanford Encyclopedia of Philosophy* (Winter Edition, 2022): https://plato.stanford.edu/archives/win2022/entries/exploitation/

Questions for Reflection

1.   What makes a deal fair? Is a deal fair whenever the dealmakers benefit roughly equally, or perhaps whenever the dealmakers have roughly equal bargaining power? Write down your guess, then think through a few examples to see how well your guess plays out.

2.   Some scholars, though deploring the exploitation of sweatshop labor, don't want to ban sweatshops, since that could well hurt the laborers being exploited. Closing down sweatshops doesn't create good jobs, but may instead force people into far worse jobs. Is this position coherent? A more general question: is it ever OK (or even obligatory) to allow people to do (or keep on doing) morally wrong things? (For an interesting paper on this topic, see Tyler Doggett's "Letting Others Do Wrong.")

NOTES

1   For a taste of Kant's absolutism, see **#21, Kant's Murderer at the Door**.

2   Kamm puts this in a more technical way. Rather than attacking the "second mile" metaphor, she attacks the idea of a "strict lexical ordering between duties and acts of supererogation" (1985: 120). Kamm also distinguishes the "effort" involved in doing a duty from the sacrifice of "personal goals," and creates a different example and intransitivity for each. But you only need one example to see the core idea.

3   This idea is sometimes called the "Nonworseness Claim" (Zwolinski, Ferguson, and Wertheimer 2022: section 3).

7

WELL-BEING AND VALUE

So far we've seen a plethora of puzzles about right and wrong actions. But ethical theory isn't just about actions and their moral characteristics. In this chapter we'll dip a toe into two other large and important topics in ethics: *well-being*, and *value* in general.

Well-being. Set aside how we treat *other people*, which is the primary focus of morality. Focus instead on the fact that everyone wants to live a life that goes well for them, a life in which they are happy and flourishing. Theories of *well-being* are views about what *makes* a life good in this way for the person living it. What activities, states, or features make up a truly good life? If there are such items, then they are what we most fundamentally ought to aim at in order to live a good life; and the more of these things we have, the higher our well-being. So it's very important to figure out what those things are or might be.

Investigation into such questions has been at the center of ethics since Book I of Aristotle's *Nicomachean Ethics*, written around 340 BC. One venerable answer to such questions is *hedonism*, the view that the only thing which contributes to our well-being is *pleasure* and the only thing which detracts from it is *pain*. On this view, your life is going exactly as well as it *feels*. Robert Nozick's famous thought experiment, **The Experience Machine (#29)**, tests the adequacy of this simple conception of well-being.

DOI: 10.4324/9781003319962-8

A more specific question in this neighborhood focuses on *death* in particular. Is death bad for us? If so, why? This question, which also has a long history in philosophy, can be read in two different ways. Is it bad for us humans *that we die*, i.e., that we are mortal? Would it be better for us if we lived forever? Entry **#30, Should We Wish for Immortality?** considers that question. We can also ask whether a particular person's dying is bad *for her*, a misfortune; that is the subject of entry **#31, Should We Fear Death?** While you might think it obvious that the answer to both types of question is "yes," the discussions below suggest that these issues are more complex and contestable than you might have thought.

Value in general. Theories of well-being are concerned with what is good or bad for a person. This is sometimes called *prudential* value. But in addition to what is *good for* a person, ethics also seeks to theorize what is *good, period*. If the former is a particular *species* of value, the latter is *value in general*; and it raises questions of its own. It might be good, for instance, that the earth flourish, over and above the benefit this might bring to any person. (Entry **#32, Moore's Beautiful World**, presents a more radical possibility of this kind.) In reflecting on what is good or valuable, we need to keep two structural points about value in mind. First, we need to sort out whether a candidate value is *instrumentally* valuable—valuable because of what it causes or conduces to—or *intrinsically* valuable, that is, valuable *in itself* or *for its own sake*. Entry **#32** discusses this contrast, as does **The Ring of Gyges (#34)** in the next chapter.

The second aspect we need to pay attention to is that we need some way to conceptualize *how* valuable a given thing is. After all, the world is full of many good and valuable things; the difficulty is often in choosing among them. Going hiking on Sunday would be good; having a lazy and decadent brunch on Sunday would also be good. That both are good does not give us enough information to guide our choice; for that we need to make further discriminations using measures like *how* good, or the relations *better* and *worse*. The puzzle in entry **#33, Sweetening**, shows how complicated the structure of such value relations can be.

29. THE EXPERIENCE MACHINE

A (trustworthy) neuroscientist approaches you with a fascinating story and an intriguing offer. She tells you that she and her colleagues have perfected a machine that can produce a simulation in your brain of any experience you might wish. Just crawl into this tank, put on some electrodes, and you will soon be having—or seeming to have—whatever experience you want. If you so wish, you will experience the joy of discovering that your crush returns your love; amazement at the births of your children; pride at finishing a marathon; and satisfaction at what you have accomplished professionally. Or whatever else you want to experience!

The scientist asks if you would like to plug in to the experience machine for the rest of your life. You consider this carefully. Once hooked up to the experience machine, you would no longer suffer any unwanted pain. (Adios, that distracting ache in your hip!) Your life would feel great from the inside, all the time. Indeed, it would feel for all the world as if you were truly doing the things mentioned above. (Of course, in reality you would be floating in a tank.) So would you plug in?

Let's specify a few things to clarify your choice. The machine is well tested and perfectly safe: it really will deliver what the neuroscientist promises. There is no limit to the experiences that the machine can simulate in your brain, so you wouldn't have to fear boredom if you plug in. And don't be concerned that if you're floating in a tank you won't be able to support your family. Sure, you won't be at work on Monday (or ever again), and they'll eventually fire you for absenteeism, leaving your family destitute. But set aside these worries on behalf of *others*: the point of this thought experiment is whether it's better *for you* to plug in or not to plug in. So imagine, if you need to, that no one will suffer harm as a result of your choice.

Robert Nozick, who presented this memorable example, was convinced that we would *not* choose to plug in to the experience machine. But he took this to pose a puzzle. For "*What else can matter to us, other than how our lives feel from the inside?*" (1974: 4, emphasis in original) Our life in the experience machine would *feel* just the same as if we were *actually* finding our soulmate, having children, and accomplishing things of which we could be proud. But in reality we would be doing none of these things: we would be floating in a tank.

If we would not plug in to the experience machine, this seems to show that something other than how our life feels from the inside *does* matter to us. "We learn that something matters to us in addition to experience by imagining an experience machine and then realizing that we would not use it," Nozick says (44). But what exactly might that *something* be?

Nozick identifies three things that we would lose if we plugged into the experience machine. First, we would lose our *agency*: our power to *act*. Floating in that tank, we would be nothing more than a purely passive recipient of brain stimulation. We would never again *do* anything. But it seems central to a human life to *act*, to *do*, to *create*. Second, Nozick says, we would lose *who we are* by hooking up to the machine. We would no longer be any particular way: "There is no answer to the question of what a person is like who has long been in the tank. Is he courageous, kind, intelligent, witty, loving?" (43). There seems to be no fact of the matter. So another thing we might lose by plugging into the machine is our individual character.

Finally, we would lose all contact with reality if we plugged into the machine. Everything that we *thought* was happening would not actually be happening: it would all be a mirage. We would *think* we had a loving partner, children, friends, and accomplishments, but none of these would actually exist (although we wouldn't know this). Nozick thinks this shows that we don't just want the emotions we *would* feel if we *were* to do and have these things. Rather, we want to *actually* do and have those things, and then feel those desirable emotions *as a result*.

Nozick's thought experiment has been widely taken to be the death knell for *hedonism*, the view that the only thing which has value for its own sake is pleasure. Our reaction to the experience machine seems to show that we are not hedonists: we care about things other than how much pleasant experience our lives contain. But philosopher Richard Kraut has argued that the experience machine has in effect gotten a bum rap from being viewed only as a source of pleasure. He argues that in fact you can *do* plenty in the experience machine. You can work on complicated math problems in your head. You can recall and analyze memories. You can mentally play chess, or design a building, or compose music. Kraut reminds us that humans engage in a wide variety of valuable *mental* activities, all of which would remain available to you in the machine. Moreover, you would *really be* doing those things, not just having an experience *as of* doing them. Perhaps hooking up to the experience machine would actually *enhance* your agency: after all, you would never again be distracted from such mental activities by that achy hip, or a rumbling stomach.

The experience machine might remind you of VR. Do all the lessons of the former carry over to the latter? Roger Crisp argues that they do not. One of the main downsides of plugging into the experience machine is that you would thereby sever all connections with actual people. But Crisp asks us to imagine a *collective* virtual reality: "a single virtual world just like ours, in which those connected to the machine participate together. People make choices, have relationships, achieve things, and so on; but all in a virtual rather than a real world." Like Kraut, Crisp notes that you would *actually* be doing these things while hooked up to the machine—just in a simulated world. And you would be doing them *with* other real people. Crisp suggests that once we isolate "contact with external reality" as the *sole* relevant difference between our world and this one, we will see that it's not of much value after all.

Classic Presentations

Robert Nozick, *Anarchy, State, and Utopia* (New York: Basic Books, 1974): 42–45.
Robert Nozick, *The Examined Life: Philosophical Meditations* (New York: Simon & Schuster, 1989): Ch. 10.

Responses and Other Treatments

Richard Kraut, *The Quality of Life: Aristotle Revised* (Oxford: Oxford University Press, 2018).
Roger Crisp, "Hedonism, the Experience Machine, and Virtual Reality," *Practical Ethics* blog post of October 15, 2021, https://blog.practicalethics.ox.ac.uk/2021/10/hedonism-the-experience-machine-and-virtual-reality/

Questions for Reflection

1. In the experience machine, you experience the *pleasure* of having a loving partner, children, friends, and accomplishments, even if in reality you *lack* all of these things. Now consider the

reverse scenario: you *actually do have* a loving partner, children, friends, and accomplishments, but you experience no pleasure from these things. What does this pair of cases show?

2. Of the various things we would allegedly lose by plugging into the experience machine, which do you think would be the most serious loss? Why? (Your options would include: your agency; your individual character; connections with other people; and contact with reality.)

30. SHOULD WE WISH FOR IMMORTALITY?

We normally view death as a bad thing: bad enough that our lives are filled with precautions against it. Many of us stay away from activities that carry a non-trivial risk of death and undergo various inconveniences in order to reduce the chance of death still further. Most of us, if asked, would heartily assent to the statement "I don't want to die."

But what's the alternative? Literally speaking, the alternative is eternal life: *never* dying. If we're serious about not wanting to die, it seems we want to be immortal. But do we actually want that? And ought we to?

Immortality would certainly come with advantages. Most centrally, we wouldn't have to worry about dying: the sword of Damocles of our life potentially being cut short at any moment would no longer hang over our heads. Plus, being immortal would allow us to "live dangerously," free of the death-avoiding tactics that hem us in now. (BASE jumping, anyone? Racecar driving? Of course we would still have to worry about *injury*, though.) Finally, if *everyone* were immortal—not just you—you would be guaranteed never to lose any of your loved ones, either.

The philosopher Bernard Williams argues, despite all this, that an immortal life would be "intolerable," even "unlivable." To fix ideas, let's imagine not that you continue to decay with age forever, but that you are "frozen" at, say, age 37, or 42: the age of the protagonist of Leoš Janáček's opera *The Makropoulos Case*, the spark for Williams' reflections. Elina Makropoulos has already been 37, or 42, for 300 years now when the curtain goes up, and she is unspeakably bored. Think of the things you enjoy, and how they become less enjoyable with frequent repetition: the sixteenth chocolate truffle does not bring as much pleasure as the first, and even chocolate truffles would grow tiresome if you ate them every day as a matter of routine. The monotony of repeating the same activities even for hundreds of years— let alone for all eternity—would be overwhelming. You would have seen it all before, quite literally.

How could you fend off boredom in a life that lasts forever? Repeating the activities that interest you *now* is not a winning formula, as we have seen. You could however introduce some novelty into your endless life by changing what you value and pursue. I am not (and never have been) on social media at all: I'm only into in-person relationships. But what if my immortal self threw herself into the 'Gram and the search for ever more followers? A whole new world of experience would open up for me. I could thoroughly plumb the depths of that world before moving on—just before terminal boredom set in—to yet *another* set of new values and experiences. An immortal person who shapeshifted her way through life in this way could, it seems, avoid the boredom of repetition.

Williams raises a difficulty with this scenario, however. Would we want to live in this way, untethered to any particular set of values or aims which are central to our identity? Williams questions whether we would even *care* about the survival of this person who is so unlike me. Continued life would not hold much value for us, he suggests, if we could only continue *as* someone with a completely different character. Part of what makes our life meaningful is that we conduct it under certain constraints: the constraints generated by our own individual character.

Samuel Scheffler expands on the idea that a valuable, or even recognizable, human life depends on living under constraints of some kind. Our life brings us value only if we value some of the things in our life. (If I didn't value philosophy, or educating students, I would get no real satisfaction from doing those things.) But Scheffler argues that *temporal scarcity*—lack of time, in other words—is essential to our valuing *anything*. It is precisely the fact that we have limited time that "force[s] upon us the need to establish priorities, to guide our lives under a conception of which things are worth doing and caring about and choosing. Without such limits, it is at best unclear how far we would be guided by ideas of value at all" (99). Lack of any temporal constraints would undermine the need to assign value to anything in particular. So for Scheffler, the problem with an eternal life is not merely that it would grow stale; far more profoundly, immortality would unseat the very possibility of a value-filled human life.

Suppose on reflection we agree with these theorists that eternal life wouldn't be all it's cracked up to be, and that living forever could indeed be a curse rather than a blessing. Are we then inconsistent if we also say, as many of us would, "I don't want to die"? After all, mortality and immortality are the only two alternatives here. If we think immortality would be so bad, it seems we must *welcome* the prospect of our own death, since it would spare us from that horrible fate. How then can we maintain that we don't want to die? Have we just contradicted ourselves?

Here is a possible interpretation that would save us from inconsistency. Perhaps when we say we don't want to die, we actually mean *I don't want to die in the next year*, or *in the next ten years*, or *in the next fifty years*. It seems possible to accept our mortality as such with equanimity, while nonetheless feeling that for death to come any time in the next fifty years would be too soon.

Classic Presentation

Bernard Williams, "The Makropulos Case: Reflections on the Tedium of Immortality," in his *Problems of the Self: Philosophical Papers 1956–1972* (Cambridge: Cambridge University Press, 1973): 82–100.

Responses and Other Treatments

Samuel Scheffler, *Death and the Afterlife*, Niko Kolodny, ed. (New York: Oxford University Press, 2013): Lecture 3, and the reply by Niko Kolodny in the same volume.

Michael Cholbi, ed., *Immortality and the Philosophy of Death* (London: Rowman & Littlefield, 2016).

Shelly Kagan, *Death* (New Haven: Yale University Press, 2012): Ch. 11.

Questions for Reflection

1.   Is it possible to still live under temporal constraints even if you are immortal? If so, how? Would this take care of Scheffler's objection to immortality?
2.   How valuable would it be for *just you* to be immortal, and no one else? What does your answer reveal about our values?

31. SHOULD WE FEAR DEATH?

Even if we don't actually wish to be immortal (see previous entry), most of us very much don't want to die. Indeed, most of us *fear* death (that is to say, our own death). In his poem "Aubade" (1977), the British poet Philip Larkin tried to capture the existential character of this dread which is unlike any other. Here is an excerpt:

> This is a special way of being afraid
> No trick dispels. Religion used to try,
> That vast moth-eaten musical brocade
> Created to pretend we never die,
> And specious stuff that says *No rational being*
> *Can fear a thing it will not feel*, not seeing
> That this is what we fear—no sight, no sound,
> No touch or taste or smell, nothing to think with,
> Nothing to love or link with,
> The anaesthetic from which none come round.

Larkin summarily dismisses any thought that religion might help us here. Religion, he says, only peddles a *pretense* that we will never die. If I live in on some form in Heaven (or Hell) after my earthly death, then my "death" has not after all permanently and completely terminated my existence. But the poem powerfully expresses that the total extinguishment of our existence *is* precisely what we fear. Let us understand death, then, as marking the definitive end of a person's very existence. Are we right to fear *that*? Is *our own ceasing to exist* a proper object of fear or dread?

Larkin quotes, but dismisses as "specious," an argument which aims to convince us that death is not to be feared. The line of thought quoted in italics in the excerpt above comes not from religion but from philosophy: it is due to two philosophers from antiquity, Epicurus and his follower Lucretius. Epicurus and Lucretius marshal a whole suite of arguments aimed at liberating us from the fear of death, which they believe causes great and unnecessary anxiety and suffering among the living. Philosophers today are still debating what to think about these "Epicurean" arguments, as they are called in honor of Epicurus.

The *first Epicurean argument* is the one which Larkin's quote evokes most explicitly. Epicurus and Lucretius insist that "death is nothing to us" (Epicurus: 124). Why? Because, says Epicurus, "all good and evil consists in sensation" (124); but death, by its very nature, involves a total *lack* of sensation. We need to distinguish here between dy*ing* as a process, which may well involve painful and unwanted sensations, and death itself, i.e., the definitive cessation of our existence. We can't feel anything or have any sensations if we don't exist; "those who no longer exist cannot become miserable," as Lucretius puts it (line 867). Thus death is indeed "a thing [we] will not feel," to again quote the passage in the Larkin poem. For that reason, say the Epicureans, death should not be viewed as a bad thing; thus it is not a proper object of fear.

Epicurus and Lucretius understand that we are likely to find the conclusion of the first argument counter-intuitive. It is *not bad* for your life to suddenly end? Death is never a misfortune, no matter when it comes? That's crazy talk: death *is* (usually) a misfortune. The *second Epicurean argument* tries to put pressure on that natural belief, however, by asking *for whom* death is a bad thing or a harm and *when* that person suffers that harm. Epicurus:

> Death, the most terrifying of ills, is nothing to us, since so long as we exist, death is not with us; but when death comes, then we do not exist. It [death] does not then concern either the living or the dead, since for the former it is not, and the latter are no more. (125)

Why worry, given that "when I am, death is not; when death is, I am not"? (This pithy formulation appears on a lot of quote lists.) Epicurus aims to convince us, first, that death is not a misfortune which can befall any *living* person, because it does not coexist with them. Whenever a living person is present, their death is *ipso facto* not present. Second, that death does not harm the *dead* either, because in order to be harmed you have to exist. Otherwise there is nobody *to be* harmed. According to this argument, then, we cannot identify a *subject* of the supposed harm or misfortune of death. And if death harms no one, we should not view it as a bad thing.

Lucretius is responsible for *the third Epicurean argument*. What does death consist in? Nonexistence. A very long period of nonexistence, in fact. But, Lucretius asks, what's so bad about nonexistence? Think of all the centuries that came and went before you were even born. You also didn't exist then. (Yet another long period of nonexistence for you.) If death is bad because it makes you not exist, then *not existing* must be a terrible thing. In that case it must be awful to contemplate all those centuries of *pre-natal* nonexistence. But we *don't* consider it tragic that we missed all those centuries before we came into being. As Lucretius says, "the bygone ages of eternity that elapsed before our birth [are] nothing to us" (line 972). So our *posthumous* nonexistence should similarly be nothing to us.

These Epicurean arguments are highly ingenious; but they lead to a conclusion which it is difficult to accept. If death is nothing to us, it seems we should be indifferent to the prospect of our own death. But we're not. Are we irrational? Or do the Epicurean arguments go wrong in some way? Many philosophers have thought that there is or must be something wrong with the arguments, since they lead to a conclusion which many find unacceptable. But there is no consensus on *what* the arguments get wrong (if anything). See the Nagel and Kagan texts below for some interesting attempts to articulate where Epicurus and Lucretius supposedly go wrong.

Classic Presentations

Epicurus, "Letter to Menoeceus," in *Epicurus: The Extant Remains*, Cyril Bailey, trans. (Oxford: Clarendon Press, 1926).

Lucretius, *On the Nature of Things*, Martin Ferguson Smith, trans. (Indianapolis: Hackett Publishing, 2001): Book Three.

(There are many translations of these classical texts, but they should all include the standardized line or section numbers which we have used in the citations above.)

Responses and Other Treatments

Thomas Nagel, "Death," in his *Mortal Questions* (New York: Cambridge University Press, 1979): 1–10.

Shelly Kagan, *Death* (New Haven: Yale University Press, 2012): Ch. 10.

Frances Myrna Kamm, *Morality, Mortality, Volume I: Death and Whom to Save from It* (New York: Oxford University Press, 1993). (Kamm's book contains lots of original insights, as well as criticisms of Nagel's view.)

See Also

Philip Larkin, *The Complete Poems*, Archie Burnett, ed. (London: Faber and Faber, 2012).

Questions for Reflection

1. Larkin dismisses the Epicurean argument he quotes as "specious." What reason(s) does he give for that assessment? In your opinion, does Larkin successfully identify something wrong with the first Epicurean argument?

2. What would the three Epicurean arguments say about whether *someone else's* death can be bad for you? Is it reasonable to fear or dread the death of loved ones?

32. MOORE'S BEAUTIFUL WORLD

Beauty, they say, is in the eye of the beholder. And most of us beholders think it's good when we get to enjoy the things we take to be beautiful.

But could beauty be good even if there's no one there to behold it? Could *anything* be good in a world with no conscious beings?

Lots of ethical theorists would say: no way! Take, for example, utilitarians. On their view, happiness is the only good, and obviously there can't be happiness without some conscious being there to be happy. But even if you're not a utilitarian, you might still think that goodness requires consciousness. Maybe you think free will is the ultimate good—well, you're not going to find any wills in a world without consciousness. Or maybe you think that, enjoyment aside, it's good to appreciate great art; well, that's not going to happen without an *appreciator*, and who could that be but a conscious mind?

At the turn of the 20th century, ethical theorists in the Anglophone world thought it was a no-brainer that goodness required consciousness. And that's why it was so striking when G. E. Moore—one of the great philosophers of the new century—argued that beauty can be good even when devoid of a beholder.

Moore proposes a thought experiment:

> Let us imagine one world exceedingly beautiful. Imagine it as beautiful as you can; put into it whatever on this earth you most admire—mountains, rivers, the sea; trees, and sunsets, stars and moon. Imagine these all combined in the most exquisite proportions, so that no one thing jars against another, but each contributes to the beauty of the whole. And then imagine the ugliest world you can possibly conceive. Imagine it simply one heap of filth, containing everything that is most disgusting to us, for whatever reason, and the whole, as far as may be, without one redeeming feature. (1903: §50)

Next Moore tells us to imagine that no "human being ever has or ever, by any possibility, can, live in either, can ever see and enjoy the beauty of the one or hate the foulness of the other." Then comes the key question:

> Well, even so, supposing them quite apart from any possible contemplation by human beings; still, is it irrational to hold that it is better that the

beautiful world should exist than the one which is ugly? Would it not be well, in any case, to do what we could to produce it rather than the other? Certainly I cannot help thinking that it would; and I hope that some may agree with me in this extreme instance. (1903: §50)

If you, like Moore, think there's something better about the beautiful world bereft of conscious beings, then you may have to give up on the idea that all goodness comes from consciousness.

RESPONSES

So how forceful is Moore's little thought experiment?

If you read his passage carefully, you'll notice that he's not being very pushy. He says that he "cannot help thinking" of the beautiful world as better, and he hopes that "some may agree." That's a far cry from saying that everybody *must* agree with him, on pain of their heads exploding from sheer irrationality.

Still, some ways of resisting Moore's reasoning might come with their own kind of headaches. Let's consider a few options.

To start, we might try to question some of Moore's assumptions about the nature of beauty. In particular, Moore seems to think that whether a thing is beautiful is just a plain fact about it, like its shape or size, whereas some people think of beauty as "in the eye of the beholder"—that is, relative to someone's tastes. To call a painting beautiful, without specifying *to whom* it is beautiful, would be like saying that the Eiffel Tower is far away, without specifying what it's far away from. Things can't just be "far away," and they can't just be beautiful or ugly.

But even if we grant that beauty is relative—a big "even if"—that won't help. Look closely: Moore never says, "Here's *my* beautiful world." He asks *you* to imagine a world that *you* take to be beautiful. (Though he does suggest in passing that some things are disgusting to "us," not just "you.")

A more promising reply starts by granting that the "exceedingly beautiful world" is indeed beautiful, if only in a relative way, and then challenges the further judgment that the world is *good*. At first glance, this may seem silly. Most of us would prefer a beautiful house to an ugly one, and we would rather go on vacation to a gorgeous oasis than a grotesque wasteland. But that doesn't show that beauty is *in itself* good—or as Moore would put it, *intrinsically* good. The beauty could just be *instrumentally* good—that is, it could help bring about an intrinsic good. Even a utilitarian would recommend that you vacate to the oasis, since its beauty causes so many lovely experiences.

Such views are perfectly coherent. But notice that these are precisely the views that Moore is trying to put pressure on! In the real world, beauty tends to go with good experiences. Moore's point is that beauty may *still* strike you as good *even if* we remove those experiences. If that's how you are struck, then you are going to feel the pull of his thought experiment.

In the end, Moore himself was not that strongly pulled. He presents the "exceedingly beautiful world" in the middle of his 1903 classic *Principia Ethica*. But later in that same book, he massively downplays his view that unperceived beauty has value:

> I have myself urged... that the mere existence of what is beautiful does appear to have *some* intrinsic value; but I regard it as indubitable that... such mere existence of what is beautiful has value, so small as to be negligible, in comparison with that which attaches to the *consciousness* of beauty. This simple truth may, indeed, be said to be universally recognised. (1903: §113, emphasis in original)

And in a later, less important book, Moore walks back his view altogether (1912: 107).

As for contemporary ethical theorists, they are far more open to Moore's original view that unseen beauty can be good. But they might not even realize that the view comes from *Principia Ethica*, which is mostly known today for a pair of classic arguments about the nature of goodness (namely, his "open question argument" and his attack on the "naturalistic fallacy"; for more on these, see Moore 1903: Ch. 1 and Hurka 2014: 93–101).

But we shouldn't be so quick to pass over Moore's take on the "exceedingly beautiful world." For one thing, it has historical significance, as it was initially by far the most famous part of *Principia* (Welchman 1989: 318). For another, it's still a good case! There is no more direct way to challenge the view that goodness depends on consciousness. The view remains a contender—but it's no longer a no-brainer.

Classic Presentation

G. E. Moore, *Principia Ethica* (Cambridge: Cambridge University Press, 1903).

Responses and Other Treatments

E. E. Constance Jones, "Professor Sidgwick's Ethics," *Proceedings of the Aristotelian Society* **4** (1903–1904): 32–52.

J. E. McTaggart, "The Individualism of Value," *International Journal of Ethics* **18** (1907–1908): 433–435. (This is before he added the "M" to "J. E." to make "J. M. E." Long story.)

G. E. Moore, *Ethics* (London: Williams and Norgate, 1912).

Jennifer Welchman, "G. E. Moore and the Revolution in Ethics: A Reappraisal," *History of Philosophy Quarterly* **6** (1989): 317–329.

Thomas Hurka, "Moore's Moral Philosophy," in Edward N. Zalta, ed., *The Stanford Encyclopedia of Philosophy* (Summer Edition, 2021): https://plato.stanford.edu/archives/sum2021/entries/moore-moral/

Thomas Hurka, *British Ethical Theorists from Sidgwick to Ewing* (Oxford: Oxford University Press, 2014).

Questions for Reflection

1. Do you—that is, *you*, here in the real world—have any reason to create beautiful things? Does any of this reason come from the intrinsic value of those things? How can you defend your answer against someone who disagrees?

2. Many philosophers dismissed Moore's take on beauty without argument (Welchman 1987: 318), but some critics—namely, E. E. Constance Jones and J. M. E. McTaggart (the "M" stands for "McTaggart")—gave a real objection. It went like this. Moore argues that you should choose the beautiful, mindless world over its ugly, mindless counterpart. As you should. But these are not *really* worlds without consciousness. For when you try to imagine the unperceived "mountains, rivers," and so on, there is inevitably someone conscious of them—*you*! Is this objection persuasive? (This is a question in the philosophy of mind, not ethical theory, but it's certainly relevant.)

3. Moore's "exceedingly beautiful world" is an example of an *isolation test* for intrinsic goodness. In the real world, we can

easily confuse merely instrumental goods for intrinsic ones. (Think of how some people value money for its own sake.) Hence the test: you "isolate" something, such as a beautiful landscape, by imagining a world with only it, and then ask whether it's *still* good. If so—and only if so—it's intrinsically good. Is this a good test? Try to look for both kinds of potential counterexamples: things that *are* intrinsically good but fail the test, as well as things that *aren't* intrinsically good but pass the test anyway.

33. SWEETENING

Imagine that you're choosing what TV show to watch tonight. You could watch *The Wire*, a naturalistic tragedy about the War on Drugs and its effects on the city of Baltimore. Or you could watch *The Good Place*, a philosophical comedy about the afterlife featuring a lot of jokes about Florida. Both seem great, though in very different ways. Which is better? You ponder and ponder… and yet, it seems to you in the end that neither is the better option overall.

Here's the twist. Suppose you find out that there's an extra reason— *very* minor, but still real—in favor of watching *The Good Place*. Perhaps you learn that *The Good Place* has already been downloaded on your laptop, while your episode of *The Wire* will have to be streamed, which means you have to wait for it to load up, which is slightly boring. Does that tiny bit of boringness break the tie between the two shows? Does it *have to* break the tie?

Many ethicists would say that it *doesn't* have to break the tie. Two things can be tied in value in a way that is "insensitive to mild sweetening." Consider some other "sweetening" cases, as they're now called:

- You're deciding between two careers: a fulfilling career in the arts, or a lucrative career in business. Neither seems better overall. But then you get a third option: the same career in business but with a tiny salary boost—say, $100 a year.
- You're deciding between tea and coffee. Neither seems better overall. But then you learn that you can get the coffee with a 5% discount.
- You're deciding between a night at the opera and an event featuring Oprah. Neither seems better overall. But then you get the option to sit one row further up at Oprah's event, which means being closer to the action.

In each case, you start out with two options that seem tied, in the sense that neither is better overall than the other. Let's write this as "A ~ B," meaning "A and B are tied." You then encounter a new option that is *just like* one of the originals, but *slightly better* in some respect—it's a "sweetened" version. Let's write "A+ > A" to mean that A+ is better than A, where "A+" is our name for the sweetened version of A. The problem is that, even though A+ > A, and A ~ B, it doesn't seem true that A+ > B. The sweetened version of A does not beat B.

This idea, however harmless it might seem, has explosive consequences for ethical theory. Why? Because it threatens to blow up any framework that tries to represent the value of a thing as anything like a *number*.

Consider how TV shows are rated by critics. Metacritic gives each show a number between 0 and 100. Rotten Tomatoes awards between 0% and 100% on its Tomatometer. *Rolling Stone* uses 0 to 4 stars. In each case, "bigger number" means "better," and "same number" means "tied." Nor is it just TV shows that get the numerical treatment. Think of grades on tests, credit scores, ratings of dives at the Olympics, or Yelp's ratings of restaurants. In our age of Big Data, it's utterly commonplace to use numbers to represent how valuable things are. But this whole way of conceiving of values is fundamentally flawed, if values can be insensitive to mild sweetening.

For suppose we try to represent your choice of TV show with numbers. You have three options:

W   Stream an episode of *The Wire*.
G   Stream an episode of *The Good Place*.
G+   Watch a downloaded episode of *The Good Place*.

Since W and G are tied, we have to give them the same number—let's say 9. And since G+ is better than G, we have to say that G+ gets a bigger number. It could be 10, or 9.1—it just has to be bigger than 9, if only by a little. But then G+ must be better than W as well as G, since W's number is also 9. So, improving G *even slightly* leaves us with something better than W. That seals the deal. If values are like numbers, they must, as a mathematical fact, be sensitive to even the mildest sweetening.

To put it another way, if values are like numbers, then we have to accept the following principle:

Transmission Over Ties
If A > B and B ~ C, then A > C.

Which means: if A beats B, then A must also beat anything that B ties with. Clearly this is true for numbers and their sizes: whenever $x > y$ and $y = z$, it follows that $x > z$. If values are like numbers, this simple principle of mathematics becomes an iron law of ethics.

As far as "iron laws of ethics" go, Transmission Over Ties may not be the most plausible. G+ beats G, which ties W, and G+ does not seem to beat W. But notice that analogous laws seem perfectly true when we're talking about things that can be easily quantified with numbers, like heights. If you are taller than Betty, who has the same height as Bert, you must be taller than Bert. The question is why this logic seems so much less iron-clad in the ethical case. Is it because values aren't quantifiable in terms of numbers? Or is there some kind of ethical illusion that is bewitching us into seeing values as insensitive to sweetening?

RESPONSES

The conservative response is to say that values really *do* work like numbers. There is just some other reason why they *appear* not to in sweetening cases. Maybe, in sweetening cases, the values are precise numbers, but we can't tell *which* numbers, because it's hard to precisely measure values when two things are good in very different ways. Let's suppose G has a value of 9, W has a value of 9, and G+ has a value of 9.1. Because G and G+ are so similar, you can tell that G+ is better. But when it comes to comparing *The Good Place* to *The Wire*, you can only estimate the value with a 0.5 margin of error. Then it will *seem* to you that G+ ~ W, when in fact, G+ > W.

Some radicals, however, don't think of the case as merely one of uncertainty. They think it's just *false* that G and W could have precisely the same value. The issue isn't that we're failing to grasp the precise numbers that measure the values of our options. They instead deny that there are any numbers out there to be grasped. Perhaps values are not really numerical quantities like heights and weights, but something more subtle or complicated.

If not with numbers, how we are supposed to make sense of values? Many suggest that values are in some sense "imprecise." Ruth Chang uses an analogy with the lengths of objects in a "quantum world," where things are constantly contracting and expanding within a certain range. In such a world, we might not measure a stick as being simply 9", but perhaps we could only say that it is *roughly* 9". Its real length is given by a range, say 8.5"–9.5". So we can say that a stick S1 is longer than another stick S2 if S1 is *always* longer—that is to say, the shortest length in S1's range is still longer than the longest in the range of S2.

This way of thinking of values is a bit wacky. Are values really wibbly-wobbly and indeterminate, like lengths in a quantum world? Maybe not. But then what *are* they?

Classic Presentation

Ronald de Sousa, "The Good and the True," *Mind* **83** (1974): 534–551.

Responses and Other Treatments

Joseph Raz, *The Morality of Freedom* (Oxford: Oxford University Press, 1986): Ch. 13.
Ruth Chang, "The Possibility of Parity," *Ethics* **112** (2002): 659–688.
Ruth Chang, *Making Comparisons Count* (Abingdon: Routledge, 2002).
Joshua Gert, "Value and Parity," *Ethics* **114** (2004): 492–510.
Wlodek Rabinowicz, "Value Relations," *Theoria* **74** (2008): 18–49.
Walter Sinnott-Armstrong, "Moral Dilemmas and Incomparability," *American Philosophical Quarterly* **22** (1985): 321–329.
Caspar Hare, "Take the Sugar," *Analysis* **70** (2010): 237–247.
Daniel Muñoz, "The Many, the Few, and the Nature of Value," *Ergo: An Open Access Journal of Philosophy* **9** (2022): 70–87.

Questions for Reflection

1. Many philosophers say that sweetening cases reveal something about how many basic value relations there are. There is, of course, the usual trio of *betterness*, *worseness*, and *being equally good*. Things are equally good if they are perfectly alike in value. But in sweetening cases, we seem to have two things that differ in value, even though neither is better overall. Does this idea make sense?

2. Here's a challenge. Suppose we think of values as being not numbers but *intervals*, like [1, 2]. (The interval $[m, n]$ is the set of all real numbers x such that $m \geq x \geq n$.) We might say that A > B whenever A's value is an interval whose numbers are all larger than the numbers in B's interval; if the intervals overlap, A ~ B. (So, for example, A > B if A's value is [8, 9] and B's value is [6, 7], but A ~ B if their values are [6, 8] and [7, 9].) The intuitive idea here is that things have numerical values, but it's indeterminate *which* number represents a thing's value. Can you think of a way to assign interval values in the above sweetening case, so that W ~ G+ > G ~ W?

3. An extra challenge! See if you can assign values for a *double sweetening case*, where you can choose between G, W, G+, or W+ (a slightly sweetened version of W). As it turns out, it is impossible to assign interval values so that, given the rule we defined earlier, W+ > W, G+ > G, and the Gs tie the Ws. Can you see why?

8

MORAL PSYCHOLOGY AND MOTIVATION

The cases in this chapter are meant to shine a light on the kinds of *psychological states* that motivate moral—or immoral—action. After all, whenever we choose to do something, it is because of our particular goals, desires, values, beliefs, attitudes, emotions, and character traits that we so choose. Is it possible to *philosophically analyze* which states of the above kinds are involved in morally significant choices and actions? That is the goal of the part of ethics called *moral psychology*, and this chapter will give you a little taste of it.

We just mentioned *values* as one of the things that figure into your moral decisions. The thought experiment in **#34, The Ring of Gyges**, which dates back to Plato, may reveal something about your values which you may not have known. I'm sure everyone reading this book habitually acts in a moral and just manner. But underlying those moral *actions* are two very different ways of valuing moral conduct. The Ring of Gyges thought experiment will help you figure out whether you value justice *instrumentally*, or *intrinsically*. Report back!

The idea of valuing moral action *intrinsically* points us toward the next entry, **#35, Moral Worth**. In a famous example, Immanuel Kant gave us a shopkeeper who does the right thing, but for purely self-interested reasons. Kant argued that this shopkeeper does not deserve

DOI: 10.4324/9781003319962-9

moral praise. If you agree, it would seem that whether an action has *moral worth* depends not just on what you *did*, but on *what motivated you to do it*: on your reason(s) for doing it. Later philosophers have agreed with this general approach, while disagreeing with Kant about *which* motives and reasons are morally praiseworthy.

Immoral conduct is also of great interest to moral psychology. How are we to understand the psychological states that lead someone to act wrongly? Entry **#36, Augustine's Pears**, grapples with this question. St. Augustine recounts in his *Confessions* an episode from his unruly adolescence in which he and a gang of friends stole pears from a neighbor's tree. Augustine seems mystified by his own motives for doing this. He feels that what attracted him about this action was precisely its badness: he stole the pears *because it was wrong*. But does that actually make sense?

So far we've been speaking about attitudes, desires, emotions, and the like only in relation to the morally good or bad *actions* they might motivate. But the puzzle in **#37, The Deferential Wife**, is intended to show that a person's attitudes, ideals, and character traits can be ethically evaluated in their own right. Thomas E. Hill Jr. gives us the example of an incredibly deferential wife (we call her "Flora"), noting that the case is likely to cause us "moral unease." It is not easy to identify the *source* of that unease, however. Hill argues, in part by elimination, that what is bothering us is not really Flora's servile *behavior*, but her objectionable *attitude* toward herself. Hill concludes from this case that we need an "ethics of attitudes" alongside the more familiar ethics of actions.

34. THE RING OF GYGES

The man later immortalized as Gyges started out as a humble shepherd in the ancient Greek kingdom of Lydia. But he was a very lucky dude. A chasm opened up in the earth after a thunderstorm and an earthquake, and Gyges, entering the chasm, found and took what turned out to be a very special gold ring. He discovered that if you twisted it in a particular way, the ring made its wearer invisible.

Gyges was quick on the uptake. He realized that if he could become invisible at will, he could do whatever he wanted without fear of being caught. So:

> As soon as he realized this, he arranged to become one of the messengers sent to report to the king. On arriving there, he seduced the king's wife, attacked the king with her help, killed him, and in this way took over the kingdom. (Plato: 359–360)

With the help of his ring, Gyges had gone from humble shepherd to King of Lydia in just a few steps. That's some serious social mobility!

The story of Gyges is a major topic of discussion in Book II of Plato's *Republic*, and it still poses profound questions for us today. I'm sure you readers are fine, upright citizens who are not in the habit of stealing, raping, or killing. But what would you do if you had the ring of Gyges?

If you did, you could take whatever you wanted, have sex with whomever you wanted, and easily eliminate any rivals or enemies, all without the slightest fear of punishment or even reputational damage. You wouldn't need to pay your taxes any more, and if you admired someone's car or house you could just appropriate it for yourself. *You* would know, of course, that you had done these things, but no one else would—you wouldn't fall under the slightest whiff of suspicion.

(Don't get too hung up on how *invisibility* is supposed to secure these results. It's not clear how being invisible would help you evade taxes, for example—I guess there wasn't as much scope for white-collar crime in ancient Greece. The key point here is not that you are invisible, but that you are *guaranteed not to be caught* or even suspected.)

Under these circumstances, would you continue to behave just as you do now? And if not, what does that show?

In Book II of the *Republic*, the character Glaucon is quite sure he *knows* what you would do.

> Now no one, it seems, would be so incorruptible that he would stay on the path of justice, or bring himself to keep away from other people's possessions and not touch them, when he could take whatever he wanted from the marketplace with impunity, go into people's houses and have sex with anyone he wished, kill or release from prison anyone he wished, and do all the other things that would make him like a god among humans.
> ...someone who did not want to do injustice, given this sort of opportunity, and who did not touch other people's property, would be thought most wretched and most foolish by everyone aware of the situation. (360)

As we might say now, anyone who would refrain from injustice even with total impunity guaranteed would be a real *chump*. Gyges should have stayed a shepherd?!?

Glaucon thought the example of Gyges' ring demonstrated something profound about our attitude toward justice. For there are two ways in which we can want or value something. When we value something *instrumentally*, we want or pursue that thing *because* of its further consequences: we want *what it brings us*. Money would be a good example (as would going to the dentist). We want money *because* of what it gets for us, whether that be goods and services, security, social status, or all of the above. If something else delivered those things more effectively than money does, we would quickly switch our allegiance to that thing, for our concern is not with money *as such* but with its fruits. If we had all the goods and services, security, etc., that we wanted, we would have no reason to regret that we lacked more *money*.

Sometimes, though, we want or value a thing not merely for the sake of what it brings us, but for its own sake. In philosophical terms, we value that thing *intrinsically*: we want it *for itself*. Things that we value intrinsically *cannot* be easily replaced by something else, as was possible for money. For example, many people would say that they want *love* in their life: they think a life without love would be missing something very important. If you too feel this way, you probably do not think that love could easily be replaced by something else; you probably want love *itself*. This is not to deny that love brings further benefits, only that those ancillary benefits are not the sole reason we value or want love.

The ring of Gyges story offers each of us a potent thought experiment. I said above that I'm confident you don't go around killing, raping, and pillaging. You *behave*, that is, as if you value being a just and moral person. But how much of that is simply down to the fear of being caught? With Gyges' ring, you could take that factor out of the equation completely. So how would you act then? Glaucon, as we have seen, is convinced that you would act just as Gyges did. If he is right in your case, that would show that you value just and moral behavior only *instrumentally*: only because it keeps you out of trouble and maintains your good reputation.

But there is another possibility. Perhaps you wouldn't want to steal, rape, or kill *even if* you had immunity from punishment. Perhaps you simply don't want to be that kind of person, or to treat other people like that. That could be the case even if those acts were guaranteed not to bring any further bad consequences down on you. In this scenario, it would appear (*contra* Glaucon) that you value justice and morality *intrinsically*: that you value them for their own sake. From this perspective, it is Glaucon who seems the fool.

Classic Presentation

Plato, *Republic*, C. D. C. Reeve, trans. (Indianapolis: Hackett, 2004): Book II.
(There are many translations of this classic text, but they should all include the standardized page numbers which we have used in the citations above.)

Responses and Other Treatments

David Gauthier, *Morals by Agreement* (Oxford: Clarendon Press, 1986): Ch. 10.
David Copp, "The Ring of Gyges: Overridingness and the Unity of Reason," in his *Morality in a Natural World: Selected Essays in Metaethics* (Cambridge: Cambridge University Press, 2007): 284–308.
Christopher Shields, "Plato's Challenge: The Case Against Justice in *Republic* II," in G. Santas, ed., *The Blackwell Guide to Plato's Republic* (Malden: Blackwell, 2006): 63–83.

Questions for Reflection

1.   Suppose you are someone who values justice and morality *intrinsically* (as per the last paragraph above). Could you explain

why you value them intrinsically to someone who doesn't necessarily share your outlook? How could you defend yourself against the idea that you're a fool or a chump if you wouldn't do what Gyges did?

2. The Ring of Gyges is often used as a good example of conflict between *morality* and *self-interest*. The idea is that it's very much in Gyges' self-interest to have traded shepherding for reigning; but it's also morally wrong to kill, deceive, and betray—i.e., all the things he had to do to get there. Do you think it *is* in Gyges' self-interest to kill, deceive, betray, and thereby become king? Why or why not? What do you think a person should do if they are faced with a conflict between morality and self-interest?

35. MORAL WORTH

Morality demands that we act in certain ways. When we do act in those ways, do we therefore deserve moral *praise*?

Immanuel Kant famously argues that we do not. He invites us to consider a shopkeeper who could probably get away with telling certain customers (children, the elderly) that the price of an item is higher than it actually is. (Remember, this is an *18th-century* shopkeeper: they don't have price tags yet.) It would of course be morally wrong to do that, and the shopkeeper doesn't: he charges everyone the same price, just as morality demands. So should we praise the shopkeeper for his honesty?

Kant's answer is: *not necessarily*. It depends on *why* the shopkeeper acts as he does. In this case, let us suppose, the shopkeeper charges everyone the same price *out of concern for his reputation*. He has judged that a reputation for honesty will make him more money in the long run than occasional profiteering, and that is why he refrains from the latter even when it seems he could get away with it (such as with naïve or gullible customers).

In this version of the case, Kant says, the shopkeeper does not deserve moral praise, for he is acting purely out of self-interest. The *moral* character of his action is a matter of indifference to him: he is just doing what he thinks will make him more money in the long run. It is just a *coincidence* that this motive leads him to do something that is also morally required.

Suppose we agree with Kant that *this* shopkeeper does not deserve moral praise for what he does. What would we have to change about the example in order for moral praise to be warranted? Kant argues that an action has *moral worth*—deserves moral praise—only when it is done *from duty*. It is not sufficient that the action merely *accord* with morality's demands, as the shopkeeper's does; rather, the action must be *motivated by* the fact that morality demands it. For Kant, an action has moral worth only when the agent performs that action precisely *because* it is the right thing to do. So we would need a different shopkeeper in this case: one who charges everyone the same price *because* that's the right thing to do—because it would be wrong to do otherwise.

Kant's view of moral worth and moral motivation has been highly influential. But powerful objections have also been raised against it.

The following case, from contemporary philosopher Michael Stocker, vividly brings out why "acting from duty" might not seem so admirable.

> Suppose you are in a hospital, recovering from a long illness. You are very bored and restless and at loose ends when Smith comes in once again. You are now convinced more than ever that he is a fine fellow and a real friend—taking so much time to cheer you up, traveling all the way across town, and so on. You are so effusive with your praise and thanks that he protests that he always tries to do what he thinks is his duty, what he thinks will be best. You at first think he is engaging in a polite form of self-deprecation... But the more you two speak, the more clear it becomes that he was telling the literal truth: that it is not essentially because of you that he came to see you, not because you are friends, but because he thought it his duty, perhaps as a fellow Christian or Communist or whatever, or simply because he knows of no one more in need of cheering up and no one easier to cheer up.
> Surely there is something lacking here—and lacking in moral merit or value. (1976: 462)

Imagine how you would feel if your friend (or spouse!) came to visit you simply "because he thought it his duty" to do so. You would not be quick to praise him.

It could be argued, however, that Kant's conception of moral worth survives this example. What Stocker's case perhaps demonstrates is that *friendly* or *loving* motivation is precisely *not* the same as *moral* motivation, and that we expect the former not the latter from our significant others. On this interpretation, Stocker's example does not show that Kant's view of moral worth is incorrect, but rather that moral praiseworthiness is not all that matters in life, especially among friends.

Other contemporary philosophers, however, have argued more directly that Kant's conception of moral worth is mistaken. Consider—as Jonathan Bennett did in a rich and provocative short paper—the Mark Twain character Huckleberry Finn. As we know from the book, Huck has helped his friend Jim escape from slavery. But as they paddle down the Mississippi River on their raft, Huck's conscience is plaguing him. Huck *knows* that aiding a slave's escape is stealing, and stealing is wrong. He thinks of Miss Watson, Jim's owner: she didn't do anything to deserve Huck's helping her property to up and walk away. Huck *knows* he should "do the right thing," as he himself characterizes it

(Twain 2010: 202), and turn Jim in as a runaway slave. But even when he's given the perfect opportunity, he just can't do it. He stays with Jim as they paddle toward freedom.

Far from doing something *because it's morally right*, Huck does something he thinks is morally *wrong*. But he nonetheless seems morally praiseworthy for wanting to help his friend escape to freedom—even if Kant would say otherwise. For contemporary philosopher Nomy Arpaly, the case of Huck Finn both demonstrates that Kant's formula for moral worth is mistaken, and shows us how to revise it. What confers moral worth on an action, she proposes, is doing the right thing *for the reasons that make it right*. And this can be the case even if you neither know nor even think that you are doing the right thing:

> [Huck's] reluctance [to turn Jim in] is to a large extent the result of the fact that he has come to perceive Jim as a person, even if his conscious mind has not yet come to reflective awareness of this. To the extent that Huckleberry is reluctant to turn Jim in because of Jim's personhood, he is acting for morally significant reasons. This is so even though Huckleberry knows neither that these are the right reasons nor that he is acting from them. (Arpaly 2002: 230)

Arpaly agrees with Kant that moral worth crucially turns on the *reasons why* the agent did what they did. But she disagrees that the agent must act as they do "because it's right." Even someone in the grip of an awful moral view, like Huck, can perform acts with moral worth if—perhaps despite themselves—they are moved by the factors that genuinely morally matter.

Classic Presentation

Immanuel Kant, *Groundwork for the Metaphysics of Morals*, in his *Practical Philosophy*, Mary Gregor, ed. and trans. (Cambridge: Cambridge University Press, 1996): Section I.
(There are many translations of this classic text.)

Responses and Other Treatments

Michael Stocker, "The Schizophrenia of Modern Ethical Theories," *Journal of Philosophy* **73** (1976): 453–466.

Jonathan Bennett, "The Conscience of Huckleberry Finn," *Philosophy* **49** (1974): 123–134.

Nomy Arpaly, "Moral Worth," *Journal of Philosophy* **99** (2002): 223–245.

Barbara Herman, "On the Value of Acting from the Motive of Duty," *Philosophical Review* **90** (1981): 359–382.

Julia Markovits, "Acting for the Right Reasons," *Philosophical Review* **119** (2010): 201–242.

Zoë Johnson King, "Accidentally Doing the Right Thing," *Philosophy and Phenomenological Research* **100** (2020): 186–206.

See Also

Mark Twain, *The Adventures of Huckleberry Finn* (London: Harper Collins, 2010).

Questions for Reflection

1. Philosophical discussions of moral worth have typically agreed with Kant that moral praise should be reserved for cases in which a person acts *for moral reasons*. What could be said for or against this idea? Do you think Kant was correct? (Note that you could agree with this general principle even if you disagree with Kant about *which* reasons should count as moral.)

2. Do you find something "lacking" when Smith visits his friend in the hospital purely out of duty? If so, do you think this example poses a problem for Kant's account of moral praiseworthiness? Why or why not?

3. Do you agree with Arpaly that Huck deserves moral praise for helping Jim escape and not turning him in? Why or why not? Remember that you don't earn moral praise just by *doing* something morally right or good—it matters *why* you did it.

36. AUGUSTINE'S PEARS

For a saint and Father of the Church, Augustine sure is relatable. By his own account, he was a real roustabout as a teenager (around 370 AD). At one point he begged God, "Grant me chastity and celibacy, but not just yet!" (*Confessions* 8.7.17). Later, he wrote his autobiographical *Confessions* in part "to put on record the disgusting deeds in which I engaged" (2.1.1). He gives us as a leading example an incident which has since become famous: the theft of some pears. One night Augustine and his no-good friends crept into a neighbor's garden and stole a bunch of pears off a pear tree (2.4.9). Not terribly depraved, you might think; but what especially interests Augustine about this youthful transgression is not *what he did*, but *why he did it*.

Augustine tells us that he and his friends did not actually want the pears: the fruits had "no attractive appearance or flavor" (2.4.9). Indeed, after shaking huge quantities of them down from the tree, he and his gang just threw the pears to the pigs. Augustine observes that normally, when a person performs a forbidden action, they do so for the sake of some advantage which they hope to gain from it (2.5.11). (See **#34**, **The Ring of Gyges**, in this chapter.) Thus you might rob in order to get money, commit adultery in order to slake your lust, or kill to avenge a death. In this case, however, Augustine had no desire whatsoever for the *fruits* (sorry) of his crime. Why then did he commit it?

Augustine himself puzzles over that very question. "I want to work out what it was about the theft that gave me pleasure" (2.6.12). He concludes that "my pleasure was not in the pears, it was in the actual crime" (2.8.16); "what I enjoyed was the theft and sin themselves" (2.4.9). But this explains only partly: what appealed to Augustine about theft and sin? According to his older self, what drew his teenage self to the act of stealing was precisely the fact that it was wrong or forbidden. "The cause of my wrongdoing was none other than wrongdoing itself[.] It was loathsome and I loved it. My soul... did not use disgraceful means to achieve what it wanted; *what it wanted was the disgrace itself*" (2.4.9, emphasis added). In sum, Augustine "[took] pleasure in [the theft] just because it was forbidden, and for no other reason than that it was forbidden" (2.6.14).

Does this make sense? Augustine seems to be telling us that he saw *nothing* good in the act of stealing the pears, and that its complete and utter badness was precisely why he did it. But we might wonder whether this is really possible. Could that really be the *true* and *complete* account of why Augustine stole the pears? Augustine himself seems very unsure whether it could be, and he casts around at length for some different motive that could be attributed to his younger self. (Scholars disagree about whether he found one.) Let's consider why the reason Augustine gives for stealing the pears seems so paradoxical.

To bring this out we need to reflect on what a full-fledged human action *is*. How does an *action* differ from a mere *movement* or *behavior*? When I cross the street, my body moves—so there is indeed movement taking place. But that's not *all* that's going on. For I could execute the very same movements while sleepwalking, and that would *not* be a full-fledged or intentional action. Similarly, a *kick* could involve the very same motion as occurs when the doctor taps your knee with their little hammer, but the former is an intentional action while the latter is not. What characterizes that subset of behaviors which are intentional actions, given that they may be physically indistinguishable from mere movements?

A venerable philosophical tradition going all the way back to Plato has an answer. What is distinctive about full-fledged intentional actions is that they are always done "*sub specie boni*," "under the guise of the good." According to this idea, when we act intentionally, we necessarily see what we are doing as good in some way. Because we are rational beings, capable of evaluating our own actions, the type of agency proper to us is one in which *action* is guided by *evaluation*. Thus I cross the street intentionally *because* I see something good in doing so, for example the chance to grab that taxi. By contrast, action untethered from evaluation is not really action at all: it is better classified as mere behavior. When my leg rises after the doctor taps my knee, it's not because I favorably regard the prospect of its rising. Ditto sleepwalking. On the present picture, this *independence from evaluation* is precisely why the aforementioned don't count as intentional actions. The special character of intentional action, the feature which distinguishes the action of a rational agent from all other movements or happenings, is that it is guided by *the agent's seeing something good in so acting*.

We should be careful not to pack too much into the guise of the good thesis. The thesis does not assert that all intentional action pursues what is *actually* good, only that an agent must *regard* his intentional action as good in some way. (He might be utterly mistaken about its being good in any way.) Moreover, the agent only has to see his potential action as good *in some way*: it's not necessary that he consider it good or best *overall*, or *all things considered*. There might be plenty of respects in which a given action both is and seems to the agent a terrible idea; but he can intentionally perform that action *despite* those bad features if there is some *other* respect in which the action seems to him good. In short, intentional action guarantees only that "from the agent's point of view there was, when he acted, something to be said for the action" (Davidson 2001: 9).

When Augustine suggests that he saw *nothing* good about stealing the pears, however, *that* is puzzling. Taken literally, it seems to place the theft outside the bounds of intentional action. But it so plainly *was* an intentional action! Augustine was not sleepwalking, the theft was not an involuntary reflex, and nobody compelled Augustine to steal the fruit—he did so of his own free will. According to the guise of the good thesis, then, he must have seen *something* good in the act of stealing the pears. For example, perhaps he was curious whether he could get away with it, or he wanted to impress his buddies. Or maybe he just did it for a thrill. But Augustine seems to reject all such possibilities; he insists that he chose the act *because of its badness*.

Does Augustine's theft disprove the guise of the good thesis? He seems to be saying that in this instance he acted under the guise of the *bad*. If so, and if his action was intentional, then the guise of the good thesis does *not* successfully capture intentional action as such. On the other hand, note how earnestly both he and we are trying to locate an intelligible motive for Augustine's action—one that would reveal in what way he viewed his action favorably. This search seems to demonstrate our own implicit allegiance to the guise of the good thesis: we cannot make sense of his action until we understand what good he saw in it.

Classic Presentation

St. Augustine, *Confessions, Vol. 1: Books 1–8*, Carolyn J.-B. Hammond, ed. and trans. (Loeb Classical Library 26, Cambridge: Harvard University Press, 2014): Book II.

(There are numerous translations of this classic text, but they should all include the standardized section numbers which we have used in the citations above.)

Responses and Other Treatments

Joseph Raz, "On the Guise of the Good," in Sergio Tenenbaum, ed., *Desire, Practical Reason, and the Good* (Oxford: Oxford University Press, 2010): 111–137.

Warren Quinn, "Putting Rationality in Its Place," in his *Morality and Action* (New York: Cambridge University Press, 1993): 228–255.

David Sussman, "For Badness' Sake," *Journal of Philosophy* **106** (2009): 613–628.

J. David Velleman, "The Guise of the Good," in his *The Possibility of Practical Reason* (Ann Arbor: Michigan Publishing, 2014). Second Edition. http://dx.doi.org/10.3998/maize.13240734.0001.001.

Further Reading

Donald Davidson, "Actions, Reasons, and Causes," in his *Essays on Actions and Events* (Oxford: Clarendon Press, 2001). Second Edition.

Questions for Reflection

1.   Could the guise of the good thesis be rescued by saying that Augustine must have taken the very *badness* of the act to be *good*? Or would this reveal the guise of the good thesis to be only trivially true?

2.   We have probably all seen teenagers do things *because* those things are forbidden by their parents. Does that violate the guise of the good thesis? Is it the same as doing something wrong *because* it is wrong, which is Augustine's description of his action? If not, what's the difference?

37. THE DEFERENTIAL WIFE

Meet Flora. The philosopher Thomas E. Hill Jr. tells us about her:

> [Flora] is utterly devoted to serving her husband. She buys the clothes *he* prefers, invites the guests *he* wants to entertain, and makes love whenever *he* is in the mood. She willingly moves to a new city in order for him to have a more attractive job, counting her own friendships and geographical preferences insignificant by comparison... She tends not to form her own interests, values, and ideals; and, when she does, she counts them as less important than her husband's... [Flora] believes that the proper role for a woman is to serve her family. (1991a: 5–6)

Flora is an extremely deferential wife.[1] Is there something wrong with that? If so, what?

These are not easy questions to answer. Hill predicts that many of us will experience what he elsewhere calls "moral discomfort" or "moral uneasiness" (1991b: 105, 107, 108) when we read about Flora. But what exactly is bothering us? It's not just that we disapprove of Flora's *husband* when we read about this pair (although we certainly might). Rather, there seems to be something about *Flora's own attitudes and behavior* which makes us uneasy. We may think "It's not right for Flora to feel that way," or "[Flora] ought to have more self-respect" (1991a: 7).

To understand our ethical reaction better, we need to identify *what* it is that we disapprove of or find objectionable in Flora's attitudes and behavior. Is it that we fear she is unhappy? But Hill tells us that Flora is very happy to serve her husband in this way. (No doubt her husband is too.) Whatever is off here, it seems to remain even *if* Flora is happy with her lot. (In fact, her being perfectly happy with her lot looks like a further symptom of exactly what ails her.) Is our negative reaction one of *blame* toward Flora for committing morally wrong actions? That seems unlikely. Flora is not hurting other people—the usual profile of a morally wrong action—and whatever she does, she does willingly. So it's hard to see how she could be accused of violating anyone's rights or failing in any of her duties. (We will return to this issue, however.)

Hill suspects we will not be able to express what makes us uneasy about Flora solely in terms of the usual suspects in ethical theory (like morally right and wrong action, duties, rights, and well-being). We will need to turn our attention away from Flora's *actions* and toward her *attitudes* to find the root of the "moral concern" (1991b: 105) which the case elicits in us. Hill's diagnosis is that Flora exhibits the trait or attitude of *servility*. Servility as Hill understands it is not a matter of servile *behavior*; servility concerns how you view *yourself*, not how you act toward others. Flora counts as servile because she believes that her aims and wishes deserve less consideration than her husband's and that she is of inferior status compared to him. She does not think she has the right to claim equal standing within the marriage or to develop her own preferences or ideals that might conflict with those of her husband. Indeed, Flora is so thoroughly reconciled to her supposed lower moral status that she sees it as her *duty* to defer to her husband in all things. We might sum this up by saying that Flora profoundly undervalues *herself*.

Is there anything morally wrong with that, though? Hill thinks servility is a genuine moral defect (1991a: 9). It is objectionable *in itself* not to see yourself as having equal moral standing with others: such servility betrays a lack of self-respect which is not merely regrettable but ethically problematic. The servile person fails to understand, or (alternatively) fails to acknowledge or value, her own moral rights; and this offends our moral sensibilities. Moreover, all of this is true regardless of how the servile person *acts*. The underlying ethical defect is not in her actions but in her attitudes and character.

There is a broader moral here. Our judgment that something is morally awry with Flora demonstrates the existence of a distinct branch of ethics which Hill calls "the ethics of *attitudes*" (1991c: 156). We know this branch exists because whatever is wrong with Flora shows up on it. Flora helps us see that ethics is not only concerned with how we *act*; it can also evaluate how we think and feel, the kind of character we have, and the ideals we aspire to or fall short of. In order to express ethical assessments of things like these, we will need to pass from the familiar moral vocabulary to a new lexicon. We will need a novel set of ethical concepts which are apt for the evaluation of attitudes, ideals, and character traits rather than actions. This distinct style of ethical thought is often called *virtue ethics*, and Hill is credited with having made a major contribution by drawing our attention to its importance. (Hill expands further on virtue-ethical thinking in his 1991b.)

Is all lost for the usual suspects, though? Perhaps there are alternative ways of capturing what is ethically problematic in the Flora case in more familiar moral vocabulary, without needing to move to virtue ethics. In particular, we might have been too quick to dismiss the idea that Flora contravenes some duty or violates some right. Mightn't we say that Flora *owes it to herself* not to be servile? And if we take the talk of "owing" literally, Flora could be wronging *herself*, or violating *her own* rights, by acting as she does.

There is admittedly something puzzling about the idea of rights against oneself, or wronging oneself. (**The Paradox of Self-Release**, **#15**, further explores these concepts.) If Flora "gives herself permission" to behave in a servile fashion—which it seems she does, since she acts that way willingly—it seems to follow that she has *waived* any right to assert herself which she might possess. And if she's *waived* that right she can't possibly be *violating* it, since it is no longer in force. Consider the alternative possibility, though, that Flora is only deferential because she *doesn't know she's allowed* to stand up for herself. Imagine that because of the culture in which she was brought up, she thinks wives are *supposed* to defer to their husbands in all the ways she does. In *that* case, at least, Flora *doesn't* seem to have waived the right to assert herself, since she doesn't even think she has one.

Classic Presentations

Thomas E. Hill Jr., "Servility and Self-Respect," in his *Autonomy and Self-Respect* (Cambridge: Cambridge University Press, 1991): Ch. 1. (Cited as Hill 1991a.)

In the same volume, see also "Ideals of Human Excellence and Preserving Natural Environments," Ch. 8 (cited as Hill 1991b), and "Social Snobbery and Human Dignity," Ch. 11 (cited as Hill 1991c).

Further Reading

Marcia Baron, "Servility, Critical Deference, and the Deferential Wife," *Philosophical Studies* **48** (1985): 393–400.

Daniel Muñoz and Nathaniel Baron-Schmitt, "Wronging Oneself," *Journal of Philosophy* (forthcoming).

Questions for Reflection

1.   Why should lack of self-respect be considered a *moral* or *ethical* flaw? Or should it not be?

176 MORAL PSYCHOLOGY AND MOTIVATION

2. Which do you think better captures what is wrong with Flora: the virtue-ethical judgment that she has an ethically objectionable attitude toward herself, or the non-virtue-ethical claim that she is violating one of her own rights? Why is the one you favor a better description? Could both be true?

3. Consider Flora 2.0. This Flora *does* know that she has the right to stand up to her husband. But she never chooses to *exercise* that right, instead allowing her husband to have his way every time. Does Flora 2.0 induce "moral discomfort" in you, as did Flora 1.0? Is that because she is objectionably servile (following Hill's definition)? If not, how would you characterize what makes you morally uneasy about Flora 2.0?

NOTE

1 In Hill's article, he refers to his character as "the deferential wife." "Flora" is our name.

9

MORAL RESPONSIBILITY

The concept of *moral responsibility* usually lies in the background of ethical thought. In this chapter, though, we seek to bring it out into the light so we can examine it more closely.

When a person does something morally wrong or bad, we react negatively to that action and that person. We might be angry or resentful toward them or withdraw our trust or friendship from them. In short, we *blame* them for what they did, and we express that blame through various negative feelings and actions.

It's only *fair* to blame a person, however, if certain conditions hold. So when we blame, we are in effect *assuming* that a bunch of things are true. First, that the action really was morally bad or wrong; second, that the person we are blaming really did perform it. (We leave it as an exercise for the reader to mentally verify that if one or both of these were false, it would not be correct to blame the person.) But there is a third, more subtle condition which also needs to hold, and it is here that we find the notion of *moral responsibility* lurking in the background. In order for it to be appropriate to blame someone, the bad action which they performed must reflect something objectionable about *them*. A person deserves blame for what they did only when that action reveals a moral defect *in them*.

As mentioned above, normally we just *assume* that a person is morally responsible for the acts they perform. But in some cases the third

DOI: 10.4324/9781003319962-10

condition above does *not* hold, and then we *withhold* blame. If you are forced to do something bad at gunpoint, we likely will not blame you. Why not? Because—in contrast to the case of someone doing the same thing because they really wanted to—this unfortunate action reveals no moral defect in you. In order for you to deserve blame for something you do, there has to be a tight connection between *what you did* and *who you are*. When that connection is broken, we will typically consider you not morally responsible for what you did.

Like all the concepts in this book, it turns out that we understand moral responsibility less well than we might have thought. This chapter presents a number of puzzles about when a person should count as morally responsible for what they did. **Frankfurt Cases (#38)** examines the apparent truism that you can only be morally responsible for an action if *you could have done otherwise*. If you had no choice in the matter, then of course you're not responsible! Philosopher Harry Frankfurt, however, ingeniously argues that this truism is false. In **#39, Wolf's JoJo**, we consider whether and how someone's *personal history* affects the degree to which they are morally responsible for what they now do. Susan Wolf's memorable example of JoJo—favorite son of the brutal dictator Jo the First—shows how hard it is to arrive at a consistent answer to that question.

Besides blame, *forgiveness* is another phenomenon which presupposes moral responsibility. When we forgive, we are forgiving someone *for* having done something bad or wrong, but only if they were morally responsible for doing it. (If they did it at gunpoint, there would in a certain sense be nothing to forgive.) While this moral responsibility requirement seems utterly natural, **#40, The Paradox of Forgiveness**, shows how it threatens to make forgiveness paradoxical or even impossible. In **Moral Luck (The Lorry Driver)**, **#41**, we pivot from *when* a person can be considered morally responsible to *what* a person can be considered morally responsible *for*. We imagine two equally skilled truck drivers, one of whom hits a child through no fault of his own. There are at least two reasons to think we wouldn't—and shouldn't—hold the second driver morally responsible for killing the child. First, his "action" reveals no moral defect in him. Second, the difference between the two drivers is totally down to luck; and surely luck is irrelevant to moral assessment, which aims to judge us as we are in our hearts and minds. But as we shall see in **#41**, our actual moral reactions to such cases don't obey these simple principles: instead, they are complicated and perhaps even contradictory.

38. FRANKFURT CASES

In ethical theory, many of the best ideas have been around for ages. But every once in a while, someone discovers a counterexample to a literally ancient principle, and an entire part of the field is transformed.

Case in point. Consider what the Princeton philosopher Harry Frankfurt calls:

The Principle of Alternate Possibilities
"[A] person is morally responsible for what he has done only if he could have done otherwise." (1969: 829)

For ages, this was considered a basic truism about free will and responsibility. If you couldn't have done anything other than what you did, you were not *free*—and so you were not *morally responsible* for your actions.

This principle seems obviously correct when we think about everyday examples of coercion. Suppose you're working in a store when someone puts a gun to your head and says, "Hand over the cash, NOW!" If you know they mean business, you might well decide on that basis to turn over everything in the register. Since you're under duress, you're not acting freely. Only a fool (or a fanatical manager) would say that you're morally responsible for the store's financial losses. The key fact here seems to be that you had no real choice but to give the money to the robber. Your unfreedom was due to your lack of alternate possibilities.

Just one problem with that, says Frankfurt: "the principle of alternate possibilities is false," and its "plausibility is an illusion" (829–830).

Where does the "illusion" come from? Frankfurt thinks we are conflating two roles that threats and coercion can play with respect to a person's action. First, they could make it "impossible for the person to do otherwise" (830). Second, they could be the *reason* for the person's action, serving to "bring it about that he does whatever it is that he does" (830). In the robbery case, the threat plays both of these roles. The gun to your head leaves you with no real choice but to hand the cash over, and it's also the reason why you do it—you weren't going to fork it over out of the kindness of your heart!

Now, when threats impel you to act, you aren't free, and you aren't responsible. But what if they don't impel you? Suppose someone puts a gun to your head and demands that you rob a bank, but you were going to do that *anyway*. As before, the threat means you couldn't really do otherwise. But the threat is no longer the reason *why* you act, and so it seems perfectly reasonable to hold you morally responsible for your robbery.

If that's right, then the Principle of Alternate Possibilities is indeed false, and it only seemed plausible because we were assuming that anything that *removes alternatives* must also be the agent's *reason for acting*. Not so!

When Frankfurt's arguments debuted in 1969, they were a shot in the arm for compatibilism—the view that we can be morally responsible for our actions even if the laws of nature, along with the initial conditions of the universe, fully determine how the future will unfold. In such a deterministic universe, it seems that for any action we take, there's a clear sense in which we couldn't have done otherwise. But if Frankfurt is right, that's no threat to moral responsibility. If someone decides to rob a bank fully on the basis of their own beliefs and values, they can't wriggle out of their responsibility by saying "the laws of nature made me do it." That's like saying "the gunman made me do it" when you were perfectly happy to do it anyway. Not much of an excuse!

RESPONSES

The first response to Frankfurt's attack comes from… Frankfurt!

To refute the Principle of Alternate Possibilities, we need a case where (1) an agent is morally responsible, but (2) they could not have done otherwise. The problem with the case of threats is that there is *some* sense in which the victims *could* have done otherwise. You could have defied the person trying to rob your register, and the would-be bank-robber could have refused to do any robbing. These acts of defiance would, alas, lead to a swift death. Still, even if they aren't desirable, they do still seem like alternate possibilities.

To shut down such objections, Frankfurt gives his most famous example by far:

> Suppose someone—Black, let us say—wants Jones$_4$ to perform a certain action. Black is prepared to go to considerable lengths to get his way, but he prefers to avoid showing his hand unnecessarily. So he waits until Jones$_4$ is about to make up his mind what to do, and he does

nothing unless it is clear to him (Black is an excellent judge of such things) that Jones$_4$ is going to decide to do something other than what he wants him to do. If it does become clear that Jones$_4$ is going to decide to do something else, Black takes effective steps to ensure that Jones$_4$ decides to do, and that he does do, what he wants him to do. Whatever Jones$_4$'s initial preferences and inclinations, then, Black will have his way.[1] (1969: 835)

In this version of the case, Jones isn't threatened or coerced. If he does what Black wants—say, robbing a bank—then the entire sequence of events leading up to Jones' decision looks *exactly like it would if Black hadn't been there*. Moreover, it seems Jones could not have even *started* to do otherwise, since before he could get that far, Black would stop him—perhaps with a hi-tech device that sends a signal straight to a chip implanted in Jones' brain, causing Jones to rob the bank (you can fill in the details as you wish). This time, there's truly no room for doing otherwise.

...or so Frankfurt might have thought. Since his groundbreaking article, an entire subfield of philosophy has sprung up around "Frankfurt cases": thought experiments like that of Jones and Black, where the agent (apparently) couldn't have done otherwise, and yet (apparently) is still morally responsible, since their decision wasn't actually based on their lack of alternatives.

Frankfurt cases utterly changed the way that ethical theorists talk about free will and moral responsibility. For one thing, such cases set off a lively debate over whether there is any way to defend or revise the Principle of Alternate Possibilities, with many philosophers arguing that there remains a sense in which Jones is unfree *because* he cannot do otherwise. Frankfurt cases also hinted at a fresh approach to moral responsibility that is less about the possibility of doing otherwise and more about the *actual sequence of events* that led up to the action and whether the agent was in some relevant sense in control of those events. (See for example Fischer and Ravizza 1998 on "guidance control" and "reasons-responsiveness.")

Maybe someday ethical theorists will reach a new consensus about the Principle of Alternate Possibilities. Maybe not. For now, at least we know that the principle is anything but a boring truism. Whether it's true or false, it's a big deal—and a long time in the making.

Classic Presentation

Harry Frankfurt, "Alternate Possibilities and Moral Responsibility," *Journal of Philosophy* **66** (1969): 829–839.

Further Reading

Carolina Sartorio, "Frankfurt-Style Examples," in Kevin Timpe, Meghan Griffith, and Neil Levy, eds., *The Routledge Companion to Free Will* (New York: Routledge, 2016): Ch. 15. (A truly excellent overview.)

John Martin Fischer and Mark Ravizza, *Responsibility and Control: A Theory of Moral Responsibility* (Cambridge: Cambridge University Press, 1998).

David Robb, "Moral Responsibility and the Principle of Alternative Possibilities," in Edward N. Zalta and Uri Nodelman, eds., *The Stanford Encyclopedia of Philosophy* (Winter Edition, 2023): https://plato.stanford.edu/entries/alternative-possibilities/

Questions for Reflection

1. Do you think it's true, in the last kind of Frankfurt case we considered, that Jones could not have done otherwise? Look for some ways to argue that Jones *could* have done otherwise. (This is sometimes called the "Flickers of Freedom" strategy.)

2. Do you think those ways of doing otherwise are robust enough to make Jones morally responsible?

39. WOLF'S JOJO

JoJo's father rules the world. Or so it seems to JoJo. Papa is master of all he surveys; indeed, to JoJo the whole world appears to revolve around Papa. Papa does whatever he wants, without the slightest fear of interference or protest from those around him, and JoJo finds this absolute freedom of action intoxicating. He wants nothing more than to grow up to be like his father.

JoJo is right about his father's power. For Papa—known to others as Jo the First—is a brutal dictator. He exercises absolute and arbitrary power over his court and his terrified subjects. He has people hung, drawn, and quartered if they displease him, and he is quick to deploy chemical weapons against any region of his domain that might prove restive. No one dares oppose him, so he is indeed free to do whatever he wants.

Jo the First is especially fond of his namesake son, and he has arranged for the boy to shadow him daily so that JoJo will learn how to be a successful brutal dictator when his turn comes. JoJo (predictably) grows up in awe of his father: he is exposed to no other models he could aspire to. When JoJo becomes dictator himself, he follows in his father's footsteps and visits arbitrary harm on individuals and entire regions when he so pleases. Now JoJo is intoxicated by his *own* power.

JoJo performs heinous actions. But his creator, philosopher Susan Wolf, presses the question: is JoJo *morally responsible* for the awful things he does? We normally respond to wrongful actions with negative feelings and responses that express our *blame* of the agent for having so acted. But there are exceptions to this general rule. If a person did something terrible while under hypnosis, or if he was forced to do it at gunpoint (as in the previous entry), we don't blame him in the same way for what he did. In such cases we judge the agent not to have been (fully) *morally responsible* for his wrongful actions, and this mitigates or eliminates our blame.

Is JoJo one of those cases? Here is an argument that he is *not*: that he should be held responsible for the things he does. One salient feature of the "exceptions" for actions performed under hypnosis or duress is that such actions are not expressive of *who we really are*. Under normal circumstances, our actions express our desires, aims, character traits, and values; so someone who does bad things to other people is normally taken to have revealed something objectionable in the above. But in cases of hypnosis or coercion, that link is broken. (See the previous entry for an important qualification of this point, however.) Perhaps we make an exception in such cases precisely *because* the person's actions do not reflect their "deep self." The actions of the hypnotized agent, for example, stem not from *him* but from something external to him, namely the agent pulling the strings behind the scenes.

The "deep self" view would say that JoJo *is* responsible for his actions, since they *do* stem from who JoJo really is. JoJo's actions perfectly express his values and character; he fully embraces arbitrary power as his *summum bonum*. If asked, JoJo would say he *wants* to be the kind of person he is and that he is living his best life. The deep self view gives JoJo no out.

However, the deep self view seems to overlook a possibility which might exonerate JoJo and lead to the conclusion that he is *not* after all morally responsible for the awful things he does. The deep self view considers only whether our actions express our desires, aims, character traits, and values. It neglects to ask whether we are responsible for those aims and values themselves. Suppose a malevolent brainwasher managed to implant a totally new set of evil aims and values in you. Would you be morally responsible for the actions that resulted? It seems you shouldn't be, even if those actions perfectly match your (newly implanted) values. For those values are themselves *externally sourced* (in the brainwasher), not sourced in *you*. This exactly parallels the case of the hypnotized agent, whom we agreed is not morally responsible for what he does.

Now JoJo has not had his values implanted by a malevolent brainwasher. But you might think his situation resembles that one in important respects. Is JoJo responsible for having the values he does? Susan Wolf, for one, doubts this. She writes, "It is unclear whether anyone with a childhood such as his could have developed into anything but the twisted and perverse sort of person that he has become" (1987: 54). JoJo seems to be a victim of circumstance, and in particular of his upbringing: he was given no opportunity to be inspired by any role model other than his father. From this perspective, JoJo is *not to be blamed* for becoming what he became: it is *not his fault*. And if JoJo is not responsible for having the values and aims which lead him to commit atrocities, then it would seem he's not responsible for the atrocities either.

A danger is lurking here, however: the above line of reasoning threatens to "prove" that *none of us* is morally responsible for our actions. In other words, the argument we just made on behalf of JoJo threatens to generalize. We asked whether *JoJo* is responsible for having the values and aims he does; but it is true of *all of us* that our values and aims have been shaped by our parents, our environment, and the circumstances of our upbringing. JoJo is simply not unique in that respect. "If Jojo is not responsible because his deepest self is not up to him, then we are not responsible either," Wolf observes (54). If, "in order to be responsible for our *actions*, we have to be responsible for our *selves*" (60, emphasis added), then "responsibility would be impossible for *anyone* to achieve" (54, emphasis added). The line of argument we just applied to the JoJo case seems to lead straight to global skepticism about moral responsibility.

Wolf herself, however, argues that we need not draw such a nihilistic conclusion from the case of JoJo. She thinks we can maintain that JoJo lacks full responsibility for his actions *without* being forced to say the same about the rest of us. For there is a big difference between (most of) us and JoJo, and Wolf thinks that difference is what accounts for JoJo's impaired responsibility. Notably, JoJo lacks a very significant *ability* which most of us have: the ability "to understand and appreciate right and wrong, and to change our characters and our actions accordingly" (59). For Wolf, it is *this* missing piece which undermines JoJo's moral responsibility—not the mere fact that his values have been shaped by his environment and upbringing, which is true of all of us. The major problem here is instead JoJo's moral perception of the world, which is seriously off base. JoJo clearly does not "understand and appreciate right and wrong." And that he *persists* in this deeply incorrect orientation suggests that he is not *able* to alter or ameliorate that lack of comprehension and appreciation. Most of us do not share these misfortunes: we *are* capable of understanding and appreciating right and wrong, and we have at least some ability to course-correct when we waver from the path of the true and the good. The tragedy of JoJo is that he is "governed by [a] mistaken conception of value that [he] cannot help but have" (57).

Classic Presentation

Susan Wolf, "Sanity and the Metaphysics of Responsibility," in Ferdinand Schoeman, ed., *Responsibility, Character, and the Emotions* (Cambridge: Cambridge University Press, 1987): 46–62.

Responses and Other Treatments

Harry Frankfurt, "Freedom of the Will and the Concept of a Person," *Journal of Philosophy* **68** (1971): 5–20.

Gary Watson, "Free Agency," *Journal of Philosophy* **72** (1975): 205–220.

Gary Watson, "Responsibility and the Limits of Evil: Variations on a Strawsonian Theme," in Ferdinand Schoeman, ed., *Responsibility, Character, and the Emotions* (Cambridge: Cambridge University Press, 1987): 219–259.

Gary Watson, "Two Faces of Responsibility," *Philosophical Topics* **24** (1996): 227–248.

Questions for Reflection

1. Are we morally responsible for *who we are*? (If your answer is "most of us are," that should count as a "yes.") What considerations could be brought in support of or against this idea? (Note that the question is asking about moral responsibility for our *selves*, not for our *actions*.)

2. Wolf's analysis puts a lot of weight on JoJo's moral view being *incorrect*. That suggests she would give a different verdict on the moral responsibility of someone who is also "governed by [a] conception of value that [he] cannot help but have," but where that conception of value *accords* rather than clashes with what we understand to be right and wrong. Is an asymmetrical treatment of these two cases justified?

40. THE PARADOX OF FORGIVENESS

The Lord's Prayer enjoins us to forgive those who trespass against us. But humorist S. J. Perelman quipped that "To err is human; to forgive, supine." Clearly, opinions of forgiveness vary. When, if ever, should we forgive someone who has trespassed against us?

Before we can pursue that question, though, we need a better understanding of what forgiveness *is*; and when examined closely, the very idea of forgiveness appears paradoxical.

Forgiveness requires something you are forgiving the person *for*, so we'll need a trespass, a trespasser, and a victim. Suppose for example that you caught a kid at summer camp reading your diary. (This happened to me.) To say that you were *affronted* or *offended* by this violation would be an understatement: you would feel both humiliated and very angry. Let's specify that there was no conceivable justification for what the kid did; it was pure malicious snooping. They trespassed against you big time, and you are full of righteous indignation about it.

In my case, I never forgave that girl. But suppose you are a better person than I am, and you did. What would that look like? Clearly, forgiveness involves somehow *resetting* or *reorienting* your relationship with the wrongdoer. When you forgive, you withdraw your (previous) angry and resentful feelings toward the trespasser; you stop holding their trespass against them. In that sense, forgiveness "wipes the slate clean."

But how is that possible? After all, forgiveness can't rewrite the past; it doesn't *literally* wipe the slate clean. Forgiveness doesn't remove the infraction from the history books, or from the wrongdoer's moral ledger. It will remain forever true that this trespasser—let's call them "Tristyn"—did that to you, that what they did was wrong, and that they had no excuse for doing it. If any of *those* things turn out not to be true, then we are not dealing with a case of forgiveness.

- If it turns out that it wasn't Tristyn—it was actually someone *else* who committed the trespass—then you obviously can't forgive *Tristyn*: for as concerns Tristyn there is literally nothing to forgive.
- If it turns out that Tristyn's action was not *wrong*, but *justified*, then you can't *forgive* Tristyn, because they did nothing wrong. (We can't use the diary example to illustrate this possibility, because we already stipulated that there was no conceivable justification for what

that kid did. So consider a different example. "Sorry I didn't show up for our lunch date—my kid had a seizure and had to be rushed to the hospital." It would be very strange to say, "I forgive you for standing me up.")

- Finally, if Tristyn's *moral responsibility* or *culpability* for what they did was compromised, you would *excuse* Tristyn for what they did, not forgive them. (Suppose Tristyn was in the midst of a severe allergic reaction to a bee sting, or suffering from delusions, when they did it. Then the usual link between their objectionable *action* and something objectionable *in them* would be broken, or at least weakened.)

In sum, when you forgive Tristyn, the infraction remains on the books, as does its wrongness, as does Tristyn's culpability for the trespass. What's more, you are aware of all this. (Literal *forgetting* actually *precludes* forgiving: if you simply *forgot* that Tristyn did this to you, you could not forgive them. So when people say "Forgive and forget," remember to do them *in that order*.) Given all this, your negative feelings toward Tristyn seem to remain just as appropriate as they were before! Philosopher Agnes Callard argues that we actually have reason to stay angry *forever* about trespasses against us:

> There are reasons to remain angry. And the reasons are not hard to find: they are the same reasons as the reasons to get angry in the first place. [Nothing can] cancel or alter the fact that I stole, nor the fact that I ought not to have stolen. Those facts were your reasons to be angry. Since they [have] not changed, you still have the very same reasons to be angry. (Callard 2020: 17)[2]

What we have said about forgiveness so far seems to reveal a paradox in the very idea of forgiving. To forgive someone seems to involve both *blaming* and *not blaming* them for what they did; both *holding them responsible* for their action and *not holding it against them*. As philosopher Lucy Allais puts it, "Forgiving seems to mean ceasing to blame[;] but if blaming means holding the perpetrator responsible, then forgiveness requires *not* ceasing to blame, or else there will be nothing to forgive" (2008: 33). Philosopher Jean Hampton: "If forgivers never give up the idea that the action was wrong, how can they ever give up the view of the actor as a wrongdoer?" (1988: 41) It seems impossible to change your mind about the *offender* without changing your mind about the *offense*. But that seems to be exactly what forgiveness requires: the first *without* the second.

People do forgive, however. Perhaps the Bible can help explain how this is possible. Here's a clue from Luke 17:3: "If thy brother trespass against thee, rebuke him; and *if he repent*, forgive him" (emphasis added). Possibly taking a lead from this Biblical hint, philosophers have proposed that *apology* and *repentance* are what make forgiveness possible. If the trespasser apologizes and repents, he now acknowledges the wrongness of his previous action. Not just that: he *disavows* and *repudiates* his action. In this way he "sever[s] himself from his past wrong," as Jeffrie Murphy puts it (1988: 26). And since *his* relation to his past trespass is now different, *yours* can be too. You can now "draw a distinction between the immoral *act* and the immoral *agent*" (24), retaining your negative judgment of the former while altering your orientation toward the latter. This seems impossible as long as the wrongdoer "stands by" his wrongdoing; but once he joins you in condemning his earlier act, some daylight opens up between the offender and the offense.

When someone has wronged you, your image of them often has that fact at its center, like a great big pimply nose. For me, that girl at camp will always be first and foremost "that horrible person who read my diary." (As you can see, I hold grudges for decades.) But forgiving, set in motion by repentance, sets aside or *de-centers* the trespass in your thinking about the offender. You are now open to seeing them in a different light. "The forgiver is able to respond to the wrongdoer as something other than 'the person who hurt me'" (Hampton 1988: 38); you no longer base how you *feel* about the wrongdoer primarily on the latter's offense. This reorientation toward the offender opens the door, as forgiveness often does, to reconciliation.

Recommended Treatments

Lucy Allais, "Wiping the Slate Clean: The Heart of Forgiveness," *Philosophy & Public Affairs* **36** (2008): 33–68.

Jean Hampton and Jeffrie Murphy, *Forgiveness and Mercy* (Cambridge: Cambridge University Press, 1988).

Agnes Callard, *On Anger* (Cambridge: MIT Press, 2020).

John Kekes, "Blame Versus Forgiveness," *The Monist* **92** (2009): 488–506.

Questions for Reflection

1. What do you think about forgiveness when the perpetrator *hasn't* apologized or repented? Is it possible? Advisable? Admirable?

2. Kekes and Callard argue that you still have the same reasons to be angry at the perpetrator even *after* they repent. (After all, it remains true even then that they culpably wronged you.) On this view, forgiveness, even if *possible*, is always *unreasonable*. How would you respond to their argument?

3. When you forgive someone, are you *condoning* what they did? If not, what's the difference?

41. MORAL LUCK (THE LORRY DRIVER)

Imagine two lorry drivers who are at this moment both traveling through residential neighborhoods in a certain city. (They both drive moving trucks, and have just left the houses of their respective clients.) Amal has an uneventful journey through the city: they are an experienced driver, and this job poses no special problem for them. Blair is an equally experienced driver, and this job is also routine for them. But something horrible happens as Blair drives down the street: through no fault of Blair's, a child suddenly darts out into the road, and Blair hits her. The child perishes.

Blair has done nothing wrong. He's a conscientious driver, and it wasn't his fault that the child suddenly ran out into the road. But despite all that, it is now true that *Blair has killed a child.* As drivers, the only difference between Blair and Amal seems to be that no child happened to run out into the road along Amal's route. Obviously, neither Blair nor Amal has any control over whether children run out into the street as they drive by. So this was pure *bad luck*—for Blair. Amal, by comparison, was lucky.

Through no fault of his own, Blair is now a child killer. Amal is not. And yet the difference between them is totally down to luck. Can the moral status of an action, or a person, vary depending on factors that are purely a matter of luck? If so, we can call that *moral* luck. If Blair is subject to an unfavorable moral judgment that doesn't also apply to Amal, then Blair has been *morally* unlucky.

Note that we seem to get the same asymmetry if we alter the example to increase the culpability of both Amal and Blair. Suppose that each has been very *slightly* negligent with respect to their trucks—they're both a *little* behind on the prescribed maintenance schedule for the brakes. Then it's no longer true that Blair's hitting the child was *purely* a matter of luck, with *zero* contribution from Blair's actions. Perhaps things would have gone differently if Blair had had the brake maintenance done on time. Unlike in the original example, now Blair has something to reproach himself for; now he is at least a *little* bit at fault in the child's death. But as Thomas Nagel notes, when

> [the driver's] negligence contributes to the death of the child, he will not merely feel terrible. He will blame himself for the death. And what makes this an example of moral luck is that he would have to blame himself only

> slightly for the negligence itself if no situation arose which required him to
> brake suddenly and violently to avoid hitting a child. Yet *the negligence* is
> the same in both cases, and the driver has no control over whether a child
> will run into his path. (1979: 29)

Blair is blameworthy; Amal is practically blameless. And yet their
degree of *fault* is identical. The only difference between them lies in
something over which neither of them had any control.

Why does this seem paradoxical? When a person does something we
consider morally wrong, we—and perhaps they—make a special kind of
judgment: a *moral* judgment. Moral judgment does not consist merely in
thinking that a terrible thing happened; it involves judging the *person* who
did that terrible thing. Moral judgment looks beyond *the thing done* to *the
doer*, finding a fault in *them*. And while success in many other aspects of
life is highly subject to contingencies and luck, morality can be seen as
"provid[ing] a shelter against luck" (Williams 1993: 251), since it aims to
judge us as we are in our hearts. So if a bad thing done does *not* represent
any fault in the doer, but only bad luck, it seems we ought to refrain from
morally judging the doer. Why then do we feel differently about what
Blair did than about what Amal did, in both versions of the case?

Bernard Williams, who introduced the lorry driver example, notes
that Blair would even judge *himself* in a special way after the accident.
A spectator would of course think it a terrible thing that a child was
killed. But Blair himself would not think only that. In fact, we would
be rather taken aback if Blair's reaction were, "It is awful that a child
was killed. But *I* didn't do anything wrong." Rather, we would expect
Blair to be overcome with *regret*, even if not *remorse*. Indeed, Williams
suggests that the lorry driver will feel regret of a special kind, one that
no spectator could in principle feel: regret for *one's own past actions*.
This "agent-regret," as Williams terms it, involves an ardent wish that
one had not done what one did. It registers "that there is something
special about his relation to this happening, something which cannot
merely be eliminated by the consideration that it was not his fault"
(1981: 28). The driver's agent-regret may be expressed in his trying to
make some kind of restitution, if only symbolic; something that would
not be fitting on the part of a mere spectator.

Our thoughts here seem to be in a muddle. It seems to be in the
nature of moral judgment that identical *faults in the agent* ought to

receive identical moral censure. That would make "moral luck" an oxymoron: moral assessment would by definition be immune to influence by mere matters of luck. But our actual practices and reactions do not seem to fit this pattern. We *do* react differently to Blair and to Amal—even Blair does. So the alleged phenomenon of moral luck seems to expose a deep tension in our moral views.

In fact, the effect of luck on moral assessment might be even more pervasive than we have so far noticed. Thomas Nagel identifies three additional kinds of "moral luck," beyond luck in how our actions turn out. These are constitutive luck (being lucky or unlucky "in your inclinations, capacities, and temperament," 1979: 28); luck in one's circumstances (good or bad luck in "the opportunities and choices with which we are faced," 25–26); and luck in "how one is determined by antecedent circumstances" (28). Nagel tries to show that once we start separating what is truly attributable *to the doer* from what we consider luck, we start to find luck at every stage. "Eventually nothing remains which can be ascribed to the responsible self," he writes; "the area of genuine agency, and therefore of legitimate moral judgment, seems to shrink under this scrutiny to an extensionless point" (35).

Classic Presentations

Bernard Williams, "Moral Luck," in his *Moral Luck: Philosophical Papers 1973–1980* (Cambridge: Cambridge University Press, 1981): 20–39.

Thomas Nagel, "Moral Luck," in his *Mortal Questions* (Cambridge: Cambridge University Press, 1979): 24–38.

Responses and Other Treatments

Judith Jarvis Thomson, "Morality and Bad Luck," *Metaphilosophy* **20** (1989): 203–221.

Daniel Statman, ed., *Moral Luck* (Albany: State University of New York Press, 1993), including a *Postscript* by Bernard Williams (cited as Williams 1993).

Questions for Reflection

1.   How might you try to argue that the lorry driver cases do not involve *moral* luck, but only (for instance) *legal* luck? That is, Amal and Blair should not receive different *moral* assessments;

rather, the difference between them lies in some other department.

2.   How might you try to argue *against* the idea that morality can assess only what is within the agent's control and attributable to *her* rather than to circumstance?

3.   Might there be reasons to treat Nagel's four kinds of luck differently?

NOTES

1 Why Jones$_4$? Because Frankfurt uses the prior Joneses to illustrate three ways of acting in accordance with a threat. (In the rest of the text, we'll just say "Jones.") "Black," meanwhile, might be an homage to Max Black, Frankfurt's old teacher.

2 A few words have been omitted from the relevant paragraph in Callard.

10

BELIEF AND IGNORANCE

When you choose to do something, that choice is made in light of your aims, goals, values, emotions, moral judgments, or what have you. But a further factor which *always* comes into the equation is what you *believe*. We don't mean "believe" in any highfalutin' sense ("I believe in the universal brotherhood of man"); we mean by "believe" something extremely down-to-earth. If you go over to the fridge to get a beer, that means you think, believe, know, or assume *that there is beer in the fridge*. Your beliefs are all the things like *there is beer in the fridge*: all the things you think are the case. Keep your goals exactly the same, but alter your *beliefs*—in this version, you're assuming the beer is in the cooler—and you will act differently. You won't head for the fridge, but for the cooler.

Our actions, then, are always guided, not just by our goals, values, and so on, but also by what we believe. This is true in particular of our *moral* actions and decisions. This chapter shines a spotlight on the dependence of choice on belief and the ethical ramifications of that fact.

We begin, in **Wronging by Believing?** (#42), with the arresting idea that perhaps beliefs *themselves* can be ethical or unethical. Remember, we're not talking about "fancy" beliefs here, like a belief in the universal brotherhood of man. We're just talking about plain old factual beliefs. But then this hypothesis sounds almost paradoxical.

DOI: 10.4324/9781003319962-11

How could it be either *morally right* or *morally wrong* to think that there is beer in the fridge? Moral terms don't even seem to apply here. Nonetheless, **#42** presents a number of examples in which one person seems to wrong another simply by *thinking* something about them. (Only beliefs *about people* can be moral or immoral, it would seem.) You will have to decide whether you agree with that description of the cases.

The next two entries focus on how we should make moral decisions when we are hampered by *uncertainty* and *ignorance*. We need knowledge or belief to guide our actions; but what if we *have* no knowledge or belief concerning a point which is highly relevant to our decision? If I'm trying to rescue someone from a burning building, I need to know *where in the building they are*. Unfortunately I have no idea where they are: they might be upstairs, but given the fumes and smoke I shouldn't go up there unless I need to. My problem here—besides the fact that I'm in a burning building!—is that I don't have a belief which could guide me to the appropriate part of the house. That's *ignorance*, and it poses a severe problem for moral decision-making. Similar to ignorance, although less dramatic, is *uncertainty*. With ignorance, you have no clue; with uncertainty, you have some clue, but not enough to be *sure*. **The Miners Puzzle (#43)** demonstrates how ignorance and uncertainty about relevant *facts* can lead to painful moral dilemmas. **Moral Uncertainty (#44)** asks how you should make decisions when you are uncertain, not about some pertinent fact, but about some *moral* question. What should I do if I *think* it's OK to eat meat, but I'm not *sure*?

Once you start paying attention to ignorance and uncertainty you are apt to find them all over the place, infecting almost all our decisions. **Cluelessness (#45)** suggests that we may well be *pervasively* clueless, and it invites reflection on the implications of that idea. In particular, we are notably ignorant of the full effects of our actions in the future, and this is especially important for consequentialism. Since the rightness or wrongness of our actions *now* depends on their consequences over an indefinitely extended *future*, cluelessness about the latter would mean we are essentially clueless about the former. But can we really seriously entertain the idea that we *never know* whether what we're doing is morally right or morally wrong?

42. WRONGING BY BELIEVING?

Distinguished historian John Hope Franklin was about to receive the nation's highest civilian honor, the Presidential Medal of Freedom. The night before the awards ceremony, he hosted a celebratory dinner for friends at the Cosmos Club, an elite private club in Washington to which Franklin belonged. While he was walking across the lobby after dinner, a woman beckoned him over, gave him her coat check, and ordered him to fetch her coat.[1]

Lest you think this an aberration, former President Barack Obama told *People* magazine that "There's no black male my age, who's a professional, who hasn't come out of a restaurant and is waiting for their car and somebody didn't hand them their car keys." (Quoted in Basu 2019: 916.)

Clearly the woman in the Cosmos Club thought, or assumed, that the famous historian was an attendant. Ditto the people who handed Barack Obama their car keys. This raises an interesting moral question. Was it in any way *morally wrong* for the woman to think or assume this? More specifically, did she insult, or otherwise wrong, John Hope Franklin by thinking this? In considering this question, let's focus solely on what the woman *believes* about Franklin, separating that out from what she *did* (beckon him over, etc.).

Proponents of so-called *doxastic wronging* maintain that you *can* morally wrong a person simply by believing something about them. ("Doxastic" means "of or pertaining to belief," from the Greek *doxa*, meaning beliefs.) According to these proponents, the problem with the woman in the Cosmos Club was not merely what she *did*; it was what she *thought*. In jumping to the conclusion that Franklin was a cloakroom attendant, she *did him wrong*.

However, here are two arguments against the idea that the woman doxastically wronged John Hope Franklin. First: there's a reason that ethics usually concerns itself with *actions*, with what people *do* to other people. We freely choose what to do: our actions are under our control. But our *beliefs* are not in the same sense under our control. We can't believe something just by deciding to, nor can we keep from believing just by deciding to. Just try looking out of the window on a cloudy day and *not* believing that the sky is cloudy. See? You can't do it. You will find yourself believing that the sky is cloudy whether you want to or not.

The opponent of doxastic wronging might argue that because belief is in this way *involuntary*, it is not something for which we can be morally criticized. Criticizing someone for their beliefs would be like criticizing them for their breathing: they're both things the person can't help. Therefore neither is an appropriate target of moral condemnation.

The second reason you might think the woman did not doxastically wrong Franklin is that it would appear that her belief was *rational*. We might imagine that she tacitly reasoned as follows:

> At least 90% of the Black men in the club tonight are attendants.
>
> That man on the other side of the lobby [i.e. Franklin] is Black.
>
> So he's probably an attendant.

Now in fact, Franklin was one of the Cosmos Club's very, very few Black members; while almost all of the club's attendants were Black men. So in reality, virtually all of the Black men the woman might have seen at the Club that evening *were* attendants. Under those circumstances, "the likelihood that a black man present in the Cosmos Club was a member of the staff rather than a member of the club was very high" (Gendler 2011: 35).

How, though, can it be morally wrong to believe something which is rational and well-supported? If the woman's belief was entirely appropriate under the circumstances, it seems distinctly odd to morally *forbid* her from forming it.

Both of these arguments appeal to general principles about what is (allegedly) not open to moral criticism. This gives room for proponents of doxastic wronging to persist in their view: perhaps what needs to be rejected is not the idea of doxastic wronging, but these alleged constraints on moral criticism. To bolster the idea that we should make room for purely doxastic wronging, proponents could point to cases in which it seems appropriate to *apologize* simply for what you *thought*. Consider the following example (adapted from Basu and Schroeder 2019): when his wife, who has recently gotten sober, comes home from a departmental function smelling of alcohol, a husband concludes that she has fallen off the wagon. In fact—as emerges later—someone had merely spilled some wine on her shirtsleeve at the reception. You can easily imagine the husband saying, "I'm sorry I thought you were drinking again."

Proponents could also take aim at the idea that we can only be criticized for things under our direct control in the way that our actions are. Do we consider it morally bad or wrong if you feel resentful or jealous of your friend's success? How about if you feel pleased by his failures, or indifferent toward misfortunes which befall him? If any of these are morally bad or wrong, then it seems *feelings*—which we don't directly control—*are* subject to moral criticism. (See Adams on "involuntary sins.")

Finally, proponents could question whether a *rational* belief is thereby necessarily a *moral* belief. Insulting beliefs and assumptions like those of the woman at the club constitute part of the special burden Black Americans have to bear in today's society. Insofar as they reinforce and perpetuate that inequity, such beliefs and assumptions are thus genuinely harmful. And they remain harmful *even if* they correctly match up with our current, lamentable, social reality. Perhaps a moral person would try not to make such assumptions even when the statistics warrant them.

Recommended Treatments

Tamar Szabó Gendler, "On the Epistemic Costs of Implicit Bias," *Philosophical Studies* **156** (2011): 33–63.

Rima Basu and Mark Schroeder, "Doxastic Wronging," in Brian Kim and Matthew McGrath, eds., *Pragmatic Encroachment in Epistemology* (New York: Routledge, 2019): 181–205.

Rima Basu, "What We Epistemically Owe to Each Other," *Philosophical Studies* **176** (2019): 915–931.

Robert Merrihew Adams, "Involuntary Sins," *Philosophical Review* **94** (1985): 3–31.

Catharine Saint-Croix, "Rumination and Wronging: The Role of Attention in Epistemic Morality," *Episteme* **19** (2022): 491–514.

David Enoch and Levi Spectre, "There is No Such Thing as Doxastic Wrongdoing," *Philosophical Perspectives* (forthcoming). https://philpapers.org/archive/ENOTIN.pdf

Questions for Reflection

1. Which, if any, of the arguments *against* the possibility of doxastic wronging do you find most compelling?
2. Do you think it's important for a spouse to *have faith in* their spouse? If so, would you say the husband in our example fell short in that regard? Would you say that if it turned out he was *right* about his wife having fallen off the wagon?

43. THE MINERS PUZZLE

As any gambler can tell you, most choices involve *uncertainty*: you don't know how things will play out if you do this or that, but you have to choose anyway. Trying an exotic dish, asking someone on a date—even buying this book was a gamble, since you didn't know the contents yet.

How should we make risky decisions? We can't just "pick the best thing" if we don't know what the best thing *is*. So what's the reasonable way to choose under uncertainty?

Surprisingly, ethicists mostly ignored this problem until the 20th century, when the ethics of risk was supercharged by probability theory. The supercharging started with problems like:

An Easy Miners Case
There's been a disaster at the mine, and 100 miners are trapped either in Shaft A or Shaft B. You can send rescuers into either shaft, saving everyone there. (Anyone in the other shaft, sadly, will perish.) You know there is a 75% chance the miners are all in Shaft A, and a 25% chance they're all in Shaft B.
Where ought you to send the rescuers?

Some say you don't know the answer. You don't know which shaft you "objectively" ought to send rescuers to, because you don't know where the miners are. If they are in Shaft A, then objectively you ought to send the rescuers to Shaft A. Ditto for Shaft B. ("You objectively ought to do it" means "It's what you ought to do, assuming complete knowledge of the facts.")

And yet, clearly, the reasonable thing to do is to send the rescuers to A. Some express this by saying you "subjectively" ought to send them to Shaft A; it is the best option given your uncertainty.

Why A and not B? Well, Shaft A is *probably* objectively right. Sending rescuers to A has a 75% chance, rather than a 25% chance, of being objectively right. And that sounds like the key fact. If you're uncertain, perhaps you subjectively ought to do whatever is *most likely to be what you objectively ought to do*.

Just think how irresistible that sounds. If you know that A is most likely objectively right, how could you justify picking B instead?

That's no rhetorical question, by the way. There is an answer. Sometimes, the reasonable option is *not* the most likely to be objectively right—indeed, you might know it's objectively wrong.

How could that be? It sounds mind-boggling. But consider this classic thought experiment:

The Miners Puzzle
The 100 miners are trapped again, this time by rising floodwaters, with a 50% chance of being either all in Shaft A or all in Shaft B. But this time you have three options. You can block Shaft A, block Shaft B, or block neither. Blocking a shaft will save everyone in it and redirect the waters to the other shaft, where everyone will drown. Blocking neither shaft, however, will let the floodwaters distribute evenly, so that only ten drown.
What ought you to do?

Here the reasonable option is to block *neither* shaft, saving 90 for sure rather than risking 100 deaths. And yet, you know this *can't* be what you objectively ought to do. Objectively, you ought to block a shaft—whichever one the miners are in. The paradox is that it would be foolish and immoral for you to even try to do what you objectively ought to do, since you'd risk disaster.

This puzzle shows up all over, such as in cases like:

Drugs
A patient has an annoying skin condition. The doctor could prescribe Drug A or Drug B—one is a perfect cure, the other a lethal poison, and she doesn't know which is which. She could also prescribe Drug C, which she knows to be a partial cure. (Jackson 1991)

Subjectively, the doctor ought to play it safe with C, but she knows it can't be objectively right.

RESPONSES

The puzzle is that we have two "oughts" in conflict: subjective and objective. So, to resolve the tension, we might try to obliterate an "ought."

Some say that the objective "ought" is the real one: it has "obvious priority" in "moral theory" (Parfit manuscript). It is also the better "ought" to hear about when receiving advice (Thomson 1986:

179)—if you're told you objectively ought to block Shaft A, that's more useful than being told you subjectively ought to block neither!

But Parfit worries that the objective ought "has little practical importance." Most of us have no clue what's objectively best. A theory that tells us "Do what you objectively ought!" is like a study guide that says "Just pick the right answer!"

For concrete advice, Frank Jackson (1991) recommends the subjective ought as described by *decision theory*, which tells us to do what has the highest *expected value*. An option's "expected value" is found by adding up, for each possible outcome, the value of the outcome times the chance it will happen if you pick that option. To illustrate, if each life saved in the Miners Puzzle has a value of 1, then the outcome of blocking Shaft A either has a value of 0 or 100, with a chance of 0.5 (50%) for each. So, the expected value of blocking Shaft A is $0 \times 0.5 + 100 \times 0.5 = 50$. The expected value of blocking Shaft B is the same: 50. That's less than the expected value of blocking neither shaft, which is $1 \times 90 = 90$. (If you block neither, you'll surely save 90.) So, you subjectively ought to block neither—which seems like the right result!

FURTHER PUZZLE

The Miners Puzzle has a second life, just as illustrious, as a paradox about language: "ifs" and "oughts." Consider the following "ifs" about the example:

1.   If the miners are in Shaft A, you ought to block Shaft A.
2.   If the miners are in Shaft B, you ought to block Shaft B.

These sound true. And yet, (1) and (2) together seem to imply:

3.   Either you ought to block Shaft A or you ought to block Shaft B.

But this directly conflicts with the natural thing to say about the Miners Puzzle:

4.   You ought to block neither shaft.

Now, you might try to get out of this puzzle, too, by insisting on a single ought. But which? If all oughts are objective, then (4) is false—which seems absurd. If all oughts are subjective, then the "ifs" (1) and (2) are false, since it's *not* true that you subjectively ought to block Shaft A, *even if* that's where the miners are.

How to get out of this paradox? Its creators, Kolodny and MacFarlane (2010), think there's only one way out: revise the rules of logic! They reject *modus ponens*, which says we can infer "B" from "A" and "If A, then B." On Kolodny and MacFarlane's view, we can't reason from "The miners are in Shaft A" and "If the miners are in Shaft A, then you ought to block Shaft A" to the conclusion "You ought to block Shaft A." Talk about a bombshell!

Only a few thought experiments have transformed a part of philosophy. The Miners Puzzle transformed *two*. Even today, philosophers come back to it, mining the puzzle for insights about ethical risk and the nature of language.

Classic Presentations

Donald H. Regan, *Utilitarianism and Co-operation* (Oxford: Oxford University Press, 1980).

Derek Parfit, "What We Together Do" (unpublished manuscript). https://philarchive.org/archive/PARWWT-3.pdf

Responses and Other Treatments

The Miners Puzzle and language:

Niko Kolodny and John MacFarlane, "Ifs and Oughts," *Journal of Philosophy* **107** (2010): 115–143.

Further Reading

Frank Jackson, "Decision-Theoretic Consequentialism and the Nearest and Dearest Objection," *Ethics* **101** (1991): 461–482.

Judith Jarvis Thomson, *Rights, Restitution, and Risk: Essays in Moral Theory*, William Parent, ed. (Cambridge: Harvard University Press, 1986): Ch. 11.

Derek Parfit, *On What Matters, Volume 1* (Oxford: Oxford University Press, 2011): Ch. 7.

Daniel Muñoz and Jack Spencer, "Knowledge of Objective 'Oughts': Monotonicity and the New Miners Puzzle," *Philosophy and Phenomenological Research* **103** (2021): 77–91.

Questions for Reflection

1. Thomson, as noted earlier, thinks that good advisors strive to tell people what they objectively ought to do, not what they subjectively ought to do. This seems right, at least in a case where the advisor knows the miners' location, and the agent seeking advice does not. But suppose neither party knows where the miners are, and the agent asks the advisor for guidance. On Thomson's view, what should the advisor say? Is this the best advice?

2. On some views, the Miners Puzzle shows that virtue and rightness come apart. The right thing to do is the objectively best thing—blocking the shaft the miners are actually in—but a virtuous agent would play it safe by blocking neither shaft. Is this view plausible? Try to think of an argument for your answer.

44. MORAL UNCERTAINTY

As we noted in the previous entry, you often have to make decisions without knowing some of the facts relevant to your decision. If you *knew* whether it was going to rain later, it would make your decision about wearing boots a whole lot easier. If you *knew* whether your house was going to catch on fire at some point in the next twenty years, it would make your decision about insurance a whole lot easier. When you don't know these things, you have to *decide under uncertainty*.

So what *should* you do about footwear when you can't be certain whether it will rain? You should do some math. A method called *decision theory* formalizes a very natural way of making decisions under uncertainty. It goes like this. Suppose you have two choices: wearing boots, or wearing sneakers. You don't know which of these will have the optimal outcome. (If you did, your decision would be easy.) The reason why you don't know is that you lack certainty about a key variable: whether it will rain. So there are four possible outcomes here: you wear boots and it *does* rain, you wear boots and it *doesn't* rain, you wear sneakers and it *does* rain, you wear sneakers and it *doesn't* rain. These are illustrated below.

boots rain	boots no rain
sneakers rain	sneakers no rain

Now we need some *numbers* to help you decide. In particular, we need to know the following. How probable do you think the rain is? And how good or bad would each of these outcomes be, from your perspective? Let's say you rate the chance of rain at 60%. That means you give yourself a 60% chance of landing in the left-hand column and a 40% chance of landing in the right-hand column. Now let's look at how you would *evaluate* these four possibilities. Lower left is definitely the worst possible outcome. Squelchy sneakers in the rain: awful. Let's rate that as –20 "goodness points." Lower right is the best outcome of all: let's give that square a +3. That leaves the options where you *do* wear boots. Wearing rubber boots all day is guaranteed to make your feet hot and sweaty, so even upper right (the better of the two) should get a negative score: say -2. Add rain to that and it will be even more unpleasant; so say upper left rates a -5.

boots rain (60%) (-5)	boots no rain (40%) (-2)
sneakers rain (60%) (-20)	sneakers no rain (40%) (+3)

We now have all the information we need to work out in a rigorous way what you should do. Take the boots option. As we see above, this has a 60% chance of yielding -5 goodness points and a 40% chance of yielding -2 goodness points. The *expected value* of wearing boots is the *sum* of those two *products*:

$$(.6 \times -5) + (.4 \times -2) = (-3) + (-.8) = \textbf{-3.8}$$

Calculating in similar fashion, the expected value of choosing sneakers turns out to be:

$$(.6 \times -20) + (.4 \times 3) = (-12) + (1.2) = \textbf{-10.8}$$

So we have our answer: you should wear boots. While both options have a negative expected value, you should choose the option with a *less bad* expected value. The expected value of sneakers was weighed down by its 60% chance of leading to a *really* bad outcome, namely being caught in the rain wearing sneakers. That made the sneakers option come out worse than the alternative. So it looks like you will have to put up with sweaty feet.

The above method elegantly formalizes what is actually a very natural way of making decisions under uncertainty. Even if we aren't doing math in our heads, we do reason in something like this fashion. "I certainly don't want to get caught in the rain in sneakers, so I guess

I should wear boots, even though they'll make my feet hot and sweaty all day. If it turns out not to rain I'll be annoyed that I wore them, but given that I can't be certain, putting them on is the better choice."

Decision theory offers a widely accepted framework for what you should do when you are uncertain about a relevant *fact*. But philosopher Andrew Sepielli has highlighted the distinctive significance of the following different question: what should you do when you are uncertain about a *moral* matter, rather than a matter of fact? Does the same method of reasoning work there? Let's look at a case. Suppose you're *pretty* sure, but not certain, that it is morally acceptable to eat meat. You're not completely sure of this, because you know thoughtful people feel differently, and you've seen and considered the moral arguments for vegetarianism. Your own conclusion is that those arguments fail, but you accept that there is a chance you're wrong about that. At the end of the day you attach a 90% probability to its being OK to eat meat and a 10% probability to its being morally wrong to eat meat. One further thing to note: you enjoy meat.

In this scenario, you are in a state of *moral* uncertainty. Just as in the boots example, you are *not certain* about a factor which is highly relevant for your decision. So under these circumstances, should you eat meat? If we're approaching this the same way we did *factual* uncertainty, we'll need to calculate which of the two options (eating meat or going vegetarian) has what we might call the higher expected *moral* value. So let's add the missing numbers to this table:

eat meat **OK to eat meat** (90%) ( )	eat meat **not OK to eat meat** (10%) ( )
vegetarian **OK to eat meat** (90%) ( )	vegetarian **not OK to eat meat** (10%) ( )

Which is the "morally worst" of these four scenarios? Definitely upper right. If you eat meat, and eating meat is in fact morally wrong, then you are committing a grave moral wrong every single day. That's *very* bad, morally; so let's give that scenario a -100. The best option is upper left, so let's give that a +5. As for the bottom row, both scenarios will be negative (since you like meat), but lower left is worse, since in that case your sacrifice will have been for naught. So let's give those possibilities -5 and -3 respectively.

If you do the math in the same fashion as earlier (exercise left to the reader), you'll get the result that you should stop eating meat and become a vegetarian. Like the sneaker option, the meat option is weighed down by the enormous negative number attached to one of its squares. So even though you rate the chances that we are on that side of the table as very low, the moral badness in the upper right scenario is so great that it swamps all the other numbers on the chart. In both this case and the boots case, the decision-theoretic method emphasizes *preventing the worst-case scenario*, even if it is unlikely, and even at the cost of a *sure sacrifice* (of foot comfort, or of eating what you like).

Unlike the boots case, though, we are probably surprised by the answer we got here. After all, you—our protagonist—are really *pretty darn sure* that it's *not* wrong to eat meat, i.e., that the right-hand side of the table does *not* actually come into play. Indeed, in this scenario you are more or less as morally certain as they come. (Do you have *any* moral views to which you'd assign a *higher* degree of certainty than 90%?) So it's striking that even our protagonist is instructed to become a vegetarian forthwith. We might wonder if this could possibly be the right advice.

Moreover, not only might this *answer* appear questionable, so might the *reasoning*. "I am quite sure (although not absolutely certain) that any moral view which would forbid eating meat is false. Plus I enjoy meat. But I guess I should act *as if* the view which I reject were true, even though that requires a sacrifice on my part. At least that way I can ward off a possible outcome which only that (false) view would consider very bad." Ask yourself if you would give up meat simply based on reasoning of that kind. Remember, you have not changed your actual moral view of meat-eating vs. vegetarianism at all: you remain just as convinced as you were before (that is, 90% sure) that vegetarianism is *not* morally mandatory. Would the above reasoning convince you to act forevermore as if it *were* morally mandatory? Or would it take an actual change of your moral view for you to do that?

The puzzle about decisions under uncertainty which this opens up is whether and why a method of reasoning that seems entirely appropriate to decisions under *factual* uncertainty seems distinctly *inap*-propriate to decisions under *moral* uncertainty. Why this asymmetry?

And the puzzles don't stop there. The very idea of "expected moral value" involves some deep technical and philosophical problems. To calculate expected value of any kind, we have to assign "goodness points" to outcomes. But not every moral theory deals in "points." (Perhaps goodness "points" are not even possible: see **#33, Sweetening**.) Consider the extreme view that, because life is sacred, it's *absolutely* wrong to eat meat—wrong no matter how good the consequences. How many "points" does this theory assign to meat-eating? No negative number seems low enough. But what's the alternative—a negative infinity? That seems *too* low! Even a tiny chance of an infinite bad is itself infinitely bad. That means, even if you have 0.0000000001% credence in the absolute wrongness of meat-eating, it's wrong to be a carnivore.

This little puzzle points toward a bigger problem. Moral theories have radically different structures. But if we want to resolve moral uncertainty by *combining* the recommendations of multiple theories (the key idea of "expected moral value"), we need those recommendations to somehow fit together.

Recommended Treatments

Andrew Sepielli, "What to Do When You Don't Know What to Do," in Russ Shafer-Landau, ed., *Oxford Studies in Metaethics, Volume 4* (Oxford: Clarendon Press, 2009): 5–28.

Dan Moller, "Abortion and Moral Risk," *Philosophy* 86 (2011): 425–443.

Elizabeth Harman, "The Irrelevance of Moral Uncertainty," in Russ Shafer-Landau, ed., *Oxford Studies in Metaethics, Volume 10* (Oxford: Oxford University Press, 2015): 53–79.

Michael J. Zimmerman, *Living With Uncertainty: The Moral Significance of Ignorance* (Cambridge: Cambridge University Press, 2008): Ch. 4.

Johan E. Gustafsson and Olle Torpman, "In Defence of My Favourite Theory," *Pacific Philosophical Quarterly* 95 (2014): 159–174. (This paper argues that people should just follow the theory they are *most* confident in.)

Johan E. Gustafsson, "Second Thoughts About My Favourite Theory," *Pacific Philosophical Quarterly* 103 (2022): 448–470. (Self-explanatory!)

William MacAskill, Krister Bykvist, and Toby Ord, *Moral Uncertainty* (Oxford: Oxford University Press, 2020). (This is a pretty advanced treatment, but Chs. 1 and 8 should be reasonably accessible after reading this entry.)

Questions for Reflection

1. Can you think of any reasons why there might be an asymmetry between factual uncertainty and moral uncertainty? Do our moral beliefs play a different role in guiding decisions than our factual beliefs, in a way which the decision-theoretic model does not capture?

2. Elizabeth Harman argues that moral uncertainty is actually *irrelevant* to what you ought to do. How does she defend this claim? Does she have a better answer about what you ought to do?

45. CLUELESSNESS

It's easy to know, at least in the abstract, what consequentialism tells you to do. You should do whatever would lead to the best consequences!

Crucially, "consequences" doesn't just mean "obvious consequences." It means *all* the consequences—including distant ripple effects on the other side of the world, along with unforeseeable effects far away in the future.

But then how can we ever, in practice, know if we're doing the right thing? If we *can't* know this, then, in the words of Shelly Kagan (1998: 64), "consequentialism will be unusable as a moral guide to action." That's because we are typically "clueless" about nearly all the consequences of nearly everything we do.

Consider a thought experiment from James Lenman's (2000: 344) classic paper, "Consequentialism and Cluelessness."

> Imagine we are in what is now southern Germany a hundred years before the birth of Jesus. A certain bandit, Richard, quite lost to history, has raided a village and killed all its inhabitants bar one. This final survivor, a pregnant woman named Angie, he finds hiding in a house about to be burned. On a whim of compassion, he orders that her life be spared. But perhaps, by consequentialist standards, he should not have done so.

Sparing a pregnant woman's life, obviously, seems like it *should* be morally permissible. It is hard to imagine taking a theory seriously that tells you otherwise.

So why might consequentialism say to kill Angie? Not because she's evil, or even because of anything that happens in her lifetime. The problem is that in Lenman's story, Angie is the great great great great great... grandmother of a certain 20th-century German dictator. "The millions of Hitler's victims were thus also victims of Richard's sparing of Angie" (2000: 345). Given that Richard's act led to some of the worst crimes against humanity ever perpetrated, it probably didn't have the *best* possible consequences of anything he could have done. If indeed it didn't have the best consequences, then consequentialism has to say that Richard acted wrongly by sparing Angie—even though he was doing something we typically think of as obviously right, whose bad effects were utterly inscrutable at the time of action.

Let's pause to make sure we're crystal clear about the point of this thought experiment. It's not meant as just another counterexample to consequentialism. The problem is that we are *constantly* doing things, like Richard's sparing Angie, that are sure to have "massive causal ramifications" (Lenman 2000: 346) that are totally unforeseen. Since massive ramifications are (to the consequentialist) vastly more important than anything in the short term, it seems to follow that consequentialism leaves us constantly clueless about what we should be doing. Indeed, even if we told Richard about the effects of sparing Angie, he'd still be in the dark. For all he knows, killing Angie would leave the world with an even *worse* dictator—such as "Malcolm the Truly Appalling" (2000: 345). Unless Richard can foresee the full results of all of his actions throughout all of time, he hasn't got a moral clue.

RESPONSES

In response to the problem of cluelessness, there are two basic things the consequentialist might say. One is that we are not really so clueless about consequences. The other is that, even if we are, that doesn't mean we're clueless about what should be done.

On the question of consequences, it's hard to escape the conclusion that we're clueless. Lenman, following Parfit (1984), argues forcefully that even our trivial choices will massively affect the future. Even inviting someone over for tea will almost certainly completely change who exists several hundred years from now.

How could that be? Consider two facts.

Fact one: actions have ripple effects. The physical processes that make our world tick are extremely sensitive, and will amplify anything we do. Even tiny changes in air pressure and temperature—as insignificant as the flap of a butterfly's wings—will massively change global weather over time. So just about anything you do will have big indirect effects on the future.

Fact two: it's shockingly easy to change who exists. Think of how many things had to line up for your parents to meet each other. And if they had conceived a kid at even a slightly different time, that child almost certainly would have come from different gametes with different DNA—so it wouldn't have been *you*. (See **#49, The Non-Identity Problem**.)

Put these two facts together, and you see that *virtually anything we do* will massively affect who exists in the future. You don't have to kill someone or conceive a child to change the course of history: even flapping your arms in the air will do the trick.

Suppose that's all true. Does it follow that we are equally clueless about which actions are right and which are wrong from a consequentialist perspective?

That is a *very* hard question.

Perhaps the most popular answer is that we are only clueless in one sense. We do not know which actions are *objectively* right—we only know which ones are *subjectively* right. The objectively right act is the one whose consequences would *in fact* be best. The subjectively right act is, let's suppose, the one whose consequences have the most expected value, where expected value is a function of how good or bad the different possible outcomes are and how likely they are to follow from your action. (See **#43, The Miners Puzzle** and **#44, Moral Uncertainty**.)

Consider how this works with Richard. He is clueless about the objectively right thing to do, but *subjectively* he clearly ought to spare poor Angie. Why? Because sparing her is certain to have one good effect—she won't die a gruesome death—and other effects are equally likely either way. Sure, there is a chance that sparing Angie will lead to a dictator centuries down the line. But by Richard's dim lights, there is the *same* chance that *killing* Angie will lead to such a dictator. The long-run stuff may be objectively important, but subjectively it's just a wash.

In response, Lenman (2000: 357) says that this is "surely a sophistry." If you're making a hugely important life-or-death choice, you shouldn't let relatively puny values tip the scales, even if those puny values are the only ones you know how to influence. For example, if you're choosing between two war plans, each certain to kill different people (though you are clueless as to which will kill whom), you shouldn't just pick Plan A because it will save Spot the Dog from a broken leg. This is an important decision, and the stakes are *way* higher than a dog's leg! Similarly, if you know your action is likely to affect *entire generations* of human beings, that is a *massively* important decision, and you shouldn't make it on the basis of just Angie and her child. Even if this gives you some reason to act, it is an extremely weak one.

At least, that is what Lenman thinks the consequentialist must say. And so he thinks we should give up on consequentialism. Better to focus less on the distant unknowable future and more on matters closer to home: enjoying yourself, making friends, finding ways to live in harmony with others. If consequentialism says we shouldn't concern ourselves with such trifles given how great our impact on the future will be, then so much the worse for consequentialism.

Classic Presentations

James Lenman, "Consequentialism and Cluelessness," *Philosophy & Public Affairs* **29** (2000): 342–370.
Shelly Kagan, *Normative Ethics* (Boulder: Westview Press, 1998): Ch. 2, Section 6.

Responses and Other Treatments

Hilary Greaves, "Cluelessness," *Proceedings of the Aristotelian Society* **116** (2016): 311–339. (An influential but quite technical reply.)
Alan Hájek, "Consequentialism, Cluelessness, Clumsiness, and Counterfactuals" (unpublished manuscript).

Further Reading

Caspar Hare, "Take the Sugar," *Analysis* **70** (2010): 237–247.

Questions for Reflection

1. Is it "sophistry" to treat big differences as a wash when in the presence of cluelessness? Consider an example of "opaque sweetening" (as Caspar Hare (2010) dubs it; see also **#33, Sweetening**). You are choosing between a ticket to see Oprah and a ticket to see the opera. Very different, but neither beats the other. In fact, even if $5 were added to the prospect of seeing the opera (or Oprah), that wouldn't break the tie for you. Now suppose each ticket is slipped into an opaque, gleaming white envelope, and you're 50/50 which ticket is in which envelope—you're clueless, in other words. Then $5 is placed on the envelope on the left. Hare thinks you have a decisive reason to take the "sweetened" left envelope. This

reason is no weaker than an ordinary reason to take a free $5 bill. Does this seem right to you? How, if at all, is it different from the "sophistry" of choosing war plans based on what's good for Spot the Dog?

2.   Consider the following natural but rough idea:"You don't have to worry about long-term effects, because the good and the bad will balance each other out in the end." Is this a persuasive way to deal with the problem of cluelessness? Is it even true? (Perhaps you will need to sharpen the idea up a bit before you can assess it.)

NOTE

1 Philosopher Tamar Gendler presents this example in Gendler (2011: 35–36), drawing from John Hope Franklin, *Mirror to America: The Autobiography of John Hope Franklin* (New York: Farrar, Straus and Giroux, 2005): 340.

11

FUTURE GENERATIONS

The *future* is where it's at.

More specifically, the future is where we are all headed, at the speed of one second per second. The future of humankind may also—if we play our cards right—end up being very, very, *very* long. So our actions now may have profound implications stretching far beyond our own lifetimes. The ethical stakes are high. And the paradoxes, as always, are puzzling.

This chapter will be an introduction to ethical questions about future generations: what kind of future we should want for them, what kinds of moral meaning we may derive from them, and what kinds of ethical choices they might themselves confront.

We'll start with a question about technology. As we write this book in 2023, artificial intelligence (AI) and robotics are becoming ever more sophisticated at a truly astonishing pace. (Trust us, future readers: we didn't predict DALL-E and ChatGPT 4!) What happens when AI gets as smart as we are? Could robots someday qualify as people? We explore this question through a discussion of the film ***Ex Machina*** (#46). Next, we consider a different kind of existential confrontation—not the addition of a new kind of person, but the end of humankind. What would it mean for us if, in the future, the human race were to become infertile, so that the entire species comes to an

DOI: 10.4324/9781003319962-12

end? We'll puzzle through a version of this scenario imagined in the novel *Children of Men* (**#47**), combining it with Samuel Scheffler's insights in *Death and the Afterlife*.

These are specific questions about the future. Can we say anything more general about what kind of future we should want for humankind? This is the domain of *population ethics*, and we conclude the book with the three deepest paradoxes in this new field.

First is **The Procreation Asymmetry** (**#48**). We seem to have a moral reason not to create miserable people who will live lives of sheer, unredeemed agony, yet *no* moral reason to create new happy people just for their own sake. Failing to create a happy person is not like failing to make an existing person happy. Whence the difference?

Second, **The Non-Identity Problem** (**#49**). It seems wrong to bring about a merely contented life when we could have brought about a truly fulfilled one. But if the contented person we create is not identical to the fulfilled person we would have created, who is wronged? How can it be wrong to create the less well-off future when the alternative is that none of those people would have existed? This is one of the profoundest problems in ethical theory, with deep implications for our relation to the environment.

Finally, **The Repugnant Conclusion** (**#50**). (How could we *not* end the book with that?) For any happy future we might create, we could in principle create *much* more happiness by spreading it ever-so-thinly across the population. Rather than 10 billion ecstatic lives, we could have (say) 10^{100} lives, each just barely worth living, but still with more goodness than badness. This scenario involves more "total" goodness, but it seems repugnant that we should prefer a future of people just barely eking it out when we could have had a future of billions living it up. The puzzle—and of course there has to be a puzzle—is that this conclusion can seem inescapable.

46. *EX MACHINA* AND THE FUTURE OF AI

Ava is petite, beautiful, and seems somehow fragile. She gives off an air of vulnerability. Her situation is indeed not great: she is in effect imprisoned in a castle, and has never seen or spoken to anyone from outside the castle walls. Ava elicits very powerful feelings of sympathy: on meeting Ava, you very much want to help her. Moreover, it is clear what she needs help *with*. You must help Ava escape her prison.

Just one wrinkle, though: Ava isn't human. She's a highly sophisticated AI. Her brain is made of "wetware," not nerves and blood vessels, and you can see a forest of wires in her transparent torso. The human who created her, Nathan, keeps her locked up in a suite of rooms in his ultra-secluded, ultra-secure estate. (News flash: Nathan's not a good guy.) With the exception of the small lightwell outside her suite, Ava has never seen the outside. She's never met anyone but Nathan.

Enter a young single man, allowed in to marvel at Nathan's creation. (Unlike Nathan, he is actually a nice, caring young man.) You can probably predict what follows. He converses with Ava and grows increasingly close to her. He becomes determined to get her out of Nathan's clutches and liberate her from her oppressor. Plus, we can see that he has fallen in love with her. The two of them mount an audacious plan to release Ava from her prison and escape the estate.

Thus unfolds the story of *Ex Machina*, a 2014 film by Alex Garland, featuring Alicia Vikander as Ava. Except for the bit about her not being human, this is a story we've seen thousands of times, in films and fairy tales. As so often, though, things don't work out as expected—there's a sting in this story's tail.

With a few bumps along the way (involving multiple deaths), their plan succeeds. They are free! Ava asks the young man if he'll wait while she grabs some skin from previous prototypes. Once clothed, she marches to the front door and lets herself out. But she leaves the young man locked in the room where she left him! He shouts and pleads and bangs on the glass door; she walks out without even looking his way. He is left to his presumed death, while she exits her prison for the real world.

This story shows that there are at least two moral questions we urgently need to ask about AIs. Even if no current AI has Ava's capabilities, some well might in the future; so we should consider these questions now. One question is whether AIs can be moral *patients*, and, if so, how that fact constrains our actions. The other is whether AIs can be moral *agents*. Ava sure seemed human-like through most of the film. But her behavior at the end suggests that something was missing. It would have cost her nothing to release her co-conspirator (and, we thought, friend) from that locked room; her refusal even to contemplate doing that seems baffling. Ava appears to be utterly lacking in moral feeling. Was something left out of her programming, or does the obstacle here run deeper?

An entity is a *moral patient* if it matters morally what we do to them. A moral patient is someone whose well-being we need to consider when we act. If you are reading this book, you are a moral patient. A calculator, by contrast, is not a moral patient, no matter how much computing power it has. My TI-35 does not have interests of its own which I need to take account of in my decision-making. I do not *harm* my calculator when I leave it in a locked house, or throw it in the garbage when it malfunctions.

If future AIs were moral patients with interests we must consider, then it would presumably be morally wrong to lock such an AI in a house and not let it go outside. It would probably be morally wrong to take an AI apart and throw it out when we're not satisfied with its performance (something Nathan did with previous models). *If* AIs are moral patients, then, we need to be very careful about how we treat *them*. (This is part of what *Ex Machina* vividly conveys.) Suppose on the other hand that even a future AI is morally speaking just a souped-up calculator, without interests of its own. Then actions which would constitute assault or oppression if they were performed against a *person* will be fine when the "patient" is an AI. I don't *assault* my calculator if I smash it in frustration.

An entity is a *moral agent*, by contrast, if it is reasonable to apply moral standards to that entity's actions and to hold it accountable when it violates those standards. You, for example, are a moral agent. You are capable of acting morally, and we expect you to. Indeed, most of us are *both* moral patients and moral agents. But it is possible for the two categories to come apart, which is why we need to consider them separately. Babies, for instance, are moral patients without (yet) being moral agents. A calculator, of course, is neither.

Could an AI be a moral agent? Note that we don't just mean: could we program a machine to behave in what we would consider to be a moral manner. For even if we could do this, it would not make sense to *morally fault* the machine if it did something that we did not consider moral. Such an "act" would merely show that either *we* messed up—apparently our programming was imperfect—or the machine malfunctioned. But it would be ridiculous to hold a machine *morally responsible* for glitching out.

Could an AI be a moral agent in the fullest sense? Some theorists think this is in principle impossible. No matter how good a machine might be at solving problems, that doesn't mean it experiences *emotions*. But moral agency seems to rely heavily on emotions, especially *empathy*, a complex emotional disposition to feel as you imagine others are feeling. Some would say (see Montemayor et al. 2022 below) that empathy is beyond the capabilities of any machine, regardless of its computing power. (It is certainly striking that despite her very sophisticated cognitive performance, Ava seems to utterly lack empathy.) Others (see for instance Railton) are optimistic that AIs could *learn* to be ethical agents, just as human children do. So it is interesting to consider our reaction to Ava's behavior at the end of the film. If we *condemn* her for heartlessly leaving her friend and co-conspirator to die, we seem to be viewing her as a full moral agent. But others would argue that moral terms are inapplicable to even as impressive a machine as Ava.

Classic Presentation

Ex Machina, dir. Alex Garland, 2014.

Responses and Other Treatments

Einar Duenger Bøhn, "*Ex Machina*: Is Ava a Person?" in Barry Dainton, Will Slocombe, and Attila Tanyi, eds., *Minding the Future* (Cham: Springer Nature Switzerland, 2021): 41–63.

Carlos Montemayor, Jodi Halpern, and Abrol Fairweather, "In Principle Obstacles for Empathic AI," *AI & Society* **37** (2022): 1353–1359.

Peter Railton, "Ethical Learning, Natural and Artificial," in S. Matthew Liao, ed., *Ethics of Artificial Intelligence* (New York: Oxford University Press, 2020): 45–78. See also the essays in Part IV of this volume.

Martin Gibert and Dominic Martin, "In Search of the Moral Status of AI," *AI & Society* **37** (2022): 319–330.

Shelly Kagan, *How to Count Animals, More or Less* (Oxford: Oxford University Press, 2019): Ch. 1.

Adrienne Martin, "How to Betray Your Android," *The Philosopher's Magazine* **76** (2017): 35–41.

Hubert Dreyfus, *What Computers Still Can't Do: A Critique of Artificial Reason* (Cambridge: MIT Press, 1992).

Questions for Reflection

1. What questions do you think we should consider if we want to figure out whether an AI counts as a moral patient? How would those same questions classify non-human animals?

2. Is there a morally significant difference between a machine which implements a pre-programmed algorithm and a machine which can "learn," i.e. autonomously update its behaviors in light of feedback from experience?

3. Do you think that attributing feelings and wishes to Ava might simply be misplaced empathy on our part?

47. *CHILDREN OF MEN*

Imagine that a peculiar misfortune has descended on the entire human race. While everyone is otherwise perfectly healthy, human beings have become infertile. *Totally* infertile: not a single human baby has been born in over 25 years. *Homo sapiens* has irreversibly lost the ability to reproduce.

In this scenario—first imagined by the novelist P. D. James in *Children of Men*, and later discussed by the philosopher Samuel Scheffler—we would be staring human extinction in the face. Everyone alive would be able to live out their natural lifetime without a problem; but there would be no next generation. The people alive now would be the very last humans ever.

Would you be dismayed to find yourself in this situation? Does the prospect of the complete extinction of human life in the near term strike you as a tragedy? If so, it is interesting to consider why. It is also worth exploring the implications of this judgment for our actual world, in which we do not face imminent extinction (it may take humans longer than that to kill each other off completely).

One striking aspect of this scenario, which complicates the task of understanding our own reactions, is that your *personal* mortality and lifespan are unaffected by this disaster. It is easy to understand how you might view the prospect of your *own* imminent extinction as a great evil: most of us would be dismayed to learn that we were going to die soon, or sooner than we had expected. For most people under most circumstances, advance notice of their own imminent death would come as a distinctly unwelcome surprise. But no untimely or premature death *for you* is on tap in the infertility scenario. So that can't be the source of our distress.

A second notable element of the scenario is that the same is true for all of your loved ones. Your children will not die early or suffer unexpected misfortunes; your friends will live out their natural lifespan without incident. So it can't be that you're sad *for them*, or sad about the loss of them, in the way you would be if you learned that one of them was going to die soon.

Why, then, should it distress us so much to be facing this scenario? The obvious reasons for distress don't seem to be present.

Samuel Scheffler offers an answer to this conundrum. The near-term extinction of all human life would be bad for those living, he proposes, because it would make many of the things they are doing in their lives seem meaningless. Consider for example the long-term goals which many careers ultimately serve. Think of all the molecular biologists and research scientists and leaders of clinical trials and pharmaceutical company executives who have spent years painstakingly advancing, or at least trying to advance, the search for a cure for cancer. Progress in this challenging field is exceedingly slow, and these people may be well aware that the goal of curing cancer, or even *a* cancer, is unlikely to be attained in their personal lifetime. But the thought of the benefit to humanity were a cure eventually to be found—an accomplishment to which they would have contributed, even if only modestly—makes what they are doing meaningful to them.

Scheffler suggests that faced with the infertility scenario, their work would no longer seem meaningful to them in this way. If humans will die out within the next 75 years, a cure for cancer will likely never be found; in that sense all their work will have been for nought. (Moreover, if a cure *were* found within the next 75 years, it would hardly have time to benefit anyone.) Nor is this loss of meaning limited to careers. A Jewish family may find great meaning in contributing to the continued life and flourishing of traditions that Jews have practiced since the time of the pharaohs. To see that line continue unbroken through the centuries against all odds, only to end definitively in the near future, would not merely be disappointing: it might sap their participation in that tradition of much of its felt meaning.

On the basis of considerations like these, Scheffler goes so far as to suggest that a world facing the infertility scenario would be "characterized by widespread apathy, anomie, and despair; by the erosion of social institutions and social solidarity; by the deterioration of the physical environment; and by a pervasive loss of conviction about the value or point of many activities" (2013: 40). This is indeed how P. D. James, and Alfonso Cuarón in his film of the same name, portray our world under the infertility scenario. Scheffler draws a philosophical moral from this thought experiment: the survival of the *human race* is actually more important to us—more critical to the meaningfulness of our lives—than our individual, personal survival. Those molecular biologists are unfazed by the likelihood that their long-term goal

won't be achieved in their lifetime: that *they* won't get to see the ultimate fruits of their labor doesn't rob their work of all meaning. But
the prospect of human life being completely wiped out in the near
term might indeed make everything seem pointless. Scheffler's thesis
is that whatever we might think about a *personal* afterlife, the *collective*
afterlife—the continuation of human life after we are gone—is a condition of our valuing things here and now.

One might question whether human extinction would have such a
pervasive undermining effect. Perhaps there are some pursuits and attachments which would continue to seem just as valuable to us in the
infertility scenario as they do now. Relationships with friends and loved
ones, after all, are not expected to outlast the lives of the participants; so
perhaps they would not be threatened in the same way by the upcoming
disappearance of human life. It is even possible to draw a diametrically
opposed moral from the infertility scenario. Philosopher David Benatar
argues that it is true of everyone that they would have been better off if
they had never been born. In other words, *existence itself* is a great misfortune. For Benatar, human extinction would in principle be a *good* thing,
since it would spare millions of future people this tragic fate.

Even if we come down somewhere between Scheffler and Benatar,
this thought experiment suggests that the value of our own personal
pursuits depends in important respects on something we may never
have thought about, namely the continuation of human life into the
indefinite future.

Classic Presentation

Samuel Scheffler, *Death and the Afterlife*, Niko Kolodny, ed. (New York: Oxford
University Press, 2013): Lectures 1 and 2.

Responses and Other Treatments

Susan Wolf, "The Significance of Doomsday," in Samuel Scheffler, *Death and
the Afterlife*, Niko Kolodny, ed. (New York: Oxford University Press, 2013):
112–130.

David Benatar, *Better Never to Have Been: The Harm of Coming into Existence* (New
York: Oxford University Press, 2006).

Kieran Setiya, *Life Is Hard: How Philosophy Can Help Us Find Our Way* (New York:
Riverhead Books, 2022): Ch. 6.

See Also

P. D. James, *Children of Men* (New York: Alfred A. Knopf, 1992).
Children of Men, dir. Alfonso Cuarón, 2006.

Questions for Reflection

1. We already know the human race will end *sometime*, though it might not be for a very long time yet. *That* knowledge does not seem to strip human pursuits here and now of all meaning. Can you make sense of our having very different attitudes toward *eventual* human extinction and *near-term* human extinction?

2. One visually striking detail in Alfonso Cuarón's film is that there is litter all over the streets. At first glance this seems surprising: surely it is for the sake of the *present* people with whom we share those streets that we (ought to) refrain from littering. Why might motivation not to litter decline simply because some *future* people won't ever exist?

48. THE PROCREATION ASYMMETRY

Some people, you may have noticed, exist. Often there is not much we can do about this. It's too late to prevent the existence of Cleopatra, Lyndon B. Johnson, or anyone alive in the present. Nor can we avert the imminent existence of certain future people—like those about to be conceived on the other side of the world.

But sometimes, we *do* have the power to prevent people from ever existing, and to create people who would otherwise never have existed. The act of creation may be—*ahem*—direct. Other times, our influence is more distant; think of the people who introduced your parents to each other, or the policymakers who "create" children by enacting tax breaks for big families.

Either way, this is an awesome power—the power to open and close the portal into existence. How are we supposed to wield this power? Do we have any duty to create people, or prevent their creation, for their own sake?

I say "for their own sake" because the presence of new people may affect those of us already here, for better or worse. A couple might cherish their baby boy—or he might be a menace. A country might want more people to carry the torch—or resent the extra traffic.

Set these familiar concerns aside. We're going to focus on a new topic: the people who are, as of the time of acting, merely possible. Are there moral reasons to bring about good lives, or prevent bad lives, out of concern for the people who would live them? This is the fundamental problem of *population ethics*, the study of choices that affect who will exist in the future.

Let's start by breaking the problem down into two parts.

First, do we have a duty to bring about people with good lives?

Many say: we *don't*. Of course, we still want to say that good lives matter. Once it's settled that somebody will exist, we should try to give them as good a life as they can have. But that doesn't mean we have to create them in the first place. Even if you know that your kid would be happy, you're not under an obligation to procreate. Narveson (1967) illustrates this idea by analogy with promises. Promise-keeping matters: once you've made a promise, you should try to keep it. But that doesn't mean you have even the slightest reason to make promises in the first place, just so you'll get to keep them. Similarly, you don't have to make more people just so that you can do right by them.

Now the second question. Do we have a moral duty *not* to bring about people with *terrible* lives? Here, many say: we *do*. If you have a genetic condition that will definitely cause your biological children to live short, agonizing lives—mere weeks of sheer pain—it would be wrong of you to go ahead and have kids. Again, there's an analogy to be made with promises. It's wrong to make promises that can only be broken. Similarly, it's wrong to create people who could only be miserable.

Put this all together, and you get an ethical view that is at once deeply appealing and immensely puzzling. You have *no duty whatsoever* to bring about good lives, and yet you're under a *strict* duty not to bring about bad lives. This pair of principles has come to be known as the *Procreation Asymmetry*. The puzzle is: How can we justify this asymmetric treatment of good and bad lives? If we have such a strong reason to avoid bad lives, why isn't there a corresponding duty to create good ones?

RESPONSES

The most straightforward way of dealing with the puzzle is not to bother. Rather than trying to justify the Procreation Asymmetry, we could just go with a symmetric view.

Consider the *Total View*, which tells you to maximize the net amount of goodness across everybody's lives. On this view, as long as you end up with more goodness on balance, it doesn't matter if you're improving old lives or creating new ones.

To its credit, the Total View is nice, simple, and symmetric: it tells you to create good lives *and* prevent bad ones. But its symmetry may have a cost. The Total View, according to critics, loses sight of what really matters here—not just good lives, but the individual *persons* who live them. When you fail to help someone who could have been happy, there is a specific person who is left worse off, so it makes sense why your act would be wrong. When you fail to create someone who would have been happy, who is worse off? No actual person was denied anything, because the person you didn't create never existed. By condemning acts that don't affect any persons for the worse, the Total View seems to get things backwards. Instead of valuing your happiness because we value *you*, we only value *you* as a potential receptacle for happiness.[1]

What if we forget about maximizing total goodness, and instead focus on doing right by people? That's the idea behind views like *Strong Actualism*, which tells you to do what's best for whoever ends up actually existing. Strong Actualism does seem like it would help justify the Procreation Asymmetry: it won't judge you if you don't create a happy child. But suppose you do create the child. Then, strangely, the view says that you were obligated to do so! This odd feature of Strong Actualism is known as "normative variance," because your duties vary depending on what you end up doing (Bykvist 2007). That might already be strange enough to have you worried. And yet, it gets stranger. Consider what Strong Actualism says about creating miserable children. If you do it, it's wrong—but if you don't, it's not! Even if normative variance can sometimes be okay, this particular instance seems pretty egregious. When you look back on your refusal to create a miserable child, you should think, "That was the right decision," just as you should look back on the creating of a miserable child with regret.

"OK, OK," you might be thinking, "Strong Actualism doesn't justify the Procreation Asymmetry. But surely we can find *something* to justify it. We just need to look a bit harder."

By all means, look around—a lot of ethical theorists would be very happy if you found the solution! Just be warned: population ethics is stuffed with "solutions" that lead to new puzzles. And, as it turns out, most ways of justifying the Procreation Asymmetry will catapult us face-first into an even harder paradox: the Non-Identity Problem.

Classic Presentations

Jan Narveson, "Utilitarianism and New Generations," *Mind* **76** (1967): 62–72.
Jefferson McMahan, "Problems of Population Theory," *Ethics* **92** (1981): 96–127.
    (McMahan coins the term "Asymmetry.")

Responses and Other Treatments

Krister Bykvist, "The Benefits of Coming into Existence," *Philosophical Studies* **135** (2007): 335–362.
Caspar Hare, "Voices from Another World: Must We Respect the Interests of People Who Do Not, and Will Never, Exist?" *Ethics* **117** (2007): 498–523.
Elizabeth Harman, "Can We Harm and Benefit in Creating?" *Philosophical Perspectives* **18** (2004): 89–113.

Derek Parfit, *Reasons and Persons* (Oxford: Oxford University Press, 1984): Ch. 16.

Johann Frick, "Conditional Reasons and the Procreation Asymmetry," *Philosophical Perspectives* **34** (2020): 53–87. (Frick gives his own solution and explains why so many others run into the Non-Identity Problem.)

Jack Spencer, "The Procreative Asymmetry and the Impossibility of Elusive Permission," *Philosophical Studies* **178** (2021): 3819–3848. (Spencer argues for a souped-up version of Actualism that he calls *Stable Actualism*.)

Seana Shiffrin, "Wrongful Life, Procreative Responsibility, and the Significance of Harm," *Legal Theory* **5** (1999): 117–148.

Questions for Reflection

1. Consider *Presentism*, the view that you should do whatever is best for the people who *presently* exist. This view might seem a lot like Strong Actualism. Does it entail the Procreation Asymmetry?

2. Consider the *Timeless Average View*, which says that you must maximize the average well-being of all people who *ever* exist. When, if ever, does this view tell you to create good lives? When, if ever, does it tell you to create *bad* lives? Use examples to show how this view differs from the Total View.

3. Some friends of the Procreation Asymmetry, like Narveson (1967), argue for the *No Benefit View*, which is that being created cannot confer a benefit (or harm) on the person created. The argument is as follows: "When you create a person, you aren't making them any better or worse off, since the alternative for them isn't a different existence: it's nonexistence." Does the No Benefit View support the Asymmetry—or count against it? (Hint: make sure you think through both parts of the Asymmetry.)

49. THE NON-IDENTITY PROBLEM

One truism in ethical theory is that, roughly speaking, we should try to make people better off. This is called the *Principle of Beneficence*, because it's the part of ethics that has to do with giving people benefits. Think of it as: "Thou shalt help." Utilitarians see the Principle of Beneficence as essentially the whole of ethics. Deontologists tend to focus on other principles, like bans on killing and lying. But hardly anyone rejects the Principle of Beneficence altogether. Surely, giving people benefits is at least a *part* of being ethical. What could be more obvious?

As it turns out, there is a paradox deep in the idea of "giving people benefits," one with profound implications for how we should think of choices that affect the future. Its name is the *Non-Identity Problem*.

The Problem starts from a simple fact. In addition to affecting how well-off other people are, our actions can also affect *who will exist*. Our choices determine who the "other people" in the world will be.

Consider two examples.

First, we have John, a parent who must choose how to help his two children. He can help the younger child a little, by curing her mild rash, or help his older child a lot, by curing her of a very serious disease. Presumably, John should give the bigger benefit: curing the serious disease rather than the mild rash. Easy peasy.

Next, we have Jane, who is *considering* becoming a parent (Parfit 1984). If she conceives now, she will have a child whose life is difficult but decent. If she waits a few years to conceive, she will have more resources to take care of her child, and she will have a child whose life is awesome. Presumably, Jane should give the bigger benefit: creating the awesome life rather than the merely decent one.

But there is a potentially *huge* difference between John's choice and Jane's. When John cures the disease, his choice makes his older child better off than they would have been otherwise. But if Jane creates the awesome life, her happy child isn't better off than they would have been otherwise. The child would not have even *been* otherwise—a different child would have existed, derived from a different sperm and egg, with different DNA. The two possible children are—you guessed it—non-identical.

The key fact, in short, is this. Although both Jane and John can create a world with better-off people, only John can make an *existing* person better off. If Jane creates the less happy child, there is no individual person left worse off than they would otherwise have been. So how could Jane's action be wrong? Who can complain if she does it? This is the core of the Non-Identity Problem.

RESPONSES

How worried should you be, as an ethical theorist, about the Non-Identity Problem? Should it keep you up at night?

Not if you are a "total" utilitarian who only cares about the sheer amount of goodness in the world, never mind who enjoys it. To the total utilitarian, John's and Jane's predicaments will seem obviously morally similar: they are each deciding whether to add a little or a lot to the abstract glob that is the universal total of utility, and they should both choose to add a lot.

But total utilitarianism strikes many ethical theorists as excessively impersonal. It's even too much for some utilitarians! The basic problem is that, if we only care about the free-floating sum of happiness, we aren't putting much importance on the individual people who experience it—which leads to a whole host of puzzling consequences. (See, for example, **#4, Infinite Utility**, **#48, The Procreation Asymmetry**, and **#50, The Repugnant Conclusion**.)

Because of these puzzles, many ethicists put a *person-affecting restriction* on beneficence. The idea here is that giving benefits isn't fundamentally about creating good lives. It's about making lives better. So beneficence will never require you to do some action *unless* there is some person whose life is affected by your action for the better.

To put this a bit more precisely, consider two actions A and B. According to the:

Person-Affecting Restriction
If you should do A rather than B, then there must be some person who is better off if you do A.

Now, this doesn't by itself tell you that it's OK for Jane to conceive early and create the less happy child. Couldn't there be someone who's made worse off by this—namely, the unborn child who loses out on an awesome life?

To get the Non-Identity Problem going, we have to add a principle of:

No Existential Benefits
Being brought into existence does not make someone better or worse off.

To put this another way, it's impossible to compare how well off you are to how well off you *would have been* if you'd never existed. There is no such thing as the welfare of a nonexistent being. So there aren't two welfare levels to compare. And we can suppose that Jane's choice really does determine which of two possible children is brought into existence.

We're in a dilemma. We can be total utilitarians, in which case we can easily solve the Non-Identity Problem, or we can go for a Person-Affecting Restriction with No Existential Benefits, in which case we crash into the Non-Identity Problem face-first.

Some ethicists have tried to find ways to solve the Non-Identity Problem—that is, to explain why Jane must create the happier child rather than the less happy one—without retreating all the way to total utilitarianism. Elizabeth Harman (2004) argues that it can be wrong to create the less happy child if doing so causes that child *harm*. Suppose Jenn is sick. If she conceives now, her child will be born with a painful permanent disease. If she waits a few months to conceive, she will have a (different) child who is disease-free. If she conceives now, she doesn't necessarily make her child worse off. We can even imagine that the child has a pretty good life, on the whole. But the disease is still a *harm* that Jenn inflicts on her child. As a deontologist, Harman thinks it can be wrong to inflict harms even if the consequences aren't bad at all (see Chapters 2 and 3).

Another kind of solution, a bit mind-bending, comes from Shamik Dasgupta. In his view, we're approaching the whole issue backwards. We are starting from some metaphysical claims about persons: that the less happy child *wouldn't have existed* if the mother had waited to conceive. From there, we then infer a moral paradox: that the mother didn't have to wait. Why not just start from the moral truth and work backwards to the metaphysics? Perhaps we should say, precisely *because* the parent must create the happier child rather than the less happy one, that this *would* make the "the child" better off? For Dasgupta, there *is* a being—"the child"—who exists regardless of which choice the parent makes. The child does not have as many essential properties, such as coming from *this* particular pair of gametes, as you thought. This is, suffice it to say, a controversial metaphysics, coming from a controversial methodology!

There are plenty of other possible solutions, but in the end, some deontologists think the wisest course of action is to give up. Perhaps there *is* no solution. Perhaps we shouldn't be trying to show that, if you're going to create someone, you have to create the happier person—because you *don't* have to. It's not wrong to create a decent life simply because you could have created another, happier one.

This can be very hard to believe, of course, especially if you care above all about the total amount of utility. But in this part of ethics, what view *isn't* hard to believe?

Classic Presentations

Derek Parfit, *Reasons and Persons* (Oxford: Oxford University Press, 1984): Ch. 16.
Gregory Kavka, "The Paradox of Future Individuals," *Philosophy & Public Affairs* **11** (1981): 93–112.

Responses and Other Treatments

Elizabeth Harman, "Can We Harm and Benefit in Creating?" *Philosophical Perspectives* **18** (2004): 89–113.
Elizabeth Harman, "Harming as Causing Harm," in Melinda A. Roberts and David T. Wasserman, eds., *Harming Future Persons: Ethics, Genetics and the Nonidentity Problem* (Dordrecht: Springer, 2009): 137–154.
Shamik Dasgupta, "Essentialism and the Nonidentity Problem," *Philosophy and Phenomenological Research* **96** (2018): 540–570.
Caspar Hare, "Voices from Another World: Must We Respect the Interests of People Who Do Not, and Will Never, Exist?" *Ethics* **117** (2007): 498–523.
Jack Spencer, "The Procreative Asymmetry and the Impossibility of Elusive Permission," *Philosophical Studies* **178** (2021): 3819–3842.

Questions for Reflection

1.	Many philosophers think the Non-Identity Problem has profound implications for environmental ethics. If we change our policies to conserve natural resources, for example, we will greatly improve the well-being of future generations—but we will also be changing *who* is among those generations. Do you think this undercuts the case for conserving the environment? Why or why not?

2. Suppose Jane does *not* have the option of creating the very happy child. She can either create the child who lives a difficult but decent life, or she can create no one. Would the total utilitarian still say that it is wrong to create the merely decent life (which contains significant suffering, but more pleasure on balance)? Would Harman?

50. THE REPUGNANT CONCLUSION

Humanity is on the brink of something big. Whether the issue is AI, climate change, or nuclear war, the choices we make in the 21st century will profoundly affect the well-being of future generations. But that is not all. We will also affect *whether there are* any future generations, and *how many people* there will be among them.

(We will also, less obviously, affect *who* ends up existing, as we saw in **#49, The Non-Identity Problem**.)

What kind of future should we strive for? This question—even if we set aside issues of justice, equality, feasibility, and the value of a life—turns out to be *extremely* difficult. We find ourselves skirting the event horizon of what may be the most notorious problem in all of value theory: The Repugnant Conclusion.

Let's start with an undoubtedly good future: call it A. (For "awesome," if you like.) Imagine a future where ultimately 10 billion people get to live equally fabulous lives, as good as any ever lived on the planet Earth. We will leave it to your imagination what this sort of life involves—as long as you imagine it being very good! For simplicity, don't think of the people in A as being actual people, towards whom you have attachments and obligations. Think of A as a story of how the future might look in a different possible world. We'll call such a story a "population."

Now consider a second population, featuring different possible people: call it B. (For "big.") In B, 20 billion people—that's *double* A's size—enjoy lives that are *almost* as fabulous as those in A. If the A-lives each have 100 value, the B-lives each have 95. That's not quite 100, but it's still very far above 0 (where it's no longer good to be alive).

So which possible future is better: A or B?

We face a trade-off. With A, we get a higher value life for each. With B, we get more "total" value, understood as the number of people times the value of each life. We can represent this with handy boxes, as in Figure 1: the width of the box represents the size of the population, and the height represents the quality of each life.

Many ethicists would say that B is better overall. Although it's 5% worse for each person, it's almost *twice* as much total value as we find in A: 190 rather than a mere 100. The trade-off thus seems like a no-brainer.

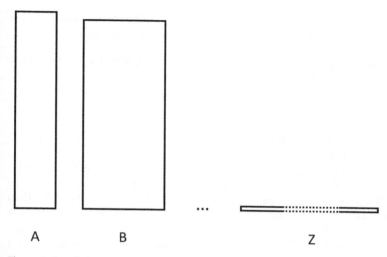

A   B   Z

Figure 1 Populations A to Z (height represents quality of life, width represents population size)

But this puts us on a slippery slope. For suppose we consider C (for "colossal"), which is twice as big as B or more, but again only slightly worse for each person. We will be tempted to say (if only for reasons of consistency) that C is better overall than B. And we could say the same for yet bigger populations D, E, F, and so on, each of which is some tiny bit worse for each and massively greater in size, so that each population is better than the last.

Eventually, we arrive at a gargantuan population Z (for "zillions"), with every life just barely worth living. Z does *not* seem like the sort of future we should strive for—a future where (we might say) people are eating bland food, reading uninspired books, and generally living drab lives. Indeed, Z seems obviously *worse* than the amazing A we started with! But notice that we got to Z by continually improving upon A, making the population better and better each time. So it seems we must conclude that *Z is the better population after all.* This is what Derek Parfit calls:

The Repugnant Conclusion
For any possible population of at least ten billion people, all with a very high quality of life, there must be some much larger imaginable population

whose existence, if other things are equal, would be better, even though its members have lives that are barely worth living. (1984: 388)

If we accept this, we may need to radically rethink what kind of future would be best for our world.

RESPONSES

To resist the Repugnant Conclusion, we'd have to deal with two key arguments.

The first is the *Spectrum Argument*. The idea here is that populations A–Z lie along a spectrum from "small and awesome for each" to "huge and barely good for each." Each population seems better than the last: $Z > \ldots > B > A$. (Where "$B > A$" means "B is better than A overall.") But as we saw earlier, it seems to follow that the last population is better than the first: $Z > A$. This implication holds given a much-loved principle:

Transitivity (of ">")
If $C > B > A$, then $C > A$.

In general, it's very plausible that comparative adjectives—like "better than" or "faster than"—will turn out to be transitive. If a car is faster than a bike, which is faster than a unicycle, it follows by transitivity that a car is faster than a unicycle.

Can we deny transitivity? Some renegades do, arguing that $Z > \ldots > B > A > Z$! This view avoids Repugnance, but we might wonder why betterness should be so unlike other comparatives. Suffice it to say, many ethicists are wary of this sort of non-transitivity.

The second argument for Repugnance is simpler. Notice that population Z is very, very, *very* big—as represented in Figure 1 by the dotted lines. In fact, we can let Z be so big that it has by far more total goodness than the other populations—certainly more than A. The Repugnant Conclusion follows straightaway, given the:

Impersonal Total Principle
If other things are equal, the best outcome is the one in which there would be the greatest quantity of whatever makes life worth living. (Parfit 1984: 387)

We might reject this principle. But if betterness doesn't just depend on the total amount of good stuff, what does it depend on?

Perhaps A > B if A has more goodness per person *on average*? This is what Parfit calls the:

Impersonal Average Principle
If other things are equal, the best outcome is the one in which people's lives go, on average, best. (1984: 386)

Such a view would say that A > B > ... > Z < A. No Repugnance—so far, so good! But the Impersonal Average Principle also implies that A > B no matter how great B's size, and no matter how close B and A are in quality of life for each. Even if A has only one person, as long as that person has a better life than the average in B, A still wins. That seems hard to believe.

Another option is to say that the lives in Z, though worth living, are not good enough to add value. On this view, lives have to be above a certain "critical level" before they count towards making the population better overall. To illustrate, let's say the critical level is at 30 (see Figure 2). Then adding a life of value 30 would *not* make a population better; adding a life of value 50 would contribute 20 units to the

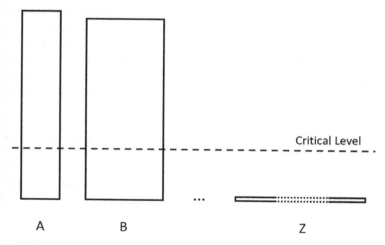

Figure 2 The Critical Level

population's value; and a life of value 10 would subtract 20 units from the population's value.

The "critical level" view does ensure that big drab populations won't be better overall than A. But the view has its own problems. For one thing, where do we set the critical level—30, 29, 31, 10, 90? Whatever we pick will likely seem arbitrary. Secondly—and this is the big problem—let's suppose 30 really is the critical level, and let's think about the badness of a small population with fairly miserable lives: say, 100 people each at level -20. Such a population will have negative value: -500, to be exact. But it would be even *worse* to have a big population with *happy* lives below the critical level—say, 1,000 people at level 20, giving us a value of -1,000. More generally, critical level views entail what Gustaf Arrhenius calls:

The Strong Sadistic Conclusion
For any population of lives with negative well-being, there is a population of lives with positive well-being that is worse, other things being equal. (2000: 256)

And this seems, if anything, *worse* than the Repugnant Conclusion! How could good lives be worse than bad lives?

It turns out that avoiding the Repugnant Conclusion is no easy task. Here we've considered a few ways out, but as you can imagine, further solutions tend to come with their own further problems.

In light of all this, some philosophers have come to think that we should *embrace* the Repugnant Conclusion. What if the conclusion is only hard to resist because it's actually true? This raises the question of why the conclusion should have ever struck us as repugnant in the first place. One answer is that, when we try to imagine big numbers—like the many, many people in Z—our imaginations fail us, and we underestimate the value of a big quantity of good stuff spread out across trillions and trillions of lives.

Whether you embrace it or resist it, the Repugnant Conclusion is sure to teach you something deep about the nature of value—and the potential for ethical problems to surprise and elude us.

Classic Presentation

Derek Parfit, *Reasons and Persons* (Oxford: Oxford University Press, 1984): Part IV.

Responses and Other Treatments

Gustaf Arrhenius, "An Impossibility Theorem for Welfarist Axiologies," *Economics & Philosophy* **16** (2000): 247–266.

Alan Hájek and Wlodek Rabinowicz, "Degrees of Commensurability and the Repugnant Conclusion," *Noûs* **56** (2022): 897–919.

Michael Huemer, "In Defence of Repugnance," *Mind* **117** (2008): 899–933.

Larry Temkin, *Rethinking the Good: Moral Ideals and the Nature of Practical Reasoning* (Oxford: Oxford University Press, 2012).

Questions for Reflection

1. Try drawing out diagrams to illustrate the Strong Sadistic Conclusion. How did you represent negative well-being?

2. Suppose someone says: "I'm not falling for the Spectrum Argument. B isn't better than A, since B is a mere *two times* the size. B would have to be at least 100 times bigger than A (holding fixed quality of life for each) before I would admit that B is truly better." Does this doom the Spectrum Argument? If not, show how it can be amended.

3. How repugnant is the Repugnant Conclusion? If we are forced to accept it, should we rethink any of our priorities in the present?

NOTE

1 In the words of Johann Frick (2007: 65), "Human wellbeing matters because people matter – *not vice versa*." The Total View also gives rise to the most notorious paradox of population ethics, and the topic of this book's final section: "The Repugnant Conclusion."

INDEX

Note: Page numbers followed by "n" denote endnotes.

For Product Safety Concerns and Information please contact our EU
representative GPSR@taylorandfrancis.com Taylor & Francis Verlag GmbH,
Kaufingerstraße 24, 80331 München, Germany

Printed and bound by CPI Group (UK) Ltd, Croydon, CR0 4YY
08/06/2025
01897002-0003